MORE THAN MEETS THE EAR

More Than Meets the Ear

Discovering the Hidden Contexts
of Old Testament Conversations

Victor H. Matthews

William B. Eerdmans Publishing Company
Grand Rapids, Michigan / Cambridge, U.K.

© 2008 Victor H. Matthews

Published 2008 by
Wm. B. Eerdmans Publishing Co.
2140 Oak Industrial Drive N.E., Grand Rapids, Michigan 49505 /
P.O. Box 163, Cambridge CB3 9PU U.K.
www.eerdmans.com

Printed in the United States of America

13 12 11 10 09 08   7 6 5 4 3 2 1

Library of Congress Cataloging-in-Publication Data

Matthews, Victor Harold.
More than meets the ear: discovering the hidden contexts
of Old Testament conversations / Victor H. Matthews.
p.   cm.
Includes bibliographical references.
ISBN 978-0-8028-0384-9 (pbk.: alk. paper)
1. Bible. O.T. — Criticism, interpretation, etc. 2. Conversation
analysis. 3. Dialogue analysis. I. Title.

BS1171.3.M38   2008
221.6′6 — dc22
2008012008

Scripture quotations are from the *New Revised Standard Version of the Bible* © 1989 by the Division of Christian Education, National Council of Churches of Christ in the United States of America. Used by permission.

Contents

Preface

During the course of writing this volume I have discovered that the biblical narrative has many ways to tell us about its social world. In particular, as I focused on embedded dialogue in biblical stories, I found that there were linguistic, syntactical, and narrative methods employed by the authors that were designed to help the ancient audience gain a richer experience when these episodes were presented orally or read. For modern readers, however, many of these social and linguistic clues are not always evident in translation. Nor is the social world that produced them familiar to us or even explicable at times. Too many wordplays and references to activities are just too foreign or unknown. With this in mind, I decided to embrace what the social sciences have been talking about for many years and utilize the methods and techniques current in sociology, critical geography, socio-linguistics, and social psychology to analyze the discourse found in the narratives of the Hebrew Bible/Old Testament.

This means that the result here is quite eclectic. I have, in fact, drawn from a wide range of studies from several disciplines. Curiously, many scholars in different fields have been doing much the same type of research, but they have attached their own labels to their methods and conclusions. Unfortunately, it is far too typical in academia today for scholars to become too insulated within their own disciplines. They seldom go down the hall to ask their colleagues in sociology, anthropology, and psychology what they have been doing or question how others' work might help illumine their own. In this volume, I have tried to cross these disciplinary divides. I have endeavored to speak with and use the methods these other research groups have developed, and thereby, hopefully, I have created a useful synthesis or at least an introduction that may spark future endeavors in biblical studies.

This is not to say that biblical scholars have been unaware of what the social sciences have to offer. Since the mid-1980s an increasing number of studies have appeared that explore the possibilities of social world studies.[1] In respect to the study of the language and dialogue contained in these texts, a number of new works have appeared utilizing various forms of communication theory, including speech act theory,[2] discourse analysis,[3] spatiality theory,[4] and cognitive linguistics.[5] In particular, the social context of speech has been touched on in a number of studies, but it deserves closer attention.[6]

Since life is filled with a constant stream of social interaction that generally takes the form of face-to-face conversations, it is not surprising to find that the biblical narratives are replete with embedded dialogues. After all, a story is more interesting if it mimics everyday life. Straight narrative is deadly dull, and in any case many of these stories originated in

---

1. Among the most recent in Hebrew Bible studies are Philip F. Esler, ed., *Ancient Israel: The Old Testament in Its Social Context* (Minneapolis: Fortress, 2006); Victor H. Matthews, "Traversing the Social Landscape: The Value of the Social Scientific Approach to the Bible," in *Theology and the Social Sciences,* ed. Michael Horace Barnes, 214-36. Annual Publication of the College Theology Society 46 (Maryknoll: Orbis, 2001); and Ronald Simkins and Stephen Cook, eds., *The Social World of the Hebrew Bible.* Semeia 87 (Atlanta: SBL, 1999).

2. Hugh C. White, ed., *Speech Act Theory and Biblical Criticism.* Semeia 41 (Decatur: Scholars, 1988).

3. See esp. for New Testament exegesis, Stanley E. Porter and Jeffrey T. Reed, *Discourse Analysis and the New Testament: Approaches and Results.* JSNTSup 170 (Sheffield: Sheffield Academic, 1999).

4. See David M. Gunn and Paula M. McNutt, eds., *"Imagining" Biblical Worlds: Studies in Spatial, Social, and Historical Constructs in Honor of James W. Flanagan.* JSOTSup 359 (London: Sheffield Academic, 2002).

5. See in particular the series of articles listed in the bibliography by Ellen van Wolde. For a more technical and hypertext approach, see Christo H. J. van der Merwe, "Biblical Exegesis, Cognitive Linguistics, and Hypertext," in *Congress Volume, Leiden 2004,* ed. André Lemaire, 255-80. VTSup 109 (Leiden: Brill, 2006).

6. For recent monographs, see two works by Raymond F. Person, Jr., *In Conversation with Jonah: Conversation Analysis, Literary Criticism, and the Book of Jonah.* JSOTSup 220 (Sheffield: Sheffield Academic, 1996); and *Structure and Meaning in Conversation and Literature* (Lanham: University Press of America, 1999).

oral tradition. Thus, when they were reproduced or edited into their written form they simply retained their communicative style. These embedded conversations are found in a variety of settings, from commercial to didactic, from political to angry, and many are very personal. Also, there are so many that no one volume could possibly catalogue or analyze all of them. As a result, I have been selective in my presentation of the text. Therefore, each pericope that is discussed here is presented as a possible model for later research. It is analyzed in terms of its social world characteristics and is illumined, where possible, by studies on its literary qualities, as well as its psychological and sociological context.

It will be the task of this volume to introduce readers briefly to the various critical communication theories currently being used by scholars in a number of fields. With these methods as a guide, it may then be possible to step more effectively into the world of ancient Israelite conversations, figuratively standing in the background and analyzing how they are a reflection of the personal status, age, gender, economic standing, and political position of the participants. But their words will not be the only things examined. The physical and social setting, current events described in the narrative or understood as historical context for that episode, the implied and present audience, as well as social and legal barriers or requirements will also be addressed. In this way the various forms of speech (spoken words, gestures, and the conscious use of positioning) will emerge from the written text and become living social artifacts of their or the author's time and social environment.

Although each chapter in this volume is designed to address a different method from the social sciences or communication theory, there will be overlap and many references within the chapters to material previously discussed. In general, however, the longer exegetical sections are intended to demonstrate how particular methods can be used to understand better the text and its social context.

Chapter 1: Introduces how embedded dialogue can be effectively analyzed using sociolinguistics and discourse analysis. Because this is the first chapter and because many of these techniques will also be applied in later chapters, it spends more time on explaining the process and the methods that have been developed primarily by scholars in the field of social psychology and sociology.[7]

---

7. Among the works I draw on are Gilles Fauconnier, *Mappings in Thought and Lan-*

Chapter 2: Drawing heavily on the theoretical studies described in the first chapter, this segment provides an extended exegesis of the story of Judah and Tamar in Genesis 38. In addition to a structural analysis, it focuses on the characteristics of a transactional dialogue, cognitive linguistics,[8] mental space theory,[9] and concepts of social identity.

Chapter 3: This chapter concentrates on the sociological theories associated with conversation analysis and, in particular, the foundational work of Harvey Sacks[10] and Erving Goffman.[11] Since both conversation analysis and discourse analysis benefit from careful attention to ethnographic, linguistic, and physical context, a synthesis of methods is illustrated here in the exegetical study of David and Michal in 2 Samuel 6 and in the social triangle story of David, Nabal, and Abigail in 1 Samuel 25.

Chapter 4: Turning to public discourse, this chapter explores the use of positioning theory as a helpful method in examining dialogue in public space.[12] In order to illustrate the shifting power relationships and the strategies employed to challenge, intimidate, or overcome opponents, I have provided an extended exegesis of the confrontation between King Ahab and the prophet Micaiah in 1 Kings 22.

Chapter 5: In this final chapter, I turn to the importance of spatial context as a creative and cognitive factor in the development of social interaction and effective storytelling. Drawing on the work of critical urban

---

guage (Cambridge: Cambridge University Press, 1997); J. Maxwell Atkinson and John Heritage, eds., *Structures of Social Action: Studies in Conversation Analysis* (Cambridge: Cambridge University Press, 1984); and a number of studies in Mark L. Knapp and John A. Daly, eds., *Handbook of Interpersonal Communication,* 3rd ed. (Thousand Oaks: Sage, 2002).

8. See esp. the studies in Vyvyan Evans and Melanie Green, *Cognitive Linguistics: An Introduction* (Mahwah: Lawrence Erlbaum, 2006); and the model described in Eve Sweetser and Gilles Fauconnier, "Cognitive Links and Domains: Basic Aspects of Mental Space Theory," in *Spaces, Worlds, and Grammar,* ed. Fauconnier and Sweetser, 1-28 (Chicago: University of Chicago Press, 1996).

9. See Gilles Fauconnier and Mark Turner, *The Way We Think: Conceptual Blending and the Mind's Hidden Complexities* (New York: Basic Books, 2002).

10. See among his works listed in the bibliography, Harvey Sacks, *Lectures on Conversation,* ed. Gail Jefferson (Oxford: Blackwell, 1992).

11. I have particularly relied on Erving Goffman, *Frame Analysis* (New York: Harper & Row, 1974).

12. A very helpful set of studies can be found in Rom Harré and Luk van Langenhove, eds., *Positioning Theory: Moral Contexts of Intentional Action* (Oxford: Blackwell, 1999).

geographers[13] and social psychologists,[14] I present a comparative analysis of the reuse of space in Isaiah 7 and 36 and discuss the spatial strategy employed by Baruch as he or his scroll traverses linked or chained spaces in Jeremiah 36.

The audience for this work is the serious student of the Hebrew Bible/Old Testament who is willing to stretch beyond traditional exegetical methods and delve into what the social sciences can provide. It may profitably be used in university and seminary contexts and for private study. Because it is not intended to address theological issues other than those that can be reconstructed about ancient Israelite worship practices and beliefs, it may be seen as a relatively neutral treatment of the materials. Numerous insets and textboxes throughout highlight information or provide background and definition of technical terms. Additional historical or archaeological materials are included, where it is deemed appropriate, to help guide the reader through the maze of names, places, and events. The volume itself should serve as a supplementary text that may best be used in conjunction with a good, one-volume Bible dictionary, an introduction to the Old Testament/Hebrew Bible, and an atlas. As always, I encourage readers to contact me with their questions or comments so that the dialogue can continue beyond the confines of the printed page.

VICTOR H. MATTHEWS
Missouri State University
Springfield, Missouri
July 2007

13. Among the works I have used are Edward W. Soja, *Thirdspace: Journeys to Los Angeles and Other Real-and-Imagined Places* (Cambridge, MA: Blackwell, 1996); Reginald G. Golledge and Robert J. Stimson, *Spatial Behavior: A Geographic Perspective* (New York: Guilford, 1997); and Setha Low and Neil Smith, eds., *The Politics of Public Space* (New York: Routledge, 2006).

14. Among them are the works of Denis E. Cosgrove, *Social Formation and Symbolic Landscape* (Madison: University of Wisconsin Press, 1998), and Stephen C. Levinson, *Space in Language and Cognition: Explorations in Cognitive Diversity* (Cambridge: Cambridge University Press, 2003).

Abbreviations

AB	Anchor Bible
ABD	*Anchor Bible Dictionary,* ed. David Noel Freedman
AJBA	*Australian Journal of Biblical Archaeology*
BAR	*Biblical Archaeology Review*
BDB	Francis Brown, S. R. Driver, and Charles A. Briggs, *A Hebrew and English Lexicon of the Old Testament*
Bib	*Biblica*
BibInt	*Biblical Interpretation*
BIW	The Bible in Its World
BJS	Brown Judaic Studies
BRev	*Bible Review*
BTB	*Biblical Theology Bulletin*
BZ	*Biblische Zeitschrift*
BZAW	Beiheft zur Zeitschrift für die alttestamentliche Wissenschaft
CBQ	*Catholic Biblical Quarterly*
EvJ	*Evangelical Journal*
HBM	Hebrew Bible Monographs
HS	*Hebrew Studies*
HSS	Harvard Semitic Studies
HTR	*Harvard Theological Review*
JANES	*Journal of the Ancient Near Eastern Society*
JAOS	*Journal of the American Oriental Society*
JBL	*Journal of Biblical Literature*
JHS	*Journal of Hebrew Scriptures*
JJS	*Journal of Jewish Studies*
JNSL	*Journal of Northwest Semitic Languages*

JSJSup	Journal for the Study of Judaism: Supplement Series
JSNTSup	Journal for the Study of the New Testament: Supplement Series
JSOT	*Journal for the Study of the Old Testament*
JSOTSup	Journal for the Study of the Old Testament: Supplement Series
MAL	Middle Assyrian Laws
MT	Masoretic Text
NCambBC	New Cambridge Bible Commentary
NEA	*Near Eastern Archaeology*
OTL	Old Testament Library
OtSt	*Oudtestamentische Studiën*
NICOT	New International Commentary on the Old Testament
SBL	Society of Biblical Literature
SBLSymS	Society of Biblical Literature Symposium Series
SBLWAW	Society of Biblical Literature Writings from the Ancient World
SJOT	*Scandinavian Journal of the Old Testament*
TOTC	Tyndale Old Testament Commentaries
VT	*Vetus Testamentum*
VTSup	Supplements to Vetus Testamentum
WBC	Word Biblical Commentary
ZAW	*Zeitschrift für die alttestamentliche Wissenschaft*

CHAPTER ONE

Analyzing Biblical Dialogue
with Sociolinguistics and Discourse Analysis

In this opening chapter we will introduce how embedded dialogue in the narratives of the Old Testament/Hebrew Bible can be effectively analyzed using sociolinguistics and discourse analysis. Of course, these formal speeches and debates, casual conversations, and commercial transactions are recorded rather than spoken live. Therefore, to examine them in a critical manner it will be necessary to introduce or further describe a variety of methods that primarily come from the social sciences: anthropology, cognitive linguistics, psychology, sociology, and spatial geography. Furthermore, in order to adapt these methods to the study of the social world of ancient Israel and the literature that it produced, it will also be necessary to employ the tools of literary criticism well known to biblical scholars. In the blending of disciplinary approaches, a working synthesis will be created that should bring the embedded dialogues off the page and breathe life into the social world that created them.

What becomes evident at first glance is that communication comes in many guises. Methods of communication can vary from a quizzically-raised eyebrow to an intricate exchange of views on a technical problem in physics. All that is required to make this a dialogue is for someone to communicate in any of the ways that humans are capable of expressing meaning and for someone else to react to that communication. This includes face-to-face, plain-spoken interaction as well as communication through the written word (author to reader).

Of course, the assumption or hope is that the other person understands the gesture or the words spoken by the first person. In effect, every word and grammatical construction has potential for meaning, but "it is only within a complete discourse or in context that meaning will actually be produced."[1] I would add to that the importance attached to the elements of the setting provided by storytellers in oral or written narratives. These elements, which include the physical domain as well as social indicators, when combined with the statements in the dialogues and the informational asides provided by the narrator function as the primary data for our study.

The cognitive linguistic process that creates meaning from setting, speech, or gesture is the result of a person's or a discourse community's recognition of grammatical and spatial cues in combination with "linguistic, contextual, and situational clues."[2] For example, it is possible to create a conceptual metaphor like "time flies" to combine otherwise unrelated temporal and physical concepts in order to manufacture a specific meaning for a discourse community. In a similar manner, metonymy can be used to make one entity stand for another. Therefore, if someone says that a group chose to "vote with their feet," the action of walking away or disagreeing with something is graphically combined with the thinking process behind that decision.[3]

Through this mental process the various forms of communication being used are assigned to specific and socially-recognized mental spaces or worlds. They in turn may elicit further speech or action (including the decision to ignore what has been said). This is not to say that every word spoken or emphasized with a gesture is always fully understood. Dialectical nuances differ, and personal vocabularies are not always the same. The personal experiences that provide the creative background for effective use of metaphor and metonymy may not have been shared by both parties in a conversation. In particular, persons of different generations, racial or ethnic backgrounds, or genders may share a common language without being able to comprehend fully every word spoken by the other. Faced with new data or expressions, it will be necessary for the speakers and/or their audience to test these words against known concepts and process and catego-

1. Gilles Fauconnier, *Mappings in Thought and Language* (Cambridge: Cambridge University Press, 1997) 37.

2. Fauconnier, *Mappings,* 38.

3. Vyvyan Evans and Melanie Green, *Cognitive Linguistics: An Introduction* (Mahwah: Lawrence Erlbaum, 2006) 167.

rize them before understanding can take place — if not always completely or satisfactorily.[4]

This means that the mental backdrop to a conversation or an embedded dialogue in a written narrative depends upon socially-recognized and agreed-upon concepts or cognitive representations. This mental backdrop allows the participants and the audience to categorize and identify the characters, the setting, and the language that they employ. Categorization operates as part of our constant and generally unconscious categorization of actions, events, words, emotions, and images to make sense of our world and to draw analogies between them or to create theories about them.[5] Therefore, it is of prime importance to the audience when the storyteller provides them with the physical location (home, palace, or field), the season of the year, and the social relationship between the characters. In this way the cognitive pathway is made clearer and the audience can both categorize the images presented and concentrate on the words being spoken without wondering who the speakers are, what their relationship to each other might be, and why they are carrying on their dialogue in this place.

Ezra's Public Address

To illustrate these points, let us briefly examine the narrative elements supplied by the author of the story of Ezra's mission to Jerusalem (Ezra 7-10, Nehemiah 8-9). While this story contains some gaps and unrealistic aspects,[6] Ezra's mission apparently reaches a climax when he assembles the Jewish people and reads from a scroll of the law.[7] His intent is to marshal support for his social and religious reforms, including the annulment of mixed marriages (Ezra 9-10), an anathema to a Jew from the exilic com-

---

4. Albert Kamp, *Inner Worlds: A Cognitive Linguistic Approach to the Book of Jonah.* Biblical Interpretation 68 (Leiden: Brill, 2004) 9.

5. George Lakoff, *Women, Fire, and Dangerous Things* (Chicago: University of Chicago Press, 1990) 6.

6. J. Maxwell Miller and John H. Hayes, *A History of Ancient Israel and Judah,* 2nd ed. (Louisville: Westminster/John Knox, 2006) 538, point to the weight of the gold and silver (30 tons) that accompanied Ezra's party from Persia to Jerusalem (Ezra 8:24-30).

7. See Cornelius Houtman, "Ezra and the Law: Observations on the Supposed Relation between Ezra and the Pentateuch," *OtSt* 21 (1981) 91-115, for a discussion of the various speculations on what might have been in the scroll read by Ezra.

munity but apparently an acceptable practice among those who have re-turned to Jerusalem.[8]

Intending to place Ezra literally on "center stage," the recorder of these events positions him on a wooden platform that is stationed in "the square before the Water Gate" (Neh 8:3-4). Several spatial elements add to the potential effectiveness of Ezra's performance and serve as cognitive triggers for his audience. First is the gate area. As we will see in a much more detailed analysis of a similar story in 1 Kings 22 (see Chapter 4), the gate in both the rural and urban setting is a place associated with legal and commercial transactions.[9] It also is tied to the defense of the city and in this case would serve as an open area where a large crowd could be assem-bled. Second, Ezra elevates himself above the people by standing on a tem-porary podium that has been constructed for this solemn occasion. This simple prop, analogous to the pulpit in modern churches, sets him apart from his audience, makes them look up to him, and aids in the projection of his voice.

A third factor here is the fact that Ezra is accompanied by an entou-rage of important officials. This gathering magnifies his personal presence and provides an image of power that a single individual would lack. Their presence also may have made his assumption of command over the city's population, based as it was on the decree of the Persian emperor, more pal-atable despite the fact that he is an outsider (Ezra 7:11-26).[10]

Ezra adds to the significance of this public address by adopting the elements of previously staged covenant renewal ceremonies.[11] However, he is hindered somewhat by the fact that Aramaic now had become the di-alect of everyday speech and the people of Jerusalem apparently had some difficulty in grasping a complete understanding of the Hebrew version of

8. See a discussion of the social tensions apparent between these two Jewish commu-nities in Victor H. Matthews, "The Social Context of Law in the Second Temple Period," *BTB* 28 (1998) 7-15.

9. See the discussion in Victor H. Matthews, "Entrance Ways and Threshing Floors: Legally Significant Sites in the Ancient Near East," *Fides et Historia* 19/3 (1987) 25-40.

10. See Lisbeth S. Fried, "'You Shall Appoint Judges': Ezra's Mission and the Rescript of Artaxerxes," in *Persia and Torah: The Theory of Imperial Authorization of the Pentateuch,* ed. James W. Watts, 63-89. SBLSymS 17 (Atlanta: SBL, 2001).

11. Victor H. Matthews, *Old Testament Turning Points* (Grand Rapids: Baker, 2005) 79-80. For previous examples of this seminal event in Israelite tradition, see Exod 24:1-8; Josh 24:1-28; and 2 Kgs 23:1-3, 21-23.

the law that he was reading. As a result, translators and interpreters of the law — in this instance, Levites who are fluent in both Hebrew and Aramaic — carefully intone the text, giving it the "exact pronunciations, intonation, and phrasing," and thereby aid in its comprehensibility.[12] The Hebrew phrase used here, *śôm śekel,* "rendered the meaning," would therefore be an attempt to explain the nuances so they people would be able to subscribe to the requirements of the covenant without question (Neh 8:5-8).[13]

Sociolinguistic Models

With these potential difficulties in mind, social scientists who work with sociolinguistic models look for examples in which language is used with the appropriate social meaning for the communication situation. Full competence in the use of a language or the modes of communication recognized within a particular culture includes knowing how to initiate and manage conversations and how to negotiate meaning with other people. It also includes knowing what sorts of body language, eye contact, and proximity to other people are appropriate, so that a person acts accordingly. For example, the rules of interaction in a market transaction may require a formal set of procedures, as is the case in the transactional dialogue between Abraham and Ephron the Hittite over the purchase of the cave of Machpelah (Gen 23:7-16). In other instances, a simple purchase of food or a piece of pottery may require no more than an indication of what is to be purchased and the required payment (Deut 2:6; Jer 13:2).

Formal Settings

In a formal setting, competent use of language requires recognized statements of greeting and welcome that are prescribed to meet the social character of the occasion and the social status of the participants. For example, when Obadiah meets the prophet Elijah, he engages in both a gesture and

---

12. Michael Fishbane, *Biblical Interpretation in Ancient Israel* (Oxford: Oxford University Press, 1985) 109.

13. See Joseph Blenkinsopp, *Ezra-Nehemiah.* OTL (Philadelphia: Westminster, 1988) 288.

in words of greeting. He "fell on his face, and said, Is it you, my lord Elijah?" (1 Kgs 18:7). Everything he does here indicates his acknowledgement of Elijah's superior status as a prophet of Yahweh. The apparently rhetorical question, "Is it you?" is a typical form of address that allows the one being addressed to identify himself formally *(ha'attâ zeh)*. In discourse analysis, this sequence of utterances is referred to as "adjacency pairs," a conversation structure that assists with turn-taking and precipitates subsequent speech and/or action.[14]

In another instance, a sequence of patterned speech occurs on the fly as Abner addresses his determined pursuer, Asahel (2 Sam 2:20-23). His opening statement, spoken as they race across the field of battle, "Is it you, Asahel?" is designed to indicate his acknowledgement of Asahel's valor and persistence.[15] However, Asahel breaks the pattern of turn-taking since this is the only statement that he will respond to, saying "Yes, it is" (2:20). The remainder of Abner's words apparently falls on deaf ears. They form the basis for his argument trying to persuade the younger man to give up the chase. Abner's repeated suggestion that Asahel choose another, safer target for his challenge also contains a political overtone since Abner does not want to incure bloodguilt by killing one of Joab's brothers: "How could I show my face to Joab?" (2:22b). In this sense, his complaint is that Asahel is forcing him to commit an act that will harm them both.[16] Faced with Asahel's silent refusal to take another path, Abner is forced to turn and kill him in order to escape. Although he will subsequently persuade Joab to give up the pursuit (2:26-28), this episode serves as the narrative context for Joab's taking his revenge at a later date (2 Sam 3:22-30).[17]

---

14. E. A. Schegloff and Harvey Sacks, "Opening Up Closings," *Semiotica* 8 (1973) 295-96.

15. A variation in this form of address is found in Jezebel's haughty statement, "Is it peace, you Zimri, murderer of your master?" (2 Kgs 9:31). While she follows the normal forms, the queen also challenges Jehu, labeling him a "Zimri" (= traitor) and suggesting that it had better be "peace" if he does not want to face her wrath and that of the people.

16. Ian Dersley and Anthony Wootton, "Complaint Sequences Within Antagonistic Argument," *Research on Language and Social Interaction* 33 (2000) 378, point to studies in which "blame and complaint can be lain at the door of the immediate recipient."

17. See Frederick H. Cryer, "David's Rise to Power and the Death of Abner: An Analysis of 1 Samuel xxvi 14-16 and Its Redaction-Critical Implications," *VT* 35 (1985) 385-94, for the redactional history of these political narratives.

Informal Settings

Informal circumstances, especially those involving social equals, allow for speech patterns that tend to be much more relaxed and less carefully phrased. For example, when Jacob arrives at the well near Haran, he strikes up a friendly conversation with the shepherds gathered there to water their sheep. In this setting, centered on a recognized resource that is not the private property of any one person, and in company with a group of men of equal status, Jacob freely asks them where they are from and whether they know his uncle Laban (Gen 29:2-5). The storyteller's presentation of quick turn-taking in the conversation is suggestive of a comfortable interaction, not dependent on social protocol such as hospitality, but merely the free exchange of information that occurs when no threat of danger is detected. A storyteller is therefore most effective when there is a seamless sense of mutual orientation by the characters during dialogue.[18]

Similarly, when Joab goes to visit Amasa and David's army he gives his old military colleague a friendly greeting, "Is it well with you, my brother?" Unfortunately for Amasa, who had recently been appointed to replace Joab as army commander (2 Sam 20:4-5), he is put off his guard and does not recognize that the greeting is a ploy. Joab uses the opportunity to murder his rival and retake command of the army himself (20:9-10). In this case, the storyteller indicates the lack of a mutual awareness of the full implications of the context of this meeting.

Analysis of Speech Patterns

To monitor further the sociolinguistic process, researchers create indexes of social characteristics in their analysis of speech patterns that are based on such categories as social class, ethnicity, and even individual neighborhoods.[19] As the fictional linguistic specialist Henry Higgins so confidently

18. Christian Heath, "Talk and Recipiency: Sequential Organization in Speech and Body Movement," in *Structures of Social Action: Studies in Conversation Analysis,* ed. J. Maxwell Atkinson and John Heritage (Cambridge: Cambridge University Press, 1984) 247, notes that "within the course of interactional activity participants themselves orient to how their actions and activities are received and attended to by their fellow participants."

19. Ronald K. S. Macaulay, *Talk That Counts: Age, Gender, and Social Class Differences in Discourse* (Oxford: Oxford University Press, 2005) 36-39.

Elisha and the Shunammite Woman

The story of Elisha and the Shunammite Woman in 2 Kgs 4:8-37 allows us to illustrate this principle of social interaction and patterned speech. When the Shunammite woman's son collapses, apparently succumbing to sunstroke or a brain hemorrhage, she seeks out Elisha for help. Seeing her approach, the prophet sends his servant Gehazi out to greet her, and when he graciously asks, "Are you all right? Is your husband all right? Is the child all right?" she simply responds, "Shalom" = "It is all right" (4:25-26). Her response contains a basic untruth or perhaps a social demur and is quite curt. It even may be an indication she does not wish to discuss her situation with Gehazi, whose social status as a servant would not equal that of the wealthy wife *(gĕdôlâ)*[1] of an established landowner. The situation is very different when she meets Elisha. Rather than speaking the standard greeting, she "caught hold of his feet," and Elisha recognized this as a signal of supplication and that she "is in bitter distress" (4:27).[2] The prophet's acknowledgement of the woman's silent

1. See Mordechai Cogan and Hayim Tadmor, *II Kings*. AB 11 (Garden City: Doubleday, 1988) 56, for this translation and usage of *gĕdôlâ* for "wealthy woman." Cf. its use for individuals in Jon 3:7 and Nah 3:10.

2. See the reaction of the two Marys, who are greeted by the resurrected Jesus. They took

states in "My Fair Lady," he could correctly identify the origin of any Englishman within six miles of his home by the quality of his speech. This is at the heart of Jephthah's linguistic test in Judg 12:5-6. While his men hold the fords of the Jordan River, he has anyone wishing to cross over into Canaan pronounce the word "Shibboleth." However, his Ephraimite opponents do not share the same dialectic pronunciation of the sibilant sound, and they mistakenly say "Sibboleth" and are promptly executed.[20]

Fortunately, not every difference in pronunciation results in such deadly consequences. However, this is a reflection of the cultural and linguistic variations that must be taken into account when examining spoken

20. For a recent analysis of the linguistic differences and possible narrative ironies involved, see Robert Woodhouse, "The Biblical Shibboleth Story in the Light of Late Egyptian Perceptions of Semitic Sibilants: Reconciling Divergent Views," *JAOS* 123 (2003) 271-89.

petition is found in his order to Gehazi to "leave her alone," not push her away, so that she can speak directly to him.[3] In this case, at least, Elisha is willing to step outside of the public persona he has created for himself, perhaps realizing he has arrogantly and too rigidly separated himself from other people (using Gehazi as a social screen).[4]

As the story progresses, it becomes clear that some situations even demand that the social graces be set aside entirely. When the prophet Elisha sends his servant Gehazi to investigate the condition of the Shunammite's son, he instructs him to make such haste that "if you meet anyone, give no greeting, and if anyone greets you, do not answer" (2 Kgs 4:29). The pragmatics of an extraordinary situation require a suspension of the normal use of language, in this case the full elimination of communication that might slow down the messenger.

---

hold of his feet and "worshipped him" (Matt 28:9). Note that after her son is revived the Shunammite once again soundlessly bows before the prophet and then departs with her son. This social gesture thus forms an inclusio in this portion of the story.

3. Cf. the episode in 2 Kgs 5:9-19 in which Elisha refuses to speak directly to Na'aman until after he has obeyed his instructions and received the cure for his leprosy.

4. See for this interpretation, Yairah Amit, "A Prophet Tested: Elisha, the Great Woman of Shunem, and the Story's Double Message," *BibInt* 11 (2003) 285-86.

or embedded dialogue. For example, speech and interpersonal communication are also governed to some extent by whether persons are members of a society that espouses "individualist" or "collectivist" views. This attitude will affect personal choice when actions or speech may have an effect on the group as a whole — that is, whether they are willing to subsume their own desires and personality to a collective set of beliefs. It will also determine whether a person is willing to engage readily in conflict or risky behavior.[21]

Ultimately, if someone's words or gestures are unintelligible, then full communication breaks down. This may result in attempts to find another

21. John A. Daly, "Personality and Interpersonal Communication," in *Handbook of Interpersonal Communication,* ed. Mark L. Knapp and Daly, 3rd ed. (Thousand Oaks: Sage, 2002) 139.

pathway to understanding — using other languages, pantomime, sign language, or seeking assistance from someone who may understand the speaker. It can be a truly disorienting experience to be in an unfamiliar locale or another country and be addressed by someone in a language that you do not understand. This often creates a sense of helplessness, fear, and a desire to remove oneself quickly to a place where "everyone speaks your language."

Still, given the social nature of humans, communication barriers generally are overcome and interpersonal communication is resumed on some level. Helpful in this regard is the realization that communication occurs through any of the senses. Agitation can be calmed through direct contact, with a hug or a firm handshake. Disagreement or passion may be expressed by a punch in the nose. Smell and taste convey meaning that can be turned into voiced statements or explained in written directions.[22] And, as they say, a picture is worth a thousand words.

With a failure to communicate at least partially alleviated, it has to be admitted that the vast majority of conversations tend to center around the broadest common cultural denominators, such as mundane exchanges remarking on the weather or the previous night's ball game.[23] While most of these exchanges are in the form of private conversations, they may also have a larger audience that may be only minimally aware of and influenced by what is said. That generally depends on whether the words or concepts are interesting enough to notice.

Public Conversations

Public conversations like those that take place on television talk shows or in public debates are intentionally designed to address both the persons immediately present as well as a wider audience. In both of these cases, power relationships will be on display. Some of these may be quite overt,

22. Ronald K. S. Macaulay, *The Social Art: Language and Its Uses* (New York: Oxford University Press, 1994) 13.

23. Richard Lapchick, "Sports and Public Behavior," in *Public Discourse in America: Conversation and Community in the Twenty-First Century,* ed. Judith Rodin and Stephen P. Steinberg (Philadelphia: University of Pennsylvania Press, 2003) 71. In addition, sports or political jargon and metaphors find their way into conventional speech, and fan loyalty can become both the source of pride and the basis for "fighting words."

such as the relationship between the moderator and the invited guests. Others are more subtle, since many conversations occur between social equals. However, culturally-determined social divisions based on such things as gender, race, or ethnicity do affect the construction of the language forms employed by both parties in every conversation.

One of the narrative episodes that display these social subtleties involves David's attempt to demonstrate how he repays his loyal allies (2 Sam 19:31-40). In this instance, David has just survived Absalom's revolt and is now performing a public ritual of rewarding those who helped him during his temporary exile and made it possible for him to return to the throne. Among those whom he especially wishes to reward is Barzillai the Gileadite, who "provided the king with food" while he gathered his forces in Mahanaim (19:32). The gift offered in this instance is the right to accompany the king back to Jerusalem and to benefit from royal patronage, as David says, to "provide for you in Jerusalem at my side" (19:33).[24]

Instead of graciously accepting this offer of royal hospitality, Barzillai demurs based on a twofold strategy. First, he says that he is an old man (80 years old) and that he realizes that he has little time left and wishes to spend it in his own land (2 Sam 19:34-36). This is certainly understandable and is not a true refusal, nor does it in any way impinge upon David's honor.[25] What is clever about his refusal of David's gift is the way in which he uses rhetorical gamesmanship to obtain a great deal more than what was initially offered. He plays on David's desire to receive public recognition and honor by reciprocating for services rendered, which is a critical aspect of the patronage system that centers on "loyalty" by both patron and client.[26]

Second, Barzillai uses self-deprecating language, referring to himself as a burden and one unworthy of such favor (2 Sam 19:35-36).[27] This height-

24. Niels Peter Lemche, "Kings and Clients: On Loyalty between the Ruler and the Ruled in Ancient 'Israel,'" in *Ethics and Politics in the Hebrew Bible,* ed. Douglas A. Knight. Semeia 66 (Atlanta: SBL, 1995) 120.

25. Erving Goffman, *Relations in Public: Microstudies of the Public Order* (New York: Basic Books, 1971) 63-65, details how interpersonal rituals have rules of performance that require proper acknowledgement of offerings but are flexible enough to allow for counterstatements while an expression of gratitude is clearly made.

26. Lemche, "Kings and Clients," 125.

27. George W. Coats, "Self-Abasement and Insult Formulas," *JBL* 89 (1970) 17-18, provides additional examples of the speech pattern from the Lachish letters and Amarna texts,

ens tension within the narrative and makes it easier for the king to accept the suggested transfer of the patronage position to the old man's son (or perhaps client; see 1 Kgs 2:7), Chimham (19:37-38). This younger man will likely enjoy the king's favor for many more years than Barzillai could have, and the place name Geruth-Chimham may well indicate the existence of a fief or land grant made to the family (Jer 41:17).[28] In this way, therefore, a gift offered to repay a political debt becomes a multigenerational grant and presumably the perpetuation of a political relationship for both families. It is also quite possible that David expected Barzillai to do this, and the old man's programmed response was part of the king's rhetorical strategy. Thus by using the rules of reciprocity to good advantage in this patterned discourse, both sides eventually obtain the solution they desired.[29]

Clearly, in formal settings such as public debate, "strategies of power" include efforts by opponents to position themselves so that they can gain an advantage (see a full discussion of positioning theory in Chapter 4). For instance, it is often the case that one speaker in a debate will exhort his opponent to "speak plainly" or "say what you really mean." As is made clear here, dialogue quite often hinges on the desire to elicit a reaction, functioning as part of a strategy such as playing for time, employing labeling as a method of flattering, weakening, or shocking one's conversation partner, or as an attempt to coerce that person and/or the audience through a variety of persuasion techniques.

Metaphors and Metonyms

We are somewhat handicapped in our desire to employ modern conversation theory in analyzing the biblical narratives because modern theory is based in large part on observable behavior as well as the current usage of language, cadence or volume of speech, the use of pauses, inflection, facial

---

as well as the biblical narrative. In particular, he points to the formula "what is your servant, the dog," expressing unworthiness (EA 201:14-16) or harmlessness (1 Sam 24:15[Eng. 14] or 2 Sam 16:9).

28. P. Kyle McCarter, *II Samuel*. AB 9 (Garden City: Doubleday, 1984) 422.

29. For further discussion of the protocols of public and private gift-giving, see Victor H. Matthews, "The Unwanted Gift: Implications of Obligatory Gift Giving in Ancient Israel," in *The Social World of the Hebrew Bible,* ed. Ronald Simkins and Stephen Cook. Semeia 87 (Atlanta: SBL, 1999) 91-104.

expressions, and gestures.[30] The dynamic nature of spoken dialogue, with its interruptions and overlapping voices, and the "mixture of redundancies and references to shared knowledge"[31] are not present in a written dialogue.

There is simply no way without direct glossing of the text (usually by employing the narrator's voice) to express such typical aspects of conversation as pauses, hand gestures, grimaces, or the use of varied inflexion or volume. As a result, "writing is unable to reproduce nonlinear, overlapping speech because of textual restraints. . . . Written conversation, by necessity, must be linear and maintain turn-taking between interlocutors."[32] If written dialogue is to flow, it is necessary for the storyteller to simulate some aspects of a live dialogue by creating a sense of disjointedness through half-voiced phrases and preemptory interruptions or commands. For example, when David questions the Amalekite who claims to have killed Saul, there is an evident raising of tensions, a sense that David is peppering the young man with accusatory questions, and an abrupt end to the proceedings with a summary execution (2 Sam 1:1-16).[33]

The fact of the matter is that none of the real-time, physical manifestations of conversation are overtly evident in the biblical narratives except through the cues provided by the storyteller or by the use of specific vocabulary or metaphors associated with emotions or sentiments such as anger.[34] Energy that is so much a part of a spoken conversation, especially when it becomes emotionally heated or intense, can lose a great deal in its translation to written form. For instance, it has been argued that people express their anger physiologically (increase in body heat and blood pressure), but these physical manifestations would be invisible to the audience of a written dialogue unless they are described for them.

A very creative aspect of written dialogue or description is the use of

30. B. Aubrey Fisher and Katherine L. Adams, *Interpersonal Communication: Pragmatics of Human Relationships,* 2nd ed. (New York: McGraw-Hill, 1994) 10-18. See also Janet B. Bavelas, Christine Kenwood, and Bruce Phillips, "Discourse Analysis," in Knapp and Daly, *Handbook of Interpersonal Communication,* 118-22.

31. Ryan Bishop, "There's Nothing Natural about Natural Conversation: A Look at Dialogue in Fiction and Drama." *Oral Tradition* 6 (1991) 60.

32. Bishop, "Nothing Natural," 61.

33. For a careful examination of other juridical dialogues and their structural and linguistic characteristics, see Asnat Bartor, "The 'Juridical Dialogue': A Literary-Judicial Pattern," *VT* 53 (2003) 445-64.

34. Paul A. Kruger, "A Cognitive Interpretation of the Emotion of Anger in the Hebrew Bible," *JNSL* 26 (2000) 183-85.

Cognition Through Metaphor and Metonym
in Speech or Writing

As a rule, poetry tends to be metaphoric while prose is more adaptable to metonymic expressions.

Metaphors are phrases that use analogy to communicate meaning. They conceptualize emotions or feelings by explaining or interpreting one thing in comparison with another. For example, the male lover in Song 4:1 passionately extols how the object of his affection has "hair like a flock of goats, moving down the slopes of Gilead." While this analogy is not one we would ordinarily use today, and that makes the metaphor less dynamic for modern readers, in the pastoral culture of ancient Israel, coupling the beauty of a beloved young woman with the prosperity associated with a fine flock of goats makes sense and provides insight into the society and the author.[1] An important strand in cognitive linguistics, associated especially with the work of George Lakoff and Mark Johnson,[2] claims that metaphor is much more than a literary ornament; it permeates much of our thinking, and hence our language.[3] It is difficult, in fact,

1. See the discussion of the relative degree of intimacy established for the "decoder" or reader by easily recognized and more esoteric or "dead" metaphors in Jutka Dévényi, *Metonymy and Drama: Essays on Language and Dramatic Strategy* (Lewisburg: Bucknell University Press, 1996) 23-24.

2. *Metaphors We Live By* (Chicago: University of Chicago Press, 1980).

3. Arthur Asa Berger, *Cultural Criticism: A Primer of Key Concepts* (Thousand Oaks: Sage, 1995) 86-87.

metaphor and metonym to provide a graphic range of meanings and to conceptualize emotions. Some claim that metaphor in fact "permeates all discourse, ordinary and special."[35] Certainly, it is an expression of worldview, and it symbolically exemplifies the manner in which appropriate comparison can be made to deepen meaning or to register a sense of heightened aesthetic or physiological emotions. Metonymic expressions also allow for representation of meaning by focusing on a single aspect or condition of an object, such as the body, to make a point. For example, after

35. Nelson Goodman, *Languages of Art* (Indianapolis: Bobbs-Merrill, 1968) 80.

to speak without using metaphors, especially ones associated with sports as in Paul's assessment: "I have fought the good fight, I have finished the race" (2 Tim 4:7). They help us structure the way we think, allow us to orient ourselves both in space and in terms of polar opposites, and provide us with a means of interpreting life through comparison with common objects.[4]

Metonymy is a figure of speech in which reference is made to something or someone by naming one of its attributes. The key to its effectiveness is whether the referent or audience shares a well-understood or easy-to-perceive aspect of that object with the author. Then when that single aspect is used to stand either for the thing as a whole or for some part of it, little conscious effort is needed for the image to work. For instance, when Ps 80:3 calls on God to "let your face shine," it is a prayer for God's favor on the people and takes into account the physiological flushing of the skin when energy is exerted or high emotions are raised.[5] Similarly, Prov 3:1 provides the injunction to "let your heart keep my commandments." In this case, the heart is viewed as the repository of the intellect and a metonym for the entire being rather than just an essential organ pumping blood to the body.

---

4. Lakoff and Johnson, *Metaphors We Live By*, 3.

5. See Zoltan Kövecses, "Anger: Its Language, Conceptualization, and Physiology," in *Language and the Cognitive Construal of the World*, ed. John R. Taylor and Robert E. MacLaury (Berlin: Mouton de Gruyter, 1995) 190-91.

Adam and Eve are expelled from the garden of Eden, they are told that if they wish to eat they will have to obtain it "by the sweat of your face" = work (Gen 3:19).

To illustrate this, George Lakoff and Zoltan Kövecses[36] employ a

---

36. "The Cognitive Model of Anger Inherent in American English," in *Cultural Models in Language and Thought*, ed. Dorothy C. Holland and Naomi Quinn, 6th ed. (Cambridge: Cambridge University Press, 1995) 196-204. According to this model, the general metonymic principle is that the physiological effects of an emotion stand for that emotion, and thus we can derive the following metonyms for body heat: "hot under the collar," "hothead," and "hot and bothered."

"container metaphor" for the process of describing how "anger is the heat that reacts to a fluid in a container." With the body serving as a container for the emotions and anger as the heat that then puts pressure on the fluids of the emotions, human action and angry speech are generated by "over-heating." Thus when Moses saw the Israelites dancing before the image of the golden calf, his "anger burned hot, and he threw the tablets from his hand" (Exod 32:19).[37] Another good example of this metaphorical and physiological process is found in Jeremiah's mournful soliloquy that expresses his despair after being abandoned by his friends and made a laughingstock by being placed in the public stocks. He angrily accuses God of "enticing" him (pittîtanî) into speaking harsh words of "violence and destruction."[38] This clearly indicates that Jeremiah felt that he had been badly used by the deity, and he is not shy in voicing his complaint. The negative reactions he has received to his oracles have made the prophet reluctant to continue his mission. However, whenever he attempts to contain God's words within him he feels a compulsion, "something like a burning fire shut up in my bones" that he cannot hold back (Jer 20:7-9).[39]

Given the restraints imposed by written dialogue, the reader must be careful to examine such narrative techniques as the use of metaphors and metonyms, stylized rhetorical devices, and graphic verbs by the author as indicators of action and speech.[40] Conventionalized conversational cues such as the use of particular vocabulary and syntax can be analyzed.[41]

---

37. For other examples, see Ps 39:3, "my heart became hot within me," and a wrathful God "speaking in my hot jealousy" in Ezek 36:5.

38. Other appearances of the Hebrew word he uses for "entice" in Exod 22:15(Eng. 16) and Hos 2:16(Eng. 14) have negative connotations of "seducing" a virgin and "tricking" a husband, respectively. See William L. Holladay, *Jeremiah 1*. Hermeneia (Philadelphia: Fortress, 1986) 552. S. D. Snyman, "A Note on *pth* and *ykl* in Jeremiah xx 7-13," *VT* 48 (1998) 562, separates the two words for "seduce" to indicate that one refers to Yahweh's prevailing over Jeremiah and the other, in v. 10, refers to the failed attempt of Jeremiah's enemies to deceive him into a misstep and thus foil God's mission.

39. Jeremiah expresses a similar compulsion to speak of God's wrath in 6:11.

40. Deborah Tannen, "Introducing Constructed Dialogue in Greek and American Conversational and Literary Narrative," in *Direct and Indirect Speech*, ed. Florian Coulmas (Berlin: Mouton de Gruyter, 1986) 323.

41. See Dennis Robert Magary, "Answering Questions, Questioning Answers: The Rhetoric of Interrogatives in the Speeches of Job and His Friends," in *Seeking Out the Wisdom of the Ancients*, ed. Ronald L. Troxel, Kelvin G. Friebel, and Magary (Winona Lake: Eisenbrauns, 2005) 283-98.

Plus, with a careful examination of the text, the reader can establish some elements of the setting, the positioning of those in a conversation, and the forms of speech they use.[42] Of course, it is also necessary to keep in mind that it is the author/editor's intentions that have framed this narrative. The speech and the reaction of the characters, and any apparent thought process or retrospective analysis by either the narrator or the characters, are a creation of the storyteller rather than a faithful transcription of the words as they were spoken.

Ultimately, it is apparent that textual perspective is defined by the contents of the narrative that represent the way the person speaks, observes, or thinks about his or her circumstances.[43] Actions or speech are therefore predicated on the propositional contents and the thought process that results when the characters sense what has been presented to them. This ongoing, evolving process drives the narrative forward based on the social interaction of the participants. Plus it is the character's cognitive process at work that serves as a further guide to the reader of what to expect and how he or she may also react to events in the narrative.[44] This can be facilitated by the storyteller when the narrator is employed to speak indirectly, portraying the character's point of view and representing the character's thinking process. For example, when the narrator notes that Moses observed a burning bush that "was not consumed," Moses' thinking process is revealed with the embedded internal speech, "I must turn aside and look at this great sight, and see why the bush is not burned up" (Exod 3:1-3). The narrator's cue also helps to guide the reader as the next episode of the story unfolds.

As we will see in subsequent chapters in this volume, temporal forms and spatial indicators in the text can combine with verbal forms to create powerful guides to textual perspective for the reader.[45] In fact, temporal

---

42. See George W. Ramsey, "Speech-Forms in Hebrew Law and Prophetic Oracles," *JBL* 96 (1977) 45-58; and Ellen Davis Lewin, "Arguing for Authority: A Rhetorical Study of Jeremiah 1:4-19 and 20:7-18," *JSOT* 32 (1985) 105-19.

43. Ellen van Wolde, "Who Guides Whom? Embeddedness and Perspective in Biblical Hebrew and in 1 Kings 3:16-28," *JBL* 114 (1995) 626.

44. Guy Cook, *Discourse and Literature* (Oxford: Oxford University Press, 1994) 46, points to this type of analysis as ethnomethodology, a form of conversation analysis that avoids imposing narrative structures on the text and instead focuses on the local level of the participants in the dialogue.

45. Van Wolde, "Who Guides Whom?" 625.

and spatial indicators can be either comforting signs of normalcy or jarring signals of abnormality. They can be used by the storyteller through the words of the narrator or the implied perspective of the character to suggest tension, danger, or fantastic situations (supernatural appearances or visions). Thus when the narrator notes in Ruth 1:22 that Naomi and Ruth had returned to Bethlehem "at the beginning of the barley harvest," the audience immediately places this story into a specific time period (mid to late April as the rainy season came to an end) and this "time cue" drives the rest of the action in the story. If the women had come to some other location, the temporal form might well have been different, since the barley harvest does not come at exactly the same time in every place.

Of course, it is the vibrant drama of the story as told that ultimately draws the audience into the action.[46] Interpretation of the text must therefore take into account both what can be learned about the authorial/editorial process as well as the words contained in the narrative and the impression they have on the audience. This also raises the caution that assumptions about what is meant by these written words may not reflect the full meaning attached to them by the ancient author or the original audience.[47]

Discourse Analysis

One method that has attempted to work with both "live" communication and with the reported or constructed voices contained in written texts is discourse analysis.[48] Although numerous methodologies are associated with discourse analysis, one of its most important purposes is to serve as "an approach to studying language's relation to the contextual background features."[49] The various methods associated with this approach require a thorough study of the use of language forms, syntax, word order, and the context in which words are used in embedded dialogue or the surrounding narrative. It includes meanings related to the physical world, social under-

46. Tannen, "Introducing Constructed Dialogue," 312.

47. Bavelas, Kenwood, and Phillips, "Discourse Analysis," 117.

48. A particularly helpful summary of the history and various strategies employed in discourse analysis is found in Robert B. Kaplan and William Grabe, "A Modern History of Written Discourse Analysis," *Journal of Second Language Writing* 11 (2002) 191-223.

49. Joan Cutting, *Pragmatics and Discourse* (London: Routledge, 2002) 1-2.

standings, as well as some knowledge of the time and place in which the statements are made.[50]

Proponents of discourse analysis are interested in establishing "patterns and regularities" in language, but they are also concerned with the people who use this language. Thus a particular usage of a pronoun, phrase, or conjunction allows for the creation of relationships between people or events that can then be represented coherently in discourse on different occasions.[51] The way in which language is used to shape a discourse also betrays ideological viewpoint or context for a story. The very ways in which the storyteller describes the world betray a social agenda and power relationships.[52]

Evidence of a discriminatory ideological and political agenda is found in the story of David's service with the Philistines. When David joins the assembly of chiefs gathered to plan a battle, several of the commanders take exception to his presence, asking why "the servant of King Saul of Israel" should be present. In this context the phrase serves as a negative label because it is spoken by the Philistines (1 Sam 29:3). Even though David has been serving for several years as a mercenary chief in their service, they do not recognize his loyalty or abilities, and they reject him as a reliable ally as they prepare to go to war against Saul (29:4-5). To bolster their argument against him, the Philistine leaders display their already heightened suspicions by citing a taunting song sung about David's prowess in killing Philistines when he was still serving Saul as a military commander (29:5; cf. 18:7 and 21:11[MT 12]). Even the strongly voiced assurances of David's value by his Philistine patron, Achish, "I have found no fault in him to this day" (29:3b, 6, 9), cannot convince them otherwise. The context of this argument betrays that David has been unable to escape completely this damaging label (enemy). Therefore the interests of the Philistine elite are best served by forcing him to stand aside as their army goes to war.[53]

When using discourse analysis it is important to classify the type of

---

50. Bavelas, Kenwood, and Phillips, "Discourse Analysis," 103-4.

51. David Nunan, *Introducing Discourse Analysis* (London: Penguin, 1993) 57.

52. Robin Wooffitt, *Conversation Analysis and Discourse Analysis* (London: Sage, 2005) 139-41.

53. As Walter Brueggemann, "Narrative Intentionality in 1 Samuel 29," *JSOT* 43 (1989) 25-27, notes, this actually spares David from direct participation in Saul's death. However, it is an excellent example of how difficult it is to escape one's reputation when there are such handy narrative mnemonics available.

communication being employed. For instance, an example of passive communication would be Ruth's diligently working in Boaz's field all day. Her silent message of determination to survive elicits a response from Boaz's foreman that she had communicated model behavior as a dutiful daughter-in-law (Ruth 2:3-7).[54] A more active form of communication would include Nathan's confronting David over his adulterous affair with Bathsheba. The prophet goes directly to the king and tells him the juridical parable of the ewe lamb. Then, following David's judgment of the case against a greedy rich man, Nathan concludes with the ringing indictment, "You are the man!" (2 Sam 12:1-7). After Nathan harangues David with a series of troubles that he will subsequently experience within his own house, David's response to this prophetic complaint against him is to say "I have sinned against the Lord" (12:7-13). Such a quick acceptance of guilt is not the typical response in situations of argumentative complaint and riposte.[55] However, David's acceptance of Nathan's accusation fits into a narrative pattern found in other prophet-king confrontations, and it serves the agenda of the editor to portray royal remorse in the face of God's judgment.[56]

Clearly, if discourse analysis is to be used effectively as a method for examining the received biblical narrative, it will involve a "commitment to the study of connected texts . . . and a concern with how people use language to accomplish social purposes."[57] Before we proceed, however, a further caution is needed since our modern Western culture is separated not only in time and space from the ancient Near East, but also in its orientation towards technology. As Ryan Bishop points out, "Western culture values things, or nouns if applicable, and interprets much of the world as 'thing' rather than process, or verb" while "many primary oral cultures . . . display biases toward processes."[58]

54. See Victor H. Matthews, *Judges and Ruth.* NCambBC (Cambridge: Cambridge University Press, 2004) 227.

55. Angela Garcia, "Dispute Resolution Without Disputing: How the Interactional Organization of Mediation Hearings Minimizes Argument," *American Sociological Review* 56 (1991) 821, points to denial as the more common response to accusation since "the absence or delay of a denial may be interpreted as an admission of/evidence of guilt."

56. For a full treatment of this motif, see Victor H. Matthews, "The King's Call to Justice," *BZ* 35 (1991) 204-16.

57. Karen Tracy, "Discourse," in *Studying Interpersonal Interaction,* ed. Barbara M. Montgomery and Steve Duck (New York: Guilford, 1991) 179.

58. "Nothing Natural," 59.

Emotions Expressed Physiologically and Linguistically

Fear: The various physiological reactions to fear are expressed by "appalled" *(hāšammû)*, "dismayed" *(nibhāltî)*, and "shuddering" *(pallāṣût)* in Job's reference to his affliction and are coupled with the physical gesture of laying the hand on the mouth (Job 21:5-6).[1]

Pride: This is generally considered an undesirable attribute that in the biblical narrative expresses insolence, selfishness, and arrogance. Its physiological manifestation may be found in the sense of "blossoming" pride *(zādôn;* Ezek 7:10)[2] that may have brought a flushing to the face or countenance (Ps 10:4) like someone who is overheated with ambition or anger (see Tob 2:14).

Grief: Among the conventional means of expressing grief and its physiological characteristics is the phrase "my eyes waste away from grief" (Job 17:7; Ps 6:7[MT 8]; 31:9[MT 10]; Lam 3:51; *ʿāšěšâ běkaʿas ʿênî)*. The swelling of the eyes caused by constant weeping and sorrow also appears in Ps 88:9(MT 10) *(ʿênî dāʾăbâ)*. Metaphorically, this emotion is said to "gnaw at the heart" like a worm through wood (Prov 25:20 NRSV).

---

1. See Jer 2:12; Ezek 27:35; 32:10 for the use of the term "shudder" *(šaʿar)* as a physical manifestation of fear or horror.

2. Daniel I. Block, *The Book of Ezekiel: Chapters 1–24*. NICOT (Grand Rapids: Wm. B. Eerdmans, 1997) 256, notes how association with *zādôn*, "pride or insolence," transforms a positive connotation of the "blossoming" rod that is usually associated with fertility and legitimate election to authority (Aaron's rod in Num 17:1-10) into one of wickedness and deceit.

Furthermore, unless the author chooses to write in a vernacular dialect,[59] written dialogue seldom includes the choppiness of normal speech patterns, the unconscious grammatical errors, or a true sense of the emotions that accompany a verbal exchange. It therefore becomes the role of the narrator to add some of the background or psychological qualities that accompany most conversations. For instance, when trying to express emo-

---

59. An example of the effort to identify variations in word usage based on class or social location is B. S. J. Isserlin, "Epigraphically Attested Judean Hebrew, and the Question of 'Upper Class' (Official) and 'Popular' Speech Variants in Judean During the 8th-6th Centuries B.C.," *AJBA* 2 (1972), 193-203.

tions such as anger, love, pride, fear, and grief, linguistic concepts play a role in showcasing these reactions by the characters.[60]

In writing a story that contains embedded dialogue, it can be assumed that the author and/or editors are attempting to communicate not only meaning, but also relevance and context.[61] To fulfill this goal the storyteller provides a cueing system that alerts the audience with shifts in tense, the introduction of new characters, locales, or temporal features.[62] For example, as the analysis of Genesis 38 that appears in Chapter 2 below demonstrates, there are repeated attempts to let the audience know that Judah did not recognize Tamar when he propositioned her and subsequently had intercourse with her. However, the significance of her wearing a veil (other than its value as a disguise) is not explained, nor is the significance of her sitting "at the entrance to Enaim." This in turn results in cognitive gaps for modern audiences of the narrative.

One sociolinguistic approach to discourse analysis allows the reader to appreciate better the nuances of a written text through what Deborah Tannen calls "involvement theory."[63] She points to the use of eight major mechanisms by the author/storyteller: rhythm, repetition, figures of speech, indirection and ellipsis, tropes, detail and imagery, dialogue, and narratives. For example, rhythm "refers to the many tempos, harmonies, beats, and intensities" that can enliven a text, build suspense, or signal action.[64] In Biblical Hebrew, a system of accents regulates junctions and pauses, thereby creating a rhythm that in turn governs the chanting of the

---

60. Zoltán Kövecses, *Emotion Concepts* (New York: Springer, 1990) 43-45.

61. One could argue over the integrity of the received text, likelihood of proper word order, or even the exact translation of each word. However, the intent of this volume, while admitting the difficulties inherent to textual criticism and the establishment of a "sound text," is to work with what is currently considered to be a stable text based on current scholarship. It is also understood, as Leroy F. Seale notes, that any edition or version cannot be totally "purified of the choices made and the interests served by the editor or interpreter"; "Emerging Questions: Text and Theory in Contemporary Criticism," in *Voice, Text, Hypertext,* ed. Raimonda Modiano, Seale, and Peter Shillingsburg (Seattle: University of Washington Press, 2004) 12.

62. See the syntactic structural approach to discourse analysis in Talmy Gívón, "Coherence in Text vs. Coherence in Mind," in *Coherence in Spontaneous Text,* ed. Morton Ann Gernsbacher and Gívón (Amsterdam: Benjamins, 1995) 59-115, esp. 81.

63. Deborah Tannen, *Talking Voices* (Cambridge: Cambridge University Press, 1989).

64. See the discussion of poetic elements including repetition and rhythmic pattern in Léo Laberge, "The Woe-oracles of Isaiah 28-33," *Eglise et théologie* 13 (1982) 157-90.

Communicative Elements in Narrative

1. Social setting of the characters
2. Gender roles of the characters involved, how they are portrayed in the story, and how that is a reflection of the culture
3. Positioning and repositioning of the characters at each point in the dialogue
4. Symbolic objects and props employed to signal social meanings
5. Realization that words, gestures, and objects may have multiple meanings and motivations based on all of the above

verses and thus regulates the meaning.[65] Repetition, such as Jeremiah's ironic threefold repetition of the phrase "the temple of the Lord" (Jer 7:4), is certainly an attention-getter, and it provides the prophet a way to mimic the chant used by worshippers as they entered the temple gateway.[66] As the readers make inferences about and interpret the text, they are more closely drawn into the world created by the storyteller.

Within narrative, the reader is guided by verbal forms (tense, person) and discourse markers that indicate to the audience when a quoted statement is about to be made or to signal the beginning of narrative frames that section off exchanges of direct speech. These discourse markers bracket units of talk and consist of conjunctions (and, but, or), interjections (oh!, lo!; *hēn*), adverbs (now, then; Deut 4:1, *wĕʿattâ*), and lexical phrases (as you know; Deut 11:30, *hălōʾ-hēmmâ;* Gen 37:13, *hălôʾ*). Because these markers are not used exclusively to introduce speech, but have an intrinsic multifunctionality, this allows them occasionally to add extra meaning or emotion to the discourse.[67]

---

65. Henri Meschonnic, "Translating Biblical Rhythm," in *Biblical Patterns in Modern Literature,* ed. David H. Hirsch and Nehama Aschkenasy. BJS 77 (Chico: Scholars, 1984) 233-39, uses this principle to discuss the rhythm found in the geographic description of Shechem in Deut 11:30.

66. Holladay, *Jeremiah 1,* 242.

67. Deborah Schiffrin, "Discourse Markers: Language, Meaning, and Context," in *The Handbook of Discourse Analysis,* ed. Schiffrin, Deborah Tannen, and Heidi E. Hamilton (Oxford: Blackwell, 2001) 56-58.

Background material, provided by the narrator, contains the role and perspective of each speaker (narrator or character).[68] Reported or quoted speech that is embedded in a narrative chronicles for the reader the statements made by characters, at least to the extent that the storyteller allows, and it provides a more personal note to the story than straight narration. It is quite likely that the reader or listener is more alert to quoted words in embedded speech/discourse than to the signals by the narrator that provide background information or indicate when a character is about to speak.

Direct speech is shaped in the narrative as dialogue between characters, which perks up our ears to listen more carefully and allows us to empathize with or identify with the speaker(s) better. In Biblical Hebrew narrative the verb *'mr* is used to signal direct speech when it is in its conjugated form, while when it appears in its infinitive form, *lē'mōr*, it signals "free direct discourse" such as "internal monologues or thoughts" and "communication acts performed by means other than speech."[69] However, when it is introduced linguistically, the construction of dialogue is a "narrative act" that allows the storyteller to construct motivations within the story rather than having to step out as a narrator to speak to the audience.[70] It is often combined with noninteractive reflections by one or both of the characters signaling through "unspeakable" sentences to the audience their nonverbalized viewpoint of events that have just occurred.[71]

Given these two forms of direct and indirect speech, the reader is much more alert to the nuances implied in the verbal exchange between Ahab and Naboth over the purchase of the latter's vineyard (1 Kgs 21:2-3) than would have been the case if the entire incident had been chronicled in

---

68. In the case of the biblical corpus, there are sufficient syntactic and stylistic differences between the material in Genesis through 2 Kings and that in the later biblical works (Chronicles, Ezra, Nehemiah, and Esther) that they may be treated separately. See Cynthia L. Miller, *The Representation of Speech in Biblical Hebrew Narrative*. HSS 55 (Atlanta: Scholars, 1996) 19-20. Her study addresses both diachronic variations that occur over time and synchronic variations of language use during the same time period (see pp. 26-29).

69. See the complete discussion of this use of *wayyō'mer* for direct speech and *lē'mōr* for free indirect discourse in Galia Hatav, "(Free) Direct Discourse in Biblical Hebrew," *HS* 41 (2000) 7-30, esp. 8-9. Compare her treatment with that in Miller, *The Representation of Speech*, 371-95.

70. Tannen, "Introducing Constructed Dialogue," 325.

71. Benjamin Lee, *Talking Heads: Language, Metalanguage, and the Semiotics of Subjectivity* (Durham: Duke University Press, 1997) 301-2.

the more sterile voice of the narrator. While the king appears to make a reasonable offer, he does not seem to be prepared for his subject's very passionate riposte, an oath declaring his refusal to give up his family's "ancestral inheritance." The king's embedded thought process is a form of noninteractive reported speech that serves as a way to indicate to the audience the internal musings that then lead to action.[72]

In this case, Ahab's personal take on Naboth's words, based in part on embarrassment and on chagrin over being stymied, becomes progressively more sullen and hostile (1 Kgs 21:4), and this adds to the overall tension in this portion of the narrative.[73] The potential for a dangerous and foolish reaction then becomes clear in the exchange between Ahab and Jezebel. Instead of providing a complete recital of Naboth's response, Ahab abbreviates it, saying only "I will not give you my vineyard" (v. 6) without any mention of Naboth's real reason for denying the king's request. Jezebel, coming from a political context in which the king's word is law, is apparently shocked and initially taunts him with a cuttingly sarcastic remark, "Do you now govern Israel?" (v. 7). While this is a statement of fact, it also contains the implication, given the tone of her later remarks that a true ruler would not be acting in such a craven fashion.[74]

Seeing that she must take charge, Jezebel treats Ahab like a child, telling him to eat his supper and cheer up because she will surely get what the king wants for him. With such a charged exchange of dialogue, the audience has been primed for high level plotting and violence and it soon follows. Naboth will become the victim of a judicially orchestrated murder that leaves Ahab with his cherished piece of land. However, all this then serves as a narrative prelude to the angry exchange between a very aggressive prophet (Elijah) and the king. The scene begins with Ahab's ironic and intrinsically guilty greeting, "Have you found me, O my enemy?" (1 Kgs 21:20).[75] Elijah matches his response to Ahab's "I have found you," and

72. Miller, *The Representation of Speech,* 37-38.

73. See the analysis of this dialogue in Meir Sternberg, *The Poetics of Biblical Narrative* (Bloomington: Indiana University Press, 1985) 431, 436.

74. Penny M. Pexman and Kara M. Olineck, "Does Sarcasm Always Sting? Investigating the Impact of Ironic Insults and Ironic Compliments," *Discourse Processes* 33 (2002) 203, discusses how the tone of voice determines whether a statement contains ironic implications, but in this case it also has to do with Jezebel's awareness of administrative practices in her father's royal court in Phoenicia.

75. John H. Leggitt and Raymond W. Gibbs, Jr., "Emotional Reactions to Verbal

then the prophet curses the king's household for such a blatant act of tyranny (21:21-24).

Final Thoughts

During the course of further discussion of discourse analysis in subsequent chapters, the various methodologies that have been discussed above, as well as others, will be employed in extended form. While the primary focus in these chapters will be on a careful analysis of select pericopes from the biblical narrative, several questions need to be kept in mind:

- What do persons actually accomplish by telling stories?[76]
- How do discourse communities (those who share common stories) preserve and use their stories to educate, socialize, and perpetuate themselves?[77]
- What do these stories tell us about their culture, their social customs, their laws, and their sense of identity?
- Given the many stories that must have existed in ancient Israel, why was a particular story told/written down in this particular manner?
- How do we overcome the handicap of our outsider (etic) perspective to get a closer glimpse into the world of the storyteller?

Irony," *Discourse Processes* 29 (2000) 3, points to strategies employed by persons, like Ahab, whose ambitions have been frustrated and so they strike out angrily using aggressive speech, including irony.

76. See Deborah Schiffrin, "Narrative as Self-Portrait: Sociolinguistic Constructions of Identity," *Language and Society* 25 (1996) 167-203.

77. See the bibliographic references on group cohesion provided by Barbara Johnstone, "Discourse Analysis and Narrative," in Schiffrin, Tannen, and Hamilton, *The Handbook of Discourse Analysis,* 641.

CHAPTER TWO

Discourse and Cognition
in the Story of Judah and Tamar

As a way to demonstrate some of the values of the methods associated with discourse analysis, and in particular cognitive linguistics, we now turn to the story of Judah and Tamar in Genesis 38. It is part of a larger unit associated with stories about Jacob and his sons, and most especially with the stories of Joseph.[1] Aaron Wildavsky suggests that the story's relevance to the Joseph narrative is in providing "a model of the right path for the Hebrew people to take," since it "teaches leaders they cannot save their people by violating the moral law."[2] The story is primarily focused on marriage customs, inheritance rights, and in particular the levirate obligation that a family owes to a deceased, childless son. Strict attention to gender roles within the context of their socio-economic function in the village culture also plays a part in the storyteller's narrative scheme.[3]

1. See Anthony J. Lambe, "Judah's Development: The Pattern of Departure-Transition-Return," *JSOT* 83 (1999) 53-55, for a survey of the literature on the chapter's placement within the Joseph cycle.

2. "Survival Must Not Be Gained through Sin: The Moral of the Joseph Stories Prefigured through Judah and Tamar," *JSOT* 62 (1994) 38.

3. See Cheris Kramarae, Candace West, and Michelle M. Lazar, "Gender in Discourse," in *Discourse as Social Interaction,* ed. Teun A. van Dijk (London: Sage, 1997) 2:122.

Structural Elements of the Narrative

The first portion of chapter 38 (vv. 1-11) provides a genealogical link to the other two sections, but also sets up the theme of procreation that runs throughout the narrative.[4] Embedded within the second section of this tale are two conversations between Judah and Tamar. One is a transactional dialogue including Judah's propositioning of a person he mistakenly believes is a prostitute, and the other contains non-face-to-face speeches that are concerned with the determination of guilt in the case of Tamar's pregnancy. Indirect communication through intermediaries[5] and the quiet presentation of irrefutable evidence ultimately resolve the tensions that have been created in the narrative and return the characters to their more normal or ordinary conditions.

> ACT ONE, SCENE ONE:
>
> v. 1 Judah "went down" from his brothers to live near Hirah the Adullamite.
>
> v. 2 Judah marries a Canaanite woman, and he "went in" to her.
>
> v. 3 Judah names his first son Er.
>
> vv. 4-5 Judah's wife bears two more sons, and she names them Onan and Shelah.
>
> v. 6 Judah "took" a wife, named Tamar, for his son Er.

> ACT ONE, SCENE TWO:
>
> v. 7 Er is wicked, and God "put him to death."
>
> v. 8 Judah orders Onan to "go in" to his brother's wife to perform the duty of levir.
>
> v. 9 Onan uses *coitus interruptus* to prevent conception and prevent giving offspring to his brother, knowing the child would not be his own.

---

4. See Esther Marie Menn, *Judah and Tamar (Genesis 38) in Ancient Jewish Exegesis.* JSJSup 51 (Leiden: Brill, 1997) 15-18, for this early section.

5. This is a form of third order positioning in which a character speaks to other persons who were not part of the original dialogue and thereby creates a personalized version of events that will be used to position that character in future actions. See Luk van Langenhove and Rom Harré, "Introducing Positioning Theory," in *Positioning Theory: Moral Contexts of Intentional Action,* ed. Harré and Langenhove (Oxford: Blackwell, 1999) 21. This method will be discussed in more detail in a later chapter.

v. 10 This displeases God, and the deity kills Onan.

v. 11 Judah orders Tamar to "remain a widow in your father's house" until his third son is old enough to perform the duties of levir — based on his fear of losing his last son.[6]

ACT TWO, SCENE ONE:

v. 12 Judah's wife dies, and after the period of mourning Judah goes up with Hirah to the sheepshearing.

v. 13 Tamar hears that Judah has gone to the sheepshearing.

v. 14 Tamar removes her widow's garments, exchanging them for a veil, and sits at "the entrance to Enaim" on the road to Timnah — doing this because Shelah, now grown, had not been sent to her.

v. 15 Judah sees her, thinks she is a prostitute, "for she had covered her face."

v. 16a Judah "went over to her" and asks "let me come in to you" — not knowing she is his daughter-in-law.

v. 16b Tamar responds, "What will you give me, that you may come in to me?"

v. 17a Judah offers a kid from the flock.

v. 17b Tamar responds, "Only if you give me a pledge, until you send it."

v. 18a Judah asks, "What pledge shall I give you?"

v. 18b Tamar responds, "Your signet and your cord, and the staff that is in your hand."

v. 18c Judah gives her these items, he "went in" to her, and she conceives.

v. 19 Tamar leaves, takes off her veil, and puts on her widow's garments.

ACT TWO, SCENE TWO:

v. 20 Judah sends Hirah with the kid to recover the pledge, but he cannot find her.

v. 21 Hirah asks the people of Enaim, "Where is the temple prostitute?" and they respond, "No prostitute has been here."

---

6. Cf. how David instructs 10 of his concubines to remain behind in his palace when he flees from Absalom's army in 2 Sam 20:3.

v. 22 Hirah reports to Judah, saying he hasn't found her, and quotes the people of Enaim.

v. 23 Judah says, "Let her keep the things . . . otherwise we will be laughed at" and justifies himself, saying, "I sent this kid, and you could not find her."

ACT THREE, SCENE ONE:

v. 24a Three months later Judah is informed that Tamar "has played the whore" and is pregnant.

v. 24b Judah orders that she be brought out and burned.

v. 25 Tamar sends word to Judah that "the owner of these . . . made me pregnant" and that he should identify "whose these are, the signet and the cord and the staff."

v. 26a Judah acknowledges ownership and issues the judgment, "She is more in the right than I, since I did not give her my son Shelah."[7]

v. 26b Judah "did not lie with her again."[8]

ACT THREE, SCENE TWO:

v. 27 At the time of delivery it is determined that she has twins in her womb.

v. 28 During labor one child puts out his hand and the midwife ties a crimson thread, saying, "This one came out first."

v. 29 After the hand is withdrawn, the other child is actually born first, and the midwife says, "What a *breach* you have made for yourself!" naming him Perez.

v. 30 The second child is born, and he is named Zerah ("brightness").

Conversational Analysis

An ancient author, when attempting to create a plausible fiction or to recount the details of a historical event, must abide by the social and cultural

---

7. Cf. the charges made against Israel's "princes," who fail "to defend the orphan and the widow's cause" (Isa 1:23).

8. Cf. David's treatment of Michal after she rebukes him for his "vulgar" display of his body "before the eyes of his servants' maids" (2 Sam 6:20-23). She is forced to remain childless, a virtual captive within his harem.

realities of his audience. Fantastic images do appear in ancient writing, especially in apocalyptic literature or fable, but they are not intended to be taken at face value.[9] Only those stories that mirror the actions, voices/vocabulary, and settings familiar to the current audience can be considered realistic and therefore comfortable to the ear or the mind's eye. One side effect of a comfortable story, however, is the high level of "insider" (emic) cultural and physical assumptions made by the author. As might be expected, there is seldom any attempt made, except by later editors, to provide cultural explanations or to enhance descriptions of everyday items. For instance, in 38:14 Tamar is said to be wearing "widow's garments," but there is no description of their appearance or style. In like manner, the sudden death of Er is given only the sketchiest explanation: he "was wicked in the sight of the Lord" (v. 7). There is no indication in the text why Judah's staff and seal are of such importance and value (v. 18). Also, Judah's summary sentence of death for the unfaithful Tamar apparently raises no legal issues or requires any justification or explanation for the ancient audience. Despite what we might consider to be cultural gaps in the story, part of the task in the analysis of the tale, and especially the conversations between Judah and Tamar, will require explanation based on comparative materials and cultural practices still evident among the traditional peoples of the Middle East.

Conversations like those found in Genesis 38 are constructed of more than an exchange of words between at least two people. The mental backdrop to the conversation includes socially-recognized and agreed-upon concepts or cognitive representations that identify the characters, the setting, and the language they employ.[10] These concepts encompass their relative power relationships based on kinship, age, gender, rank, or social status. In addition, the physical setting in which their conversation takes place and various temporal factors, such as the season of the year or the occurrence of a festival or regularly-scheduled economic activity, need to be examined. In addition to these cognitive elements, there are multiple

---

9. See Peter D. Miscall, "Biblical Narrative and Categories of the Fantastic," in *Fantasy and the Bible,* ed. George Aichele and Tina Pippin, 39-52. Semeia 60 (Atlanta: Scholars, 1992).

10. Ellen van Wolde, "Cognitive Linguistics and Its Application to Genesis 28:10-22," in *One Text, a Thousand Methods,* ed. Patrick Chatelion Counet and Ulrich Berges (Boston: Brill, 2005) 126.

Cognitive Triggers in Genesis 38

Spatial setting: The text establishes a mental base for the encounter between Judah and Tamar. In this way "the readers get access to the information through the narrator's mind."[1] Thus the roadside on the way to Enaim functions as a physical frame of reference for the conversation between Judah and Tamar. According to mental space theory (see below), the cognitive world created by this space lends it the social parameters that will direct the participants in this drama to speak and act in a specific manner, one recognizable as both plausible and correct by the audience. The elements of this particular space are contextualized; they "fit into cognitive models that are imported from background knowledge."[2] Thus, all concerned will understand that the "entrance to Enaim" *(bĕpetaḥ 'ênayim)* is a physical locale, either a fork in the road or a point along the route where one might turn into Enaim. However, since it is not within the precincts of a settlement or a field belonging to a particular individual, it is also recognized as liminal space. Its physical space is only a transition point that is neither in Enaim or Timnah. Because of its cognitive indeterminacy, not belonging to any inhabited place, it

1. Van Wolde, "Cognitive Linguistics," 135.
2. Sweetser and Fauconnier, "Cognitive Links and Domains," 11.

environmental and socially-based triggers that provide cognitive keys or directives on how a conversation will proceed.[11]

Each of these triggers helps to create specific cognitive identifiers leading the participants in the scene to speak and act in a particular manner even though the audience is aware that this is a case of mistaken identity and incorrect cognition. Coupled with these specific triggers are the forces of resistance that exist in discourse as responses to particular "strategies of power."[12] In this narrative, it will be Tamar's resistance to Judah's

11. Eve Sweetser and Gilles Fauconnier, "Cognitive Links and Domains: Basic Aspects of Mental Space Theory," in *Spaces, Worlds, and Grammar,* ed. Fauconnier and Sweetser (Chicago: University of Chicago Press, 1996) 2.

12. Michel Foucault, *The History of Sexuality,* vol. 1: *An Introduction* (New York: Pantheon, 1978) 101-2.

is a sort of social "duty free zone" in which transactions can take place and in which social identities and conventions, to some extent, may be set aside.

Pragmatic realities: The author has provided several pragmatic elements that will assist the audience by presenting a number of mental shifts that help to redefine the characters' identities and to provide a temporal and social frame for this drama:

1. **Temporal and economic factors:** It is the time of the sheepshearing and therefore spring;
2. **Biological factor:** After the death of his wife, Judah is open to or desiring of new sexual arrangements;
3. **Social status factor:** Tamar transforms herself, taking on the role of a single woman without escort sitting beside the road and therefore a liminal person, lacking the usual cognitive attributes associated with household, husband, father, and therefore approachable by a male freed of the normal social consequences.

Clothing and spatial factor: The veil and liminal setting disguise Tamar's identity, providing a cognitive viewpoint for Judah and triggering his manner of speech between the man and woman, one far different than the one that would be held if Tamar had been dressed in her widow's garments while sitting beside the road.

strategy to thwart her claim to levirate rights that will drive both action and speech. The narrative also falls within the genre of tales in which a woman is able to demonstrate how men can be fools, driven by their own desires, and thus open to be tricked by women whose sexuality they supposedly control.[13]

While Tamar shifts from her persona as a widow in Judah's household to that of a prostitute on the roadside, it is her resistance to Judah's strategy of power that precipitates their encounter. Throughout their discourse cognitive triggers determine how Judah will speak with her and in turn dictate Tamar's responses while she is playing the role of a prostitute.

13. Lila Abu-Lughod, "The Romance of Resistance: Tracing Transformation of Power Through Bedouin Women," *American Ethnologist* 17 (1990) 45.

Judah's cognitive understanding of her identity is narrowed to a single persona based on his understanding of the scene before him, although the audience is aware of both of Tamar's roles.[14]

Social Identities Governing Conversation

In this story Judah is portrayed as the head of a household. He is involved in managing its affairs or with its economic activities (arranging marriages, sheepshearing, and herding), but that recognizable social role changes during the course of the narrative. Of course, individuals can and often do "occupy a number of social positions and hence can have a number of identities that contribute to the total configuration of the self."[15] Thus Judah shifts from the married head of the household to a grieving widower to a businessman, a customer, an embarrassed dupe, a judge, and finally a morally-repentant model of proper behavior.

Tamar also is portrayed in various ways. First, she is the voiceless bride of an arranged marriage who is shuffled from one brother to another as tragedy strikes them in turn. Second, she gains a voice in the story by removing herself from her traditional role, placing herself in a situation in which she presents herself as outside the social and physical confines of the household and therefore capable of speaking with Judah as an equal as they bargain over her body. Third, after obtaining the pregnancy that she felt was her deceased husband's due, Tamar finds herself once again firmly ensconced within the boundaries of her father's house. However, she once again breaks out of the traditionally silent role she previously had played at the beginning of the story. To save her life and that of her unborn child, she speaks a private word proving that Judah is both the father of her child and the lawbreaker who has failed to carry out the levirate obligation due her. Interestingly, after obtaining sanction for her action from Judah, Tamar is silenced again by the storyteller, who writes her off as someone lacking any further importance, stating, "he [Judah] did not lie with her again" (v. 26b). Furthermore, the author gives her no voice in the naming of her twin sons.

14. Sweetser and Fauconnier, "Cognitive Links and Domains," 3-6.
15. Mary E. Roach-Higgins and Joanne B. Eicher, "Dress and Identity," in *Social Science Aspects of Dress,* ed. Sharron J. Lennon and Leslie Davis Burns. ITAA Special Publication 5 (Monument, CO: International Textile and Apparel Association, 1993) 34.

Among the methods that can be employed to analyze these shifting roles and the conversation between Judah and Tamar is mental space theory.[16] According to this method, "mental spaces and connections are built up as discourse unfolds."[17] As such, mental spaces can be thought of as temporary containers or locations for relevant information about a particular object.[18] By analyzing the viewpoint of each speaker as well as the audience, determining their spatial focus in the scene including any constraints that may exist, and keeping the "base" or social starting point for these characters in mind, it is possible to draw inferences about their constructed conversation. In this way, both Judah's and Tamar's speeches can be examined in different mental lights as their condition changes from one social role to another. Complicating this particular situation, however, will be Tamar's decision to create a false impression of herself in Judah's eyes, and this requires a separate mental space to encompass and connect her shifting public personalities.

The work of cognitive linguists has established that written and spoken language contains devices that contribute to the creation and connection of mental spaces.[19] These include:

1. **Space builders**: "A grammatical expression that either opens a new space or shifts focus to an existing space," including prepositional phrases, adverbs, subject-verb complexes, conjunctions + clause:

   "in the course of time" — 38:12
   "When Tamar was told" — 38:13
   "he thought her to be a prostitute" — 38:15

2. **Names and descriptions**: Noun phrases that "set up new elements or point to existing elements in the discourse construction" and serve as connectors capable of tying in cognitive triggers to the base or parent space and related spaces:

---

16. Gilles Fauconnier, *Mental Spaces: Aspects of Meaning Construction in Natural Language* (Cambridge: Cambridge University Press, 1994).

17. Gilles Fauconnier, *Mappings in Thought and Language* (Cambridge: Cambridge University Press, 1997) 36.

18. Seana Coulson, "Mental Space Theory," http://hci.ucsd.edu/coulson/LOT/chap1/node10.html (2002).

19. Fauconnier, *Mental Spaces,* 16-22; *Mappings,* 40-41.

Mental Space Theory

"Mental spaces are small conceptual packets constructed as we think and talk, for purposes of local understanding and action."[1] Each mental space contains a partial representation of the entities contained in a particular scenario as perceived, imagined, remembered, or otherwise understood by a speaker.[2] Because these packets of understanding are constructed during the course of dialogue, they are unique and temporary in the sense that they relate to a particular ongoing discourse. How these cognitive "bubbles" relate to or are mapped to reality allows for a variety of interpretations of what is said.[3]

Mental space theory consists of three aspects that can be either separate spaces or a single space:

Viewpoint: The space from which others are accessed and set up
Focus: The space upon which attention is currently focused
Base: The starting point for construction to which one can return

1. Gilles Fauconnier and Mark Turner, *The Way We Think: Conceptual Blending and the Mind's Hidden Complexities* (New York: Basic Books, 2002) 40.

2. Fauconnier, *Mappings*, 49.

3. Vyvyan Evans and Melanie Green, *Cognitive Linguistics: An Introduction* (Mahwah: Lawrence Erlbaum, 2006) 369.

"Er, Judah's firstborn" — 38:7
"Judah said to his daughter-in-law Tamar" — 38:11
"played the whore" — 38:24

3. **Tenses and moods**: Determine "what kind of space is in focus, its connection to the base space, its accessibility, and the location of counterparts used for identification":

Judah commands his daughter-in-law, "Remain a widow in your father's house until my son Shelah grows up." The proposition is expressed in the form of a command. The narrator indicates that this is an indirect speech act by including Judah's thinking process as a cue to the audience that he has more than one purpose: "he

Judah the herdsman and head of household is the base. When he encounters the disguised Tamar beside the road, the focus is now on a new space containing this person and setting, and Judah's viewpoint has shifted from his original purpose of traveling to the sheepshearing to encompass this newly connected space. In this way, Judah's original base remains intact, but now has connections to another mental space with its own distinct focus and viewpoint centered on the disguised Tamar.

Mental space theory also affords a way to represent information about an entity in contexts where its properties might change. In the sentence "Tamar is a widow," a certain mental space is created that supplies a portion of her identity and creates a mental space based upon the information provided and the culture's understanding of that social role. However, if we say "Tamar is a widow who has removed her widow's garments and disguised herself as a prostitute wearing a veil," then a separate mental space is created that takes into account new elements of her identity, only some of which are true to her socially-recognized identity as a widow. A "counterfactual conceptualization" has been created upon which a dialogue will be based and interpretations made.[4]

---

4. Evans and Green, *Cognitive Linguistics,* 369-70. As they note, as the context shifts, an "utterance can give rise to different counterfactual scenarios."

feared that he [Shelah] too would die, like his brothers" (38:11).[20] The linguistic indicator of Judah's motivation is the use of the conjunction *kî* ("because") prior to the speech verb *'mr (kî 'āmar).*[21]

By taking note of these linguistic and mental connections, the dialogues between Judah and Tamar can be examined from a fresh perspective.

---

20. See Joan Cutting, *Pragmatics and Discourse* (London: Routledge, 2002) 19-20.

21. Cynthia L. Miller, *The Representation of Speech in Biblical Hebrew Narrative.* HSS 55 (Atlanta: Scholars, 1996) 295.

Dialogue One (38:12-19)

Every conversation is embedded within a social setting or world with certain premises either supplied by the storyteller or distinguishable from the nature of the conversation.[22] A number of elements in this story function as catalysts and are complementary to the climax that draws the characters back into balance. Thus the action in the pericope is triggered by a series of deaths (Er, Onan, Judah's wife) and ends with the birth of twins. In addition, a series of garment shifts guide the reader through the social transformations in the narrative and function as signals of a change in social status for the characters.

Throughout the narrative the changes in Tamar's clothing function as social indicators of identity and in the second instance as a catalyst for change and deception. Structurally, an ABCBA pattern is created as she dons widow's garments, removes them, and then resumes them once the status quo is restored. I have added a final "A" to the structure, creating an inclusio pattern, given the possibility that she was allowed to resume the costume of married females.

Ancillary to the garment theme, the storyteller is careful to inform the audience of several relevant facts along the way that will influence the conversation and create mental spaces to contain and help explicate each facet of the story.

(1) Social Situation and Fertility Theme

Judah's wife had died and his period of mourning (30 days) had ended. He had resumed his work schedule, traveling to Timnah with his friend Hirah the Adullamite to inspect the work of his sheepshearers (38:12). Richard Clifford points to the use of the term *nāḥam*, "comforted."[23] He considers it to be a euphemism signaling the end of Judah's mourning period and an indicator to Judah and to the audience that he should engender more children. This could be compared to the similar use of the term in Gen 24:67, where Isaac consoles himself over the death of his mother

---

22. Compare the structure of this dialogue — ABCBA — with that in Gen 32:22-32 as noted by Jan P. Fokkelman, "Genesis," in *The Literary Guide to the Bible*, ed. Robert Alter and Frank Kermode (Cambridge, MA: Belknap, 1987) 51-52.

23. Richard J. Clifford, "Genesis 38: Its Contribution to the Jacob Story," *CBQ* 66 (2004) 529.

Shifts of Clothing as Social Markers

1. Tamar removes her normal garb as a married woman and puts on widow's garments following the death of her husband Er (implied by the fact that she is referred to as a widow in 38:11 and is wearing widow's garments in v. 14). Her social and legal status is immediately transformed.[1]

2. Tamar removes her widow's garments, and she "put on a veil, wrapped herself up" (38:14). Without a legal change of status, such as remarriage, this was a socially-inappropriate act.

3. Tamar removes her disguise and resumes her guise as a widow in her father's house (implied because she is never denounced for wearing inappropriate garb during the three months it took for her pregnancy to become evident; 38:24). In fact, she could not be charged with "whoredom" and condemned by Judah if that was her profession and she was no longer a member of his household.

4. Following Judah's acknowledgement of his own guilt and the absolving of Tamar of any criminal act, her clothing is left indeterminate. She is still a widow, but now one with children, the twins that Judah has fathered. Legally, the firstborn would be Er's heir and the younger brother would be Judah's son. Because there is no mention of Tamar's future status, it is possible that she chose to live unmarried within Judah's house, but ancient Near Eastern legal tradition (Code of Hammurapi 177) indicates that she could have chosen to marry again, which would mean a resumption of the normal clothing worn by a wife.

1. Victor H. Matthews and Don C. Benjamin, *Social World of Ancient Israel, 1250-587 B.C.E.* (Peabody: Hendrickson, 1993) 132-33.

by marrying Rebekah. Since Judah's wife is the only woman other than Tamar in the story, her death and the callous dismissal *(yāšab)* of Tamar to her father's house (38:11) triggers the next phase in the narrative. It leaves the family without an available "womb" to produce an heir and continue its existence. Of course, the youngest son, Shelah, could serve as the future progenitor of heirs, but he is never spoken of as a viable heir to

Judah.[24] Thus the theme of primogeniture and the "search for the heir" motif that are so evident in the stories about Abraham, Isaac, and Jacob continue here.[25]

Also at play in this story is its connection to the multiple examples of the barren wife motif that appear elsewhere in the ancestral narratives.[26] Tamar's enforced infertility endangers the regular flow of the inheritance of property from one generation and, on a larger scale, the inheritance due to the heirs of the covenant. Her condition is due to (1) God's unexplained anger with Er, (2) Onan's use of a self-serving birth-control method to strengthen his inheritance rights,[27] and (3) Judah's failure to send Shelah to her when this third son grew to maturity. Given the evident danger to her husband's household and the lack of strong male leadership, it will become Tamar's responsibility to act so that the period of infertility ends and the household's future is insured. Her subsequent conversation with Judah takes all of these factors into account and strengthens her moral and discursive position, even while she deceives her father-in-law.

(2) Physical Transformation and Deception

Tamar reacts to the news of Judah's departure for Timnah by making the decision to transform her appearance, using physical props that imply particular social connotations. In their encounter beside the road, she takes advantage of Judah's focus to transform his viewpoint into a desired line of perception. She will also employ a form of persuasive speech to obtain discursive authority in her dealings with Judah. Her strategy is

24. Anthony J. Lambe, "Genesis 38: Structure and Literary Design," in *The World of Genesis*, ed. Philip R. Davies and David J. A. Clines (Sheffield: Sheffield Academic, 1998) 113-14.

25. Victor H. Matthews, *Old Testament Themes* (St. Louis: Chalice, 2000) 13-15.

26. See Clifford, "Genesis 38," 528, for a list of these parallel motifs. See Melissa Jackson, "Lot's Daughters and Tamar as Tricksters and the Patriarchal Narratives as Feminist Theology," *JSOT* 98 (2002) 44-45, for a similar comparison of Tamar with other women in Genesis.

27. Note the employment of the narrator-as-informant in this instance providing the audience with Onan's thinking process, an indirect form of speech. In fact, the narrative aside here seems to be in response to a question that the audience would have asked about Onan's behavior. On this see Guy Cook, *Discourse and Literature* (Oxford: Oxford University Press, 1994) 50.

Discursive Authority

Persons may be "in authority" or be "an authority," but usually not both.

Authoritative speech is the "effect of a posited, perceived, or institutionally ascribed asymmetry between speaker and audience that permits certain speakers to command not just the attention but the confidence, respect, and trust of their audience, or . . . to make audiences act *as if* they were so."[1]

Authority both involves and often depends upon the use of nonverbal instruments and media: theatrical gestures, demeanors, costumes, props, and stage devices.

Authority may rest on the naked assertion that the identity of the speaker warrants acceptance of the speech.

The exercise of authority depends less upon the "capacity for reasoned elaboration" as on the presumption made by those subject to authority that such a capacity exists, or on their calculated and strategic willingness to pretend they so presume.[2]

When an explanation is requested, the relation of trust is suspended and the level of authority is lowered in that moment.

1. Bruce Lincoln, *Authority: Construction and Corrosion* (Chicago: University of Chicago Press, 1995) 4.
2. Lincoln, *Authority*, 6.

---

to display herself as someone who is "in authority" through her manner of speech. Of course, this is a reversal of her previous role as a voiceless, widowed daughter-in-law, who lacks any sort of authority within the household.

(a) **Cognitive Concepts Attached to Garments as Social Props**   By voluntarily removing her widow's garments (*bigĕdê 'almĕnûtāh*; a contretemps to Judah ending his period of mourning) and putting on a veil (*ṣā'îp*) to disguise her appearance, Tamar literally becomes another person in the eyes of her target audience — Judah and possibly Hirah, if he is a witness to this scene. Since clothing or dress is a form of nonverbal communication expressing social identity,[28] it can be said that two culturally-based associations are attached to Tamar's decision to change her attire. First is the matter of the widow's garments *(beged 'almānût)*. Widows were expected to wear specific and recognizable garments, just as sackcloth was considered the principal garment for mourners and those displaying their repentance (Matt 11:21; see both humans and animals in Jonah 3:6-8[MT 7-9]).

In a similar case of calculated deception, Judith combines her period of mourning with her newly-acquired status as a widow. She wears "sackcloth around her waist and dressed in widow's clothing" (Jdt 8:5). Also of interest here is the direct parallel with Judith's removal of her widow's garments and her physical and social transformation through bathing, anointing herself with ointment, combing her hair, and then attiring herself with a tiara, festive garb, sandals, anklets, bracelets, rings, and earrings "to entice the eyes of all the men who might see her" (Jdt 10:3-4; 16:7-9).

If Karel van der Toorn is correct,[29] Tamar's veil is primarily intended to differentiate her from being a widow, and it serves an ornamental purpose comparable to the finery described in Isa 3:18-23. He considers an interpretation that the veil marked Tamar as a prostitute as a "superficial reading" and suggests that it was "not unusual for a woman to wear a veil." However, the remainder of his article describes Babylonian and Assyrian laws that deal with the husband's right to veil his bride after the bride-price had been paid. It is clear that the social significance of the veil goes beyond ornamentation. The problem is differentiating between veils that were recognized in that culture as pertaining to marriage agreements or married status and those that were recognized as simple frippery.

There also is a cultural incongruity with wearing a veil, based on Middle Assyrian Law texts, but that does not have to govern Canaanite or Israelite traditions. The presumed custom of advertising oneself as a prostitute with a veil stands in contrast to the exact opposite custom in MAL A.40 that allows only married or free women the right to wear a veil when out in public. It is possible that this reflects a Canaanite custom, possibly of a bride of Baal offering herself to anyone as a fertility ritual, although we

---

28. Roach-Higgins and Eicher, "Dress and Identity," 31.

29. Karel van der Toorn, "The Significance of the Veil in the Ancient Near East," in *Pomegranates and Golden Bells,* ed. David P. Wright, David Noel Freedman, and Avi Hurvitz (Winona Lake: Eisenbrauns, 1995) 330.

have no evidence to that effect.[30] In fact, the text does not refer to Tamar as a prostitute; only Judah does this, and that highlights his limited cognitive perception rather than all possible mental concepts.

Drawing on the social implications of Tamar's shift in clothing, Anthony Lambe notes that "the change from widow's to harlot's garb reveals a change from a family role to one on the fringes of society, ironically a role used to rebuild the family."[31] Following this line of reasoning, Nelly Furman suggests that garments "function as communicative devices between the sexes"[32] — and this would add to the deception, since males and females perceive garments in different ways. Furman declares that "garments become for the women the channel they use to insert themselves into the exclusively male communicative process," and therefore Tamar's veil is her way of breaking into or jarring Judah's communication pathways and getting his attention.[33]

Despite the fact that a fertility theme is implicit in the story, this is not signified by the "harlot's veil."[34] By exchanging her widow's dress for the veil, Tamar calls attention to two social functions of garments: (1) "their use as symbols in the sexual code; and second, their use as masks and disguises."[35] In fact, a new, counterfactual mental space is created when Tamar manipulates the social connotations of her attire. Like Potiphar's wife, who strips Joseph of his garment, she "pluralizes" the meaning associated with a garment.[36] This in turn plays on the patriarchal representational system in effect in her society and makes use of symbolic codes for her own purposes.

David Gunn and Danna Nolan Fewell suggest that since the word ṣāʿîp is used for veil only in this passage and in Gen 24:65,[37] Tamar's intent is

---

30. See John R. Huddlestun, "Divestiture, Deception, and Demotion: The Garment Motif in Genesis 37–39," *JSOT* 98 (2002) 47-62, for a complete set of references on this debate.

31. Lambe, "Genesis 38," 106.

32. "His Story Versus Her Story: Male Genealogy and Female Strategy in the Jacob Cycle," in *Narrative Research on the Hebrew Bible,* ed. Miri Amihai, George W. Coats, and Anne M. Solomon. Semeia 46 (Atlanta: Scholars, 1989) 147.

33. Furman, "His Story Versus Her Story," 141.

34. Furman, "His Story Versus Her Story," 145.

35. Furman, "His Story Versus Her Story," 148. See also the widow-disguise in 2 Sam 14:2-11 used by the Wise Woman of Tekoa to provide physical evidence of her social condition when addressing David.

36. Robert Alter, *The Art of Biblical Narrative* (New York: Basic Books, 1981) 109.

37. This is Rebekah's response to her first meeting with Isaac as his betrothed bride.

actually to present herself publicly as a bride to indicate to Judah that he has failed to uphold her rights and those of her deceased husband.[38] However, this symbolic indictment of her father-in-law could have been done more effectively before the elders or the other members of the household.[39] It is an odd choice for a roadside confrontation. If Judah has so thoroughly "repressed all consciousness of such an obligation," then all he sees is an anonymous woman without a male escort publicly announcing her sexual availability.[40] As a result, Tamar's gesture has no effect on his conscious awareness of the legal matter at hand. In addition, this would suggest a very shocking action for the audience, who would perceive that she has actually enticed her father-in-law into an incestuous union (see Lev 20:12).[41]

Adding to the plausibility of Judah's mistake in determining her true identity, Roland Murphy remarks in his commentary on Prov 7:10 that "harlots did dress distinctively" ("dressed like a prostitute" — *šît*) and compares this to Gen 38:14-15.[42] Unfortunately, this wisdom text does not describe the prostitute's attire and does not mention that she is wearing a veil. Leslie A. Zebrowitz points to a "'mistaken identity' effect" that psychologically reinforces a perception of identity based on previous encounters with a specific group, body type, or facial characteristic.[43] Thus Judah's seeing a prostitute may be based on previous encounters with these individuals who resemble Tamar's dress, location, or some other trait not described in the biblical narrative.

Finally, in her examination of "dress cues" and how they relate to different types of social power, Sharron Lennon notes that "social perception is concerned with cognitive processes as they relate to people or information about people as the objects of perception."[44] These impressions are of-

38. *Narrative in the Hebrew Bible* (Oxford: Oxford University Press, 1993) 87-89.

39. See the use of a public confrontation in Deut 25:5-10, in which the aggrieved widow has the opportunity to force the issue of the levirate obligation due to her deceased husband.

40. Jan William Tarlin, "Tamar's Veil: Ideology at the Entrance to Enaim," in *Culture, Entertainment and the Bible*, ed. George Aichele. JSOTSup 309 (Sheffield: Sheffield Academic, 2000) 178.

41. Gordon J. Wenham, *Genesis 16–50*. WBC 2 (Dallas: Word, 1994) 368.

42. *Proverbs*. WBC 22 (Nashville: Nelson, 1998) 43.

43. "Physical Appearance as a Basis of Stereotyping," in *Stereotypes and Stereotyping*, ed. C. Neil Macrae, Charles Stangor, and Miles Hewstone (New York: Guilford, 1996) 102.

44. "Sex, Dress, and Power in the Workplace," in *Appearance and Power*, ed. Kim K. P. Johnson and Lennon (Oxford: Berg, 1999) 105.

ten formed during first encounters. Thus "social cognition may be seen as the way in which people jointly construct knowledge about people."[45] This is what Lauren Resnick terms "socially shared cognition."[46] In processing visual information, socially shared cognition occurs when a group of people recognizes and understands the meaning of a visual cultural icon (e.g., Santa Claus).[47] Since "directly experienced events are only part of the basis for" personal construction of a knowledge base, people often construct their knowledge base or mental impression on the statements made by others — orally, in writing, in pictures, or in gestures.[48]

(b) **Spatial Dimensions Influencing Cognition**   Ultimately, it is place that matters most in this episode. As Joan Goodnick Westenholz notes, it is not the veil, but the location that defines Tamar's "social status as a prostitute."[49] The veil only serves as a physical disguise and may have no other significance to the story. No woman other than a prostitute would be sitting beside a road, unescorted by a male, unless she was in distress, and Judah never indicates that he is offering her assistance, only employment. In that sense, it may be better to refer to this *zônâ* (38:15) as an "autonomous woman" rather than a prostitute. Although the meaning in both cases is a woman who sells her body, there is a greater sense in the premonarchic period of this practice being performed by an independent operator who wishes to "avoid servitude" and is not controlled by a male procurer or some other male agency.[50] The Levitical code does contain an injunction against a father profaning his daughter by "making her a prostitute" (Lev 19:29). However, this may refer to the practice of a debt-ridden father who finds it necessary to sell his daughter into prostitution.[51] If he has forced her into performing Canaanite cultic practices or

---

45. Lennon, "Sex, Dress, and Power," 105.

46. "Shared Cognition: Thinking as Social Practice," in *Perspectives on Socially Shared Cognition,* ed. Resnick, John B. Levine, and Stephanie Teasley (Washington: American Psychological Association, 1991) 1-20.

47. Lennon, "Sex, Dress, and Power," 105-6.

48. Resnick, "Shared Cognition," 2.

49. "Tamar, *Qĕdēšâ, Qadištu,* and Sacred Prostitution in Mesopotamia," *HTR* 82 (1989) 247.

50. Maricel Mena López, "Wise Women in I Kings 3–11," in *The Many Voices of the Bible,* ed. Sean Freyne and Ellen van Wolde (London: SCM, 2002) 25.

51. John E. Hartley, *Leviticus.* WBC 4 (Dallas: Word, 1992) 321.

idolatry in general, that would be considered a profanation of the land and the people.[52]

Sitting *(yāšab)* at the "entrance to Enaim, which is on the road to Timnah," serves as an ironic juxtaposition to "sitting" in her father's house, waiting for a male to initiate an action. Now, without asking for permission from a male, Tamar places herself in a location where she is in control of the action to come. Thus, the act of sitting does not simply imply inaction. In this case, sitting at the "entrance to Enaim" is a form of intentional positioning in significant space. In fact, the combination of physical location and the blending of a new cognitive identity for Tamar creates the charged location for the dialogue and precipitates the action in this scene that is based on Judah's misreading of cognitive cues.[53]

There is a sense of anticipation here much like Eli's role, "sitting on the seat beside the doorpost of the temple of the Lord" in Shiloh (1 Sam 1:9). In that scene he serves as a gatekeeper monitoring both those who enter and leave and those who have no business near the shrine. Interestingly, he too does not recognize the actions or the role played by a woman that he encounters there, the praying Hannah (1 Sam 1:12-14). In this case, Tamar has chosen this place because it is along Judah's route to the sheepshearing at Timnah and because it is separate from the normal domestic space that she occupies. In this way she connects her actions with Judah's, focusing his attention on her in an unfamiliar frame of reference and thereby narrowing his cognitive ability to imagine her as anything other than a prostitute.

It is implied by the narrator that Tamar has chosen this strategy because Judah's son Shelah had grown up and she had "not been given to him in marriage" (38:13-14). This should be seen in the context of Judah's promise in 38:11 that had kept Tamar waiting in social limbo until Judah's levirate obligation could be fulfilled. In addition, the intentional shift in her character role, becoming a trickster, parallels Judah's own role earlier in the story when he too functioned as a trickster figure

52. Erhard S. Gerstenberger, *Leviticus*. OTL (Louisville: Westminster/John Knox, 1996) 275-76.

53. It is possible that the misidentification of Tamar based on Judah's misreading of the scene is explained by cognitive blending theory, which attempts to create meaning out of an "emergent structure" that is created by the mental blending of the component parts of a scene, linguistic, metaphorical, and physical. See Evans and Green, *Cognitive Linguistics*, 400-10 for an overview of this approach.

(38:11).[54] The reversal of trickster figures may be compared to Jacob's turning the tables on his trickster uncle Laban (Gen 30:25-33). This situation also parallels the action of the daughters of Lot, who lack a suitable husband and are in danger of not being able to perpetuate the family line.[55] Like Tamar, they dupe a male into impregnating them (Gen 19:30-38). However, their goal is more narrowly focused — obtaining a higher social status (mother) rather than attempting to redress a legal wrong.

Tamar reaches her position at the "entrance to Enaim" ahead of Judah as he travels to Timnah. There is a pun used here based on the place name *petaḥ 'ênayim*, meaning "the opening of the eyes," which Judah seems incapable of doing. It may in fact refer to a place of justice — the gate — where Judah's failure to give Tamar her rights is judged and is open to the eyes of the audience.[56] The place name also means "spring," and Richard Clifford[57] and Robert Alter[58] both point to a well or spring as a place to find a bride, tying this back once again to the idea of Tamar as a forgotten bride. In his treatment of the text, Clifford emphasizes that the "type-scene functions to show that Tamar, no less than Rebekah and Rachel, is a fruitful 'wife' of an ancestor." A more likely scenario, however, is that Tamar, like Ruth on the threshing floor (Ruth 3:6-13), positions herself in liminal space, in essence "takes the high ground" as she prepares to confront Judah. Of course, her physical placement also creates or contributes to the illusion she wishes to be employed as either a common prostitute or a cult prostitute — if such a position actually existed in ancient Israel.[59]

One further question is, How does she reach this point ahead of him? It is possible that Judah went to the sheepshearing first and then encountered Tamar beside the road on his return home. Both Gordon Wenham[60] and Esther Menn[61] posit that Judah would have been drunk after attending

---

54. See Lambe, "Genesis 38," 107; and Wildavsky, "Survival Must Not Be Gained through Sin," 45.

55. Jackson, "Lot's Daughters and Tamar as Tricksters," 30.

56. See Gunn and Fewell, *Narrative in the Hebrew Bible*, 39.

57. "Genesis 38," 529.

58. *The Art of Biblical Narrative*, 47-62.

59. For the various arguments on this, see Karel van der Toorn, "Female Prostitution in Payment of Vows in Ancient Israel," *JBL* 108 (1989) 193-205.

60. *Genesis 16–50*, 368.

61. *Judah and Tamar*, 22.

the sheepshearing festival and that this contributed to his failure to recognize Tamar.[62] In that sense, his failure to recognize Tamar could be compared to the inebriated Jacob, who fails to recognize his substituted bride in Gen 29:22-25. Drawing on yet another example, Melissa Jackson compares Judah's lack of recognition to the inebriated Lot's lack of recognition of his daughters prior to having incestuous relations with them (Gen 19:32-36).[63]

Cognition and the Resulting Conversation

What we are left with is the narrator's statement that Judah only sees a prostitute (a *zônâ*), "for she had covered her face" (38:15). Of course, it is the author of this episode who has chosen to limit Judah's perspective of the scene in which Tamar appears. A decision has been made to limit Judah's ability to engage in a broader "imagery" of the scene. His "ability to construe a situation in alternative ways for purposes of thought or expression" is constrained in this case by the lack of information beyond the physical identification of the site and her manner of dress.[64] This construal process is implied by the language employed by the storyteller and serves as an indication of how mental impressions of the world are structured based on how the speaker "conceptualizes and portrays" a situation.[65]

As a result of this social construction of the story, the range of narrative elements provided forces Judah and, to a certain extent, the audience into this limited perspective. Judah is a widower and a man on his way to an extremely important economic activity (sheepshearing). It would be plausible to the audience that this would contribute to his rather one-track thinking. It would also invoke in the audience a series of theories or impressions that mentally categorize what it means to be a widower and a herdsman on his way to a sheepshearing.[66] Given her physical placement

---

62. See 2 Sam 13:23-29 for another instance where wine-drinking accompanies the sheepshearing and how it contributes to the assassination of Amnon by Absalom's agents.

63. "Lot's Daughters and Tamar as Tricksters," 31.

64. Ronald W. Langacker, *Foundations of Cognitive Grammar*, vol. 1: *Theoretical Prerequisites* (Stanford: Stanford University Press, 1987) 490.

65. Langacker, *Foundations of Cognitive Grammar*, 487-88.

66. See John R. Taylor, "Introduction: On Construing the World," in *Language and the Cognitive Construal of the World*, ed. Taylor and Robert E. MacLaury (Berlin: Mouton de Gruyter, 1995) 4.

and manner of dress, it seems that Tamar's primary purpose in this scene is to function as an object of Judah's passion to satisfy his sexual needs. If she is a cultic figure, she also may serve as a person who could help insure the success of Judah's shearing and herding venture in the future. His illusory, misguided perception of reality is therefore based on a mistaken inner thought process *(ḥāšab)*. This in turn ultimately permits the narrator to demonstrate to the audience how Judah's conceptual understanding of Tamar is incorrect.[67]

Charles Stangor and Mark Schaller,[68] in describing types of stereo-typing that appear to be going on here, point to the development of "group schemas":

> Schemas have broad influences upon person perception, including attention, perception, interpretation, and storage of social information, as well as judgments of and behavior toward others. At the attentional stage, schemas allow the individual to ignore what are perceived to be unrelated and unimportant details of a situation and thus reduce informational complexity, rendering more elaborative processing unnecessary.

This then translates into Judah's inability to see Tamar as anything other than a prostitute because his cognitive perception has been channeled by her clothing, her physical location, and the fact that she is an unaccompanied, "free" female. In this way, social interaction with a prostitute cannot and will not follow typical interaction with the females in his household.

In a similar way, Joshua's spies (Josh 2:1) "entered the house of a prostitute *(bêt 'iššâ zônâ)* . . . and spent the night there" because their entrance and their presence in that place would cause little or no notice since the house and its mistress carry the stereotype of a place open to free association with nonkin males.[69] Stereotyping is one of the means by which we cope with meeting new individuals. In this way we can use "social category memberships" in "an adaptive manner to draw dispositional inferences

---

67. M. Niehoff, "Do Biblical Characters Talk to Themselves? Narrative Modes of Representing Inner Speech in Early Biblical Fiction," *JBL* 111 (1992) 579.

68. "Stereotypes as Individual and Collective Representations," in Macrae, Stangor, and Hewstone, *Stereotypes and Stereotyping,* 7.

69. Phyllis A. Bird, "The Harlot as Heroine," *Semeia* 46 (1989) 127.

about the person."[70] This social shorthand is particularly useful in developing "meta-contrast" judgments between in-group and out-of-group membership.[71]

In addition, some have suggested that Tamar was actually dressed as a cult prostitute and that Judah's desire to lie with her was based not on his lack of a wife, but on his desire to have good fortune at the sheep-shearing.[72] This interpretation may be based on 38:21, where Hirah refers to the missing woman as the "temple prostitute *(qĕdēšâ)* who was at Enaim by the wayside." Either suggestion is possible since the text has provided the audience with both the fact that he is a widower and that he is on his way to the sheepshearing. However, the term *qĕdēšâ* appears only after Hirah goes looking for the woman who had lain with Judah (38:20-23), and Judah does not dispute the label when Hirah quotes the townspeople of Enaim.[73] Jan William Tarlin suggests that, while Judah's response to seeing Tamar as a prostitute is socially based and controls his actions toward her, it is equally constraining on Tamar, who must play the role, never voicing her legal case to Judah, even in a place of judgment.[74] She is in fact "manipulated by the veil" and the spatial situation herself.[75]

Discussing the additional explanatory readings found in the LXX and the Vulgate of this passage, John Huddlestun suggests that Tamar's actions "relate more to concealment than deception per se, although the former is central to the success of the latter."[76] Thus Judah fails to recognize her, "although ironically he is later identified in this fashion."[77] Judah's failure to "know" Tamar marks him as a fool, a fact that is certified later when he gives her his pledge items, and is only mitigated in the text when he acknowledges that she is more righteous than he.[78] Adding to the comic mood of this episode and playing on the apparent stereotyping of the char-

70. Stangor and Schaller, "Stereotypes as Individual and Collective Representations," 20.

71. See John C. Turner, *Rediscovering the Social Group: A Self-Categorization Theory* (Oxford: Blackwell, 1987) 46-48.

72. Gerhard von Rad, *Genesis*. OTL (Philadelphia: Westminster, 1961) 359.

73. Lambe, "Genesis 38," 117, n. 18.

74. "Tamar's Veil," 177. Cf. the public voice given to a widow in Deut 25:5-10 so she can publicly demand her levirate rights.

75. Tarlin, "Tamar's Veil," 178.

76. "Divestiture, Deception, and Demotion," 58.

77. Huddleston, "Divestiture, Deception, and Demotion," 58.

78. Jackson, "Lot's Daughters and Tamar as Tricksters," 40.

acters, Johanna W. H. Bos points out that all of the men in this story are "bunglers, who don't see straight."[79]

Judah Speaks First

With the scene set, the conversation between the characters can begin. Of course, the storyteller could have just presented this as straight narration without embedded dialogue, but that would not be as vibrant or interesting to the audience. Instead, what we have here is constructed speech or dialogue that follows established cultural and language patterns.[80] Thus, Judah's perceived identification of Tamar as an available, free female is made clear to the audience when he makes the abrupt offer: "Come, let me come in to you" (38:16a; *bô ',* using the particle of entreaty, *nā'*). Such a bold statement, without preliminary or apparent courtesy, suggests that this may be the universally accepted offer or euphemism tendered to prostitutes.[81]

Language such as this is an indication of preexisting knowledge or experience.[82] While it does not provide a total look at Judah's thinking process, it could plant the suggestion in the minds of the audience that he is familiar with prostitutes and may have dealt with them in the past. In any case, Judah would have been culturally restrained from speaking in this way to Tamar if he knew that she was his daughter-in-law. Only Amnon seems capable of such a social gaff when he boldly says to the other Tamar, his half-sister, "Come, lie with me, my sister" (2 Sam. 13:11). However, there are political considerations at play in that demand that are not present in Genesis 38.[83]

While drawing on Phyllis Bird's work on the meaning of *zônâ* as "a

---

79. "Out of the Shadows: Genesis 38; Judges 4:17-22; Ruth 3," in *Reasoning with the Foxes,* ed. J. Cheryl Exum and Bos. Semeia 42 (Atlanta: Scholars, 1988) 48-49.

80. Deborah Tannen, "Introducing Constructed Dialogue in Greek and American Conversational and Literary Narrative," in *Direct and Indirect Speech,* ed. Florian Coulmas (Berlin: Mouton de Gruyter, 1986) 311.

81. Cf. Judg 16:1, where Samson "went in" to a prostitute in Gaza.

82. Van Wolde, "Cognitive Linguistics," 125.

83. See Victor H. Matthews and Don C. Benjamin, "Amnon and Tamar: A Matter of Honor (2 Sam 13:1-38)," in *Crossing Boundaries and Linking Horizons,* ed. Gordon D. Young, Mark Chavalas, and Richard E. Averbeck (Baltimore: CDL, 1997) 349-55.

kind of legal outlaw,"[84] Tarlin suggests a reading in 38:15 of "wild woman" rather than professional prostitute. He notes that Judah "does not approach her with a business proposition, but with an unadorned sexual request: *hābâ nā' 'ābô' 'ēlayik* — "permit me to come (in) to you."[85] It is possible that this perception applies to apparently unaffiliated persons, such as the "uncivilized" Enkidu of the Gilgamesh epic, who does not know social mores. Of course, it simply may be a further indication of Tamar's "unattached status," again pointing to the only profession open to a woman without a household.

It is possible that the abruptness of Judah's demand is designed to shock the "knowing" audience, who would recognize that what is about to be violated is an incest taboo prohibiting a father from having sexual relations with his son's wife (Lev 18:15). While we cannot be certain, it is probably safe to assume that this taboo existed in the time period of the ancestors or when this narrative was composed. This could help explain why the narrator is so careful to add the explanation that "he did not know that she was his daughter-in-law" (38:16b), even though in the previous verse it had been made clear that he did not recognize her.

There is also some legal uncertainty in Israelite law whether the father, like the deceased's brothers, can serve as the levir.[86] Hittite Law no. 193 indicates that this is possible in some legal codes,[87] but there is no direct biblical parallel. The obvious dependence of this narrative on the garment motif that governs the Joseph cycle of stories suggests that the mental and physical transference of a woman in "widow's garments" to a veiled unattached female is a major key to the entire episode.[88] However, the story also seems to be tied to the motif of the "birth of a savior" by incest, and like the story of Ruth contains a link to David. Adding a further di-

---

84. "The Harlot as Heroine," 125.

85. Tarlin, "Tamar's Veil," 179.

86. See Dvora E. Weisberg, "The Widow of Our Discontent: Levirate Marriage in the Bible and Ancient Israel," *JSOT* 28 (2004) 415-16.

87. Martha Tobi Roth translates the law: "If a man has a wife, and the man dies, his brother shall take his widow as wife. (If the brother dies,) his father shall take her. When afterwards his father dies, his (i.e., the father's) brother shall take the woman whom he had"; *Law Collections from Mesopotamia and Asia Minor.* SBLWAW 6 (Atlanta: Scholars, 1995) 236.

88. For a full discussion of the garment motif, see Victor H. Matthews, "The Anthropology of Clothing in the Joseph Narrative," *JSOT* 65 (1995) 25-36; and Huddleston, "Divestiture, Deception, and Demotion," 47-62.

mension is Judah's prominent role in the Joseph cycle as the spokesman for his brothers before the disguised Joseph (43:3-5, 8-10). This provides a possible reason why there is no approbation about his actions in this narrative other than to conclude that Tamar is "more righteous" than he is over this matter (38:26).[89]

Tamar's First Riposte

Playing along with Judah's acceptance of her identity, Tamar responds to Judah's request: "What will you give me, that you may come in to me?" (38:16b). Tamar's response is designed to position herself in a dominant role, magnifying her discursive authority. Instead of the tone of cooperation and compliance that might be expected of a female when addressed forcefully by a male,[90] she establishes the strongest position possible for herself based on Judah's perception of her identity as a prostitute.[91] In fact, her speech follows the traditional transactional protocol of a riposte following a request/demand that is more common between males.[92]

Positioning oneself within conversation is based not only on what is said, but on the nuances of the words, the emotional and physical situation, and the reaction of the other participants in the conversation.[93] By confronting Judah in a manner more like another male in a bargaining session, Tamar positions herself to succeed while reinforcing her disguise as a prostitute, who cannot be expected to speak or act like a "typical" female member of the household. It is interesting that, instead of setting her own price, she demands that the man make an offer. There will be a counterproposal on her part, but it is based on the fact that Judah does not currently have the means to pay her immediately upon delivery of services.

Note also that the storyteller has constructed this narrative world in which Tamar's widowed condition and Judah's reluctance to provide her with the fulfillment of her levirate obligation give her a voice. The audience, if not Judah, recognizes that this voice is not "her own," but rather

89. See Weisberg, "The Widow of Our Discontent," 416.
90. See Kramarae, West, and Lazar, "Gender in Discourse," 130, for gender-based restrictions on discourse in patriarchal societies.
91. Tarlin, "Tamar's Veil," 179.
92. See the transactional dialogue between Abraham and Ephron in 23:7-16.
93. Van Langenhove and Harré, "Introducing Positioning Theory," 17.

Transactional Scheme in Genesis 23:7-16

Tamar's response does contrast with the much longer and perhaps more traditional transaction narrative in Gen 23:7-16. In that narrative the following scheme is followed:

Abraham: Demand, offer, demand + offer (vv. 7-9)
Ephron: Offer (vv. 10-11)
Abraham: Offer + demand (vv. 12-13)
Ephron: Setting of price (vv. 14-15)
Abraham: Acceptance of price and completion of the transaction before witnesses (v. 16)

---

that of a disguised person. In pointing to this reluctance or "anxiety" on the part of males to fulfill the levirate obligation, Dvora Weisberg supports the idea that "Tamar is given a voice; after her husbands' deaths, she becomes her own advocate."[94] Of course, Tamar does not do this before the elders like the widow in Deut 25:7. Apparently her options, in a premonarchic setting, are limited and therefore require a more creative response. Thus Tamar takes the more radical course of removing her widow's garments and at least temporarily abandoning her social identity in order to deceive Judah. The irony of this choice is that ultimately, to pay her price, Judah will be coerced into yielding "his symbols of status and authority." In this way, "Tamar's temporary change of status results in Judah's loss of the same."[95]

Judah's Offer

Trapped within a rhetorical web and driven by his own sexual desires, Judah makes an offer: "I will send you a kid from the flock" (38:17a). This is a truly generous offer, and it represents a financial sacrifice.[96] There is a

---

94. Weisburg, "The Widow of Our Discontent," 414.
95. Huddleston, "Divestiture, Deception, and Demotion," 56-57.
96. Cf. Gideon's offering of a kid to his angelic visitor in Judg 6:19.

sense of desperation on Judah's part in his offering such a high price for Tamar's favors. This may be based on the combination of the death of his wife and the completion of the traditional mourning period (38:12). His sexual passions may have been raised by a period of abstinence and by the availability of sexual favors implicit in Tamar's position beside the road and Judah's perception of her as a prostitute.[97] In essence, Tamar has become what Slavoj Žižek calls a "spectre: an obscenely enjoyable fantasy object" for Judah.[98]

Given the many parallels between the Joseph narrative and the story of Judah and Tamar, as outlined by Alter,[99] it is not surprising to find the inclusion here of an animal from the flock. In this episode as well as in the first installment of the Joseph story, an animal functions as part of the deception, although in 37:31 it only supplies the blood needed to deceive Jacob into thinking Joseph had been killed.

One interesting parallel to Judah's offer is Samson's bringing a kid with him when he goes to visit his Philistine wife in Judg 15:1. While this may be a peace offering after the fiasco of the riddle contest with the wedding guests, it could serve as a genuine attempt on his part to show that he has the financial ability to support a wife. While it is possible that Judah is offering marriage rather than a prostitute's fee, that seems unlikely, given the spatial context of the story. Like Samson, he may be asserting his ability to pay by offering a valuable commodity. The bottom line, however, is that this is an offer that requires Tamar to perform on faith, and few prostitutes are going to operate on "credit."

Tamar's Second Riposte

Tamar remains within the protocol of a transactional dialogue by countering Judah's proposition and stating: "Only if you give me a pledge, until you send it" (38:17b). In this way she is able to maintain her masterful posi-

---

97. See the list of sexual metaphors associated with lust and associated with the power of sexuality on speech and action compiled by George Lakoff, *Women, Fire, and Dangerous Things: What Categories Reveal About the Mind* (Chicago: University of Chicago Press, 1987) 409-15.

98. *Mapping Ideology* (London: Verso, 1994) 15-30. For a more extensive discussion of the use of Žižek's concept of "faulty vision," see Tarlin, "Tamar's Veil," 177-80.

99. *The Art of Biblical Narrative*, 3-11.

tion in this situation and is free to rebuke him and his offer. She demands a pledge that will eventually cost him much more than a kid. Mieke Bal ties the Joseph narrative and Genesis 38 together at this point, saying that "deceit is committed with the help of an object used as a pledge or as proof" to strip away a "significant part of the victim's outfit."[100] She is correct to the extent that both Joseph and Judah are literally stripped of their identifying paraphernalia, but in Judah's case he voluntarily relinquishes his staff and seal while Joseph has his clothing torn from him by force. Certainly, Tamar will make good use of them as "the visual markers of a father (or master) and son relationship" in order to save herself from the charge of "whoredom" (38:24-25). As we will see, the legal and social importance of the items she obtains will have significant value in the upcoming "paternity suit."[101]

Again turning to the possibility that Judah is offering marriage and Tamar is negotiating the terms of the bonding, then a pledge in the form of items that are public aspects of his identity is appropriate since she will be joining his household and sharing his identity. The question is, can a woman do this? She has removed her widow's garments and replaced them with more "normal" garb including a veil, signaling to all comers that this woman is unattached, lacks a household representative, and is asking for offers of marriage. Tamar's leaving her father's house against Judah's orders constitutes a declaration of her freedom from the social constraints imposed by both households. In a similar situation in which the survival of her husband's household is at stake (1 Sam 25:18-19), Abigail takes independent action by loading up donkeys with peace offerings and does not inform her husband of her departure to meet with David in the nearby hill country. In this case, however, it seems more likely that Tamar is making a legal claim to maternity and the inheritance rights of her deceased husband Er rather than seeking a new husband for herself.

The evident theme of reversed social and gender roles in this narrative is not unique. Another example of an assertive female dealing with a pacified male is found in the verbal confrontation between Caleb and his daughter Achsah.[102] The judge's daughter "dismounted from her don-

---

100. "One Woman, Many Men, and the Dialectic of Chronology," in *Lethal Love* (Bloomington: University of Indiana Press, 1987) 95.

101. Furman, "His Story Versus Her Story," 145.

102. Cf. also Jephthah's daughter asking for a brief reprieve before her sacrifice in Judg 11:35-38.

key,"[103] causing Caleb to respond, "What do you wish?" (Judg 1:14). She then demands a "present," meaning an addition to her dowry so that the land in the Negeb given to her will also have water sources (1:15). Here, as in the Judah and Tamar story, setting and situation are triggers to conversation and transaction.

There is real irony in this episode that combines a disguised widow operating as a person outside the normal social constraints for females with a head of household who is a law-breaker. In this context, a delicious reversal of cognitive roles occurs when the *widower* supplies an animal in pledge. Surely the audience is aware of Job's list of the misdeeds of the wicked in which he says that the evil ones "take the widow's ox for a pledge" (Job 24:3b). The storyteller may have brought some knowing smiles to the ancient audience at this point.

Judah's Acceptance of Terms

Forced into a position of weakness, Judah does not contest Tamar's demand, but only responds, "What pledge shall I give you?" (38:18a). His statement represents a total surrender. By verbally accepting the role of supplicant, Judah has placed himself into a position that temporarily transforms his identity and cognitive attributes from a male head of household with full authority over other people's lives into a powerless client completely at the mercy of his transactional partner. Is the "product" so precious, so desirable, so necessary that Judah is willing to leave it up to an "unknown" prostitute to set the price? More likely, this is simply part of the transactional protocol as seen in Genesis 23 where the owner of what is being purchased is "forced" to set the price.

Lambe sees Judah's quick acquiescence here as evidence of his general alienation from the traditions of his family (i.e., his "turning aside" from dwelling with his brothers). If he sees Tamar as a cult prostitute, this would mean that he has accepted the validity of Canaanite ritual activity. In fact, Lambe states, the "abandonment of the insignia . . . represents a deeper rejection of his heritage and identity, consummating a process of separation and alienation."[104] While I am willing to see Judah as a nonconformist in

103. The Hebrew is uncertain here, but some form of social gesture must be meant by her action.

104. Lambe, "Judah's Development," 57.

some sense given his marriage to a Canaanite woman, I doubt that he has totally distanced himself from the rest of his extended family. However, if Lambe is correct about Judah's self-alienation, then his mental space — in essence his personal world as head of a household — is connected to a separate and quite alien space that is recognized by his brothers and possibly by other households in the community, identifying him as a nonconformist.

The term used here for pledge (*ʿērābôn*) appears only in this passage and in Job 17:3 instead of the usual legal term, *ḥābal*.[105] However, another form of the verb *ʿārab* also appears in Gen 43:9 and 44:32. In these passages Judah agrees to serve as "surety" for the life of Benjamin.[106] It is possible that the storyteller is using this unusual term as a signal to the audience. By employing such a term as part of Judah's actions here, it could be a cue that the tribe of Judah will stand as "Israel's pledge" in the future. In that way, the cognitive position of Judah and its most famous member, King David, takes on the traditional servant role often assigned to political leaders whether it is a valid label or not (see 1 Kgs 12:7).[107]

Tamar's Third Riposte

Having verbally imposed her will over her interlocutor, Tamar completes the transaction by setting her price: "Your signet and your cord, and the staff that is in your hand" (38:18b). Huddlestun[108] compares "in your hand" (*yād*) here with other usages in the Joseph narrative (39:1, 3-4, 6, 8, 12-13, 22-23), and Gunn and Fewell add the dimension of sexual innuendo, suggesting Judah has an erection and Tamar is taunting his rampant physical condition in a pun.[109] If her statement is based on such a gross physical signal of Judah's sexual arousal, then it is a further indication to the audience of his inability to govern his own emotions, something that ordinarily would be expected of the head of household.[110]

---

105. See Exod 22:26; Deut 24:17; and Amos 2:8 for other texts in which garments are taken in pledge.

106. See BDB, 786.

107. See Moshe Weinfeld, "The King as the Servant of the People," *JJS* 33 (1982) 189-94; and James Ian Harris, "The King as Public Servant," *JTSA* 113 (2002) 61-73.

108. "Divestiture, Deception, and Demotion," 59.

109. *Narrative in the Hebrew Bible*, 40.

110. See the admonition for "self-control" in Prov 25:28. In modern psychological

Whatever the case, this is an incredible demand.[111] Seeing that she has the ascendancy here, Tamar presses her advantage and requests that Judah give her every physical symbol of his identity short of the clothes on his back.[112] It is like asking today for someone's driver's license, social security card, and passport — an open invitation to identity theft. Why does Judah not balk at such an outlandish request? Either he is totally besotted with desire or, if she is a cultic figure, he may feel he is in need of a god's favor, given his bad fortune with his sons and the recent loss of his wife.

This completed transaction provides a legal fiction for the audience that strips Judah of his identity as Tamar's father-in-law. As a result, when he does have sexual relations with her and "she conceived by him" (38:18c) the incest issue is laid to rest. Of course, it also sets up the legal case she will make against him in 38:24-26. To be sure, the cognitive range of their identities has already been expanded by the verbal exchange and one more is not out of the question.

Final Narrative Structuring

The pericope ends with an inclusio: Tamar once again acts on her own and returns to her traditional place in her father's household, takes off her veil, and adorns herself in widow's garments (38:19).[113] The question could be asked why no one ever sees her come or go and why the first witness to anything out of the ordinary is three months later when it is reported to Judah that Tamar has "played the whore" and is pregnant (38:24a). But such mundane social realities have been suspended throughout this narrative, and it would be out of character for the storyteller to inject them suddenly.

---

analysis of emotions, the conclusion is drawn in Richard A. Shweder and Jonathan Haidt, "The Cultural Psychology of the Emotions: Ancient and New," in *Handbook of Emotions*, ed. Michael Lewis and Jeannette M. Haviland-Jones, 2nd ed. (New York: Guilford, 2000) 397, that "the character and meaning of particular emotions are systematically related to the kind of ethic (autonomy, community, or divinity) prevalent in a cultural community."

111. Alter, *The Art of Biblical Narrative*, 9, likens it to the "ancient Near Eastern equivalent of all a person's major credit cards."

112. See Paul R. Noble, "Esau, Tamar, and Joseph: Criteria for Identifying Inner-biblical Allusions," *VT* 52 (2002) 229. Cf. Delilah's pressing Samson to reveal his innermost secrets in Judg 16:4-17.

113. Menn, *Judah and Tamar*, 23.

Therefore, it is quite natural for the author to indicate the completion of the transactional portion of the narrative by reversing the order of the verbs that had been used in 38:14 from "clothing, actions and locations" to location, action, and clothing.[114]

Comic Relief

The follow-up to this episode is the comic attempt on the part of Judah's Adullamite friend to locate what Judah refers to as "the woman" (hā'iššâ) rather than the prostitute (zônâ) and which Hirah refers to as a cult prostitute (qĕdēšā) when he questions the people of Enaim (38:20-22).[115] Bird suggests that Hirah is using "polite speech" in referring to the woman as a cult prostitute rather than as a whore — a euphemism instead of a direct label of shame that might tarnish his friend's honor.[116] Westenholz counters that Hirah is in fact "denying the affair and pretending to take the kid to the קדֵשָׁה [qĕdēšā] for a sacrifice, as in Hos 4:14."[117] This is possible, but it would erode the comic character of the episode. Compounding the rhetorical game playing, Judah chooses to use a term that means both woman and wife. Hirah, who may be making a value judgment on the affair, uses a cultic term, as do the people of Enaim, who are pleased to be able to deny any such person exists as a way of staying out of the whole thing.

Judah's retrospective evaluation of these events is found in 38:23. Obviously wishing to put this whole episode behind him or wish it away, he tells Hirah to give up the search for her. In fact, Tamar can keep "the things," for "otherwise we will be laughed at." Judah's guilty reaction can be described as both a face-saving gesture and a part of a "shame-anger sequence in which the anger is directed back at the self."[118] With no other recourse available, he must accept the divestiture that has removed a portion of his identity (again a direct parallel to the multiple divestitures in the Joseph narrative). In the end, of course, Tamar voluntarily returns the items

---

114. Lambe, "Genesis 38," 116.

115. See Gunn and Fewell, *Narrative in the Hebrew Bible,* 40-41, on this change in vocabulary. See Lambe, "Genesis 38," 117, n. 18, on the alternative ways to translate qĕdēšā.

116. "The Harlot as Heroine," 126.

117. "Tamar, Qĕdēšā, Qadištu, and Sacred Prostitution in Mesopotamia," 248.

118. Thomas J. Scheff and Suzanne M. Retzinger, *Emotions and Violence: Shame and Rage in Destructive Conflicts* (Lexington, MA: Lexington, 1991) 13.

to him as proof of her innocence and righteousness in the affair, but that is only after three months have passed.[119] Throughout the narrative, her discursive authority allows Tamar to remain in control of the sequence of events until she obtains the necessary pregnancy that will insure the survival of her husband's, and in fact Judah's, households.

Resolution Through Intermediary Speech

The final resolution of these events comes in a moment of crisis for Tamar, but this time the embedded dialogue that signals the emotions and reactions of the characters is addressed to and through intermediaries. Cognitively, the scene hinges upon two words: *zônâ* and *ṣaddîq*. They function as the two facets of Tamar's perceived character and demonstrate that "meaning is a conceptual phenomenon," serving as "cognitive domains" within which understanding of the terms used falls within a spectrum of possible meanings.[120] As discussed above, the cognitive domain that encompasses the word *zônâ* includes a range of meanings within the context of illicit sexual behavior, but the specifics of this case require a meaning of adulteress because of her legal tie to Shelah. The other significant term, *ṣaddîq*, also has a spectrum of meanings ranging from "righteous" of character (Noah in Gen 6:9) to a technical, legal connotation of "innocent" (see Exod 23:7; Deut 25:1).[121]

The moment of truth comes after three months when her pregnancy can no longer be disguised. This time factor is comparable to the temporal indicator associated with Judah's traveling to Timnah for the sheepshearing following his period of mourning (38:12).[122] It is a narrative trigger, and it also closes a loop in the story that had begun with death and infertility (the death of Judah's wife) and ends with the announcement of a pregnancy. At that moment in time, Tamar's swelling belly precipitates the charge made against her of "whoredom," better translated as adultery in

119. See Huddlestun, "Divestiture, Deception, and Demotion," 60-61.

120. Ronald W. Langacker, "Possession and Possessive Constructions," in Taylor and MacLaury, *Language and the Cognitive Construal of the World*, 52.

121. Wenham, *Genesis 16–50*, 52.

122. See Albert Kamp, *Inner Worlds: A Cognitive Linguistic Approach to the Book of Jonah*. Biblical Interpretation 68 (Leiden: Brill, 2004) 19, for a discussion of time as a significant cognitive factor in interpreting biblical narrative.

this instance.[123] Interestingly, the narrator chooses to employ indirect speech here, transcribing what the accusers say to Judah rather than having a named character speak in direct dialogue with Judah.[124]

Judah now at last is allowed to play the role expected of him, exercising the speech pattern associated with one "in authority." He speaks in a short, choppy manner, with a marked tone focusing solely on this charge without any request for evidence or extenuating circumstances.[125] This speech pattern can be compared favorably to his initial command to Tamar to "let me come in to you" (38:16). Never once addressing Tamar face-to-face and without a trial, Judah summarily orders that she be publicly executed by burning (38:24b). His order to "bring her out," using the Hebrew imperative form *hôṣî'ûhā*, linguistically displays his heightened emotions and publicly displays his anger.[126] Such a precipitate strategy may be his way of showing moral outrage while eliminating a long-standing family problem as quickly as possible.

The result of Judah's unbridled rage is that Tamar is once again forced by circumstances to leave the normal confines of the household. The command that she be burned is unusual since the more common form of execution is stoning (Lev 20:27; Num 15:32-36; Deut 22:21). The only other situation in which burning is required for a young woman is in the case of the daughter of a priest, who "profanes herself through prostitution" (Lev 21:9). Despite this fact, there is no outcry by other members of the household. Once again the storyteller is narrowing the audience's focus, leaving Judah on center stage and withdrawing Tamar's accusers from the scene.

Since Tamar is not brought before Judah for judgment, she cannot physically respond to the charges in his presence or in public. As a result, her response must come through intermediaries, a form of indirect speech, addressed to those who were charged with "bringing her out." The accused's message is accompanied by a set of physical evidence that cannot

123. Wenham, *Genesis 16–50*, 368-69.

124. See Charles N. Li, "Direct Speech and Indirect Speech," in Coulmas, *Direct and Indirect Speech*, 37-39, on functional differences between direct and indirect speech.

125. Gary Long, "The Written Story: Toward Understanding Text as Representation and Function," *VT* 49 (1999) 170-72.

126. Zoltán Kövecses, "Anger: Its Language, Conceptualization, and Physiology," in *Language and the Cognitive Construal of the World*, ed. John R. Taylor and Robert E. MacLaury (Berlin: Mouton de Gruyter, 1995) 181.

be disputed.[127] These objects, as much as her words, convey the implications of what Judah has done. The staff and seal therefore function as a form of nonverbal communication evoking a cognitive response from the one person most likely to understand their full meaning.[128]

Further strengthening her appeal, Tamar adds a private message to Judah, saying, "It was the owner of these [a staff, seal, and cord] who made me pregnant." Since these items would have been well known to everyone in the household and the community, Judah has little choice but to acknowledge them and her (38:25). This simple statement shames Judah into accepting his levirate obligation to Tamar and legitimizing her children (twins). Of particular importance is the fact that Tamar does this in a private manner rather than shouting out accusations to anyone who would listen. Instead of publicly denouncing Judah as he had done to her, she allows him and his household to save face.

It is possible that the storyteller chooses this form of response because it is one that the audience would approve. In many traditional cultures the socialized role of the female is to be supportive.[129] Even though Tamar's evidence is embarrassing to Judah personally, his position as head of the household is not endangered. In turn, Judah does not directly confront Tamar, choosing instead to speak also to the intermediaries who had brought the objects to him. By stating, "She is more in the right than I," Judah certifies to witnesses that Tamar is innocent *(ṣaddîq)* of all charges (38:26; cf. Saul's statement in 1 Sam 24:17[MT 18]). She is absolved of all guilt, and her actions are accepted as appropriate behavior.

In evaluating this narrative resolution, Wildavsky concludes that "Tamar is saved because she acts to achieve an honorable purpose albeit through dishonorable means."[130] When Judah "recognizes" *(wayyakkēr)* these personal identity items and chooses to receive them back, he has little choice but to spare Tamar. In terms of the larger narrative that includes the Joseph cycle of stories, this provides "the prerequisite for a future rec-

---

127. See Deut 22:13-21 for another example of a narrative that centers on the display of physical evidence.

128. Judee K. Burgoon and Gregory D. Hoobler, "Nonverbal Signals," in *Handbook of Interpersonal Communication,* ed. Mark L. Knapp and John A. Daly, 3rd ed. (Thousand Oaks: Sage, 2002) 243.

129. John A Daly, "Personality and Interpersonal Communication," in Knapp and Daly, *Handbook of Interpersonal Communication,* 141.

130. "Survival Must Not Be Gained through Sin," 46.

onciliation with his brothers and father and a preparation for his role as family spokesman."[131]

Postscript: The Ordinary as a Factor in Storytelling

What is remarkable in reading the story of Judah and Tamar is the degree of detail that it contains. Most personal experiences do not elicit such detail, and in fact we tend not to see most of what goes on around us. We are too busy being employed in "being ordinary" either to take note of what is remarkable or even to want to experience it to any great degree.[132] Why should we be interested in taking more than casual note of the color of the sky, the feel of the wind on our face, or the majority of other sensory sensations that are available to us all the time? Our world is peopled by the expected — both the characters and the scenery. In an urban setting, we expect certain sounds and smells, the honking of horns and the rush of cars and people. However, we would find these experiences totally incongruous in a rural setting. Do we in fact really hear the constant roar of sound in the big city? If it suddenly stopped, would we be alarmed, or would we instead do a mental exercise designed to discount the current reality and instead replace it with the expected phenomena? Thus when we do see something out of the ordinary, we often wish to transform it into the ordinary. For example, when Lot warns his sons-in-law of the imminent demise of Sodom and Gomorrah, they refuse to believe him, choosing instead to assume that only the ordinary ever happens until they are struck in the face by the extraordinary (Gen 19:14).[133]

Might it be, therefore, that good storytelling is the presentation of the extraordinary as a way of exciting or waking up our senses to the possibilities that may exist when people choose to or are forced to act outside the ordinary? In fact, it may not be possible to write a plausible story without requiring the characters to step periodically beyond the ordinary. Otherwise, every story would be the same — an endless series of expected experiences, an endless response to the senses that "nothing much"

131. Lambe, "Judah's Development," 58.
132. Harvey Sacks, "On Doing 'Being Ordinary,'" in *Structures of Social Action: Studies in Conversation Analysis*, ed. J. Maxwell Atkinson and John Heritage (Cambridge: Cambridge University Press, 1984) 418-19.
133. Sacks, "On Doing 'Being Ordinary,'" 419-20.

happened. Likewise, conversation within a story is driven by the desire to draw the audience into a world that goes beyond their ordinary existence while at the same time playing off of ordinary events and expectations. The storyteller generally is not trying to create the fantastic, except in apocalyptic or visionary scenes. Instead, the goal is to create staged, reciprocal conversations that sound "normal" or ordinary, but actually have a richer subtheme of meaning or dimension that exists side by side with the ordinary. When the audience discover this subtheme, they are awakened to the talents of the author and are entertained, shocked, or at least temporarily drawn away from their comfort area and into the world created by the author.

This takes us back to the scene in which Judah encounters Tamar alongside the road to Enaim. In a sense, what he encountered was exactly what was expected, a prostitute or a priestess (either serves the function of the story, depending on the intent of the author — prurient satisfaction for a new widower or opportunity to obtain a god's good will through a fertility ritual) who is open to his invitation that they have intercourse. There is no physical danger implicit in this scene, and Tamar shows no sense of threat, although the audience, of course, who have been clued in by the narrator, know full well the danger Judah is about to encounter. They know he is a "law-breaker" or at least a noncompliant father of a household. They know that Tamar has taken an extraordinary step, leaving her ordinary existence, transforming her appearance, and placing herself in a position that she would never ordinarily occupy. Unlike Judah, the audience are already aware of the subtheme and are completely cognizant of social elements that are contributing to this drama. What has actually happened is that the audience have been given the extraordinary ability to see beyond the surface. Instead of being constrained by the normal mode of "seeing" a scene or "hearing" the conversation between the two parties, which by its nature fails to take in all of its details and only recognizes the expected elements, the audience have been invited to take note of unusual details thereby enriching their overall experience of the story.

Now if Judah had seen his daughter-in-law in her widow's garments sitting beside the road, his reaction would have been very different. He would never have perceived her as an object of sexual desire or as a means of obtaining good fortune during the sheepshearing. More likely, he would have assumed that she was injured, had been attacked and left beside the road, or some other "ordinary" explanation. Thus the catalyst for a particular type of conversation between them is the setting (the entrance to Enaim) plus the costume, which does not permit him to recognize Tamar. She does not "look like Tamar," and therefore she cannot be Tamar.

With regard to which character is dominant in this scene, it could be argued that Tamar is the more dominant because she is the one who sets the scene. She elicits Judah's invitation to her by positioning herself in this place and by portraying herself in a guise that he would recognize immediately. Having "set the scene" and established a specific cognitive frame for his mind's eye, she does not have to speak first. Her initial, nonverbal statement is made by her clothing and her location. The bargaining actually begins when Judah sees her as an acceptable object of sexual desire and turns aside from his journey.

At the same time, there is nothing entirely unbelievable about this story. Its basic elements involve recognized and acceptable behavior. The conversation between Judah and Tamar that follows their encounter on the road does not involve extraordinary procedures, requests, demands, or fantastic events. It is simply a transactional dialogue, a service solicited from a person who is perceived as regularly supplying that service. The price is determined ahead of time and, given Judah's inability to pay his debt immediately, a "marker" is provided to insure future payment. It is not likely that the audience will be disturbed to any great extent by any of these ordinary speeches or actions, especially given the storyteller's narrative cues. In other words, they will accept the likelihood that they themselves could experience these events and thus will feel an entitlement to the surface story presented here.[134] Where they may become a bit uncomfortable is in Tamar's breach of social protocol in removing herself from the ordinary and taking extraordinary steps to obtain a child in the face of Judah's obstructionism. However, the return to normalcy following the birth of the twins restores social identities, and the cognitive frame is once again set on the themes of covenant, inheritance, and the future of the nation.

---

134. Sacks, "On Doing 'Being Ordinary,'" 428.

CHAPTER THREE

Conversation Analysis and Embedded Dialogue

In this chapter we will explore some of the methods of conversational analysis and in particular how context influences dialogue.[1] Conversation analysis, at its heart, is "the systematic analysis of the talk produced in everyday situations of human interaction: *talk-in-interaction*."[2] Its purpose is to examine both the ordinary conversations that take place constantly between people and the occasional extraordinary dialogues that occur spontaneously or as part of staged performances. Thus it embraces interaction in every context, including those that occur in more formal situations or within an institutional/work context that requires a restricted or directed form of discourse.[3] Conversation analysis is one of many methodologies that fall within what are called constructionist approaches. In particular, conversation analysis relates to the constructionist principle that "language derives its significance in human affairs from the way in which it functions within patterns of relationships."[4]

The assumption that is made in conversation analysis is that interac-

1. See Charles Goodwin, "Conversation Analysis," *Annual Review of Anthropology* 19 (1990) 283-307, for a helpful summary of the origins of this method and its usefulness to the social sciences.

2. Ian Hutchby and Robin Wooffitt, *Conversation Analysis: Principles, Practices and Applications* (Cambridge: Polity, 1998) 13.

3. Robin Wooffitt, *Conversation Analysis and Discourse Analysis* (London: Sage, 2005) 68.

4. Kenneth J. Gergen, *Realities and Relationships: Soundings in Social Construction* (Cambridge, MA: Harvard University Press, 1994) 52-53.

tion is "highly organized and orderly and . . . that the specifics of meaning and understanding in interaction would be impossible without this order-liness."[5] Therefore, when people talk, whether it is in a live conversation or in embedded dialogue in a narrative, they are not only communicating their thoughts, bits of information, or accumulated knowledge. They are also communicating their identities and their relative positions, and they are engaging in active social interaction: making others feel comfortable or nervous or scared, offering an invitation, or negotiating a point.[6] The process therefore provides a key to the study of their society through its forms of conversation.

Oral vs. Written Conversation Analysis

One of the earliest developers of conversation analysis was Harvey Sacks. Working originally with accounts of callers to suicide hot lines, he ultimately broadened his research to include categories within conversational organization: turn-taking, overlapping of dialogue, the initiation of conversation topics, greetings and invitations.[7] Eventually, to insure closer attention to detail, he advocated the use of recorded data. This practice was designed to eliminate the inaccuracies that result from after-the-fact reconstructions or transcriptions of speech and to provide ease of study through as much iteration as desired.[8] While this practice is not possible when dealing with the reported conversations contained in the biblical narrative, I suggest that having written accounts serves much the same purpose as recorded speech and is subject to the same caveat that people and authors do not always give voice to their full story.[9]

5. Paul Drew and John Heritage, "Introduction," in *Conversation Analysis*, vol. 1: *Turn-Taking and Repair*, ed. Drew and Heritage (London: Sage, 2006) xxii.

6. John Shotter and Kenneth Gergen, "A Prologue to Constructing the Social," in *Constructing the Social*, ed. Theodore R. Sarbin and John I. Kitsuse (London: Sage, 1994) 1.

7. See a comprehensive discussion of his various areas of research in Harvey Sacks, *Lectures on Conversation*, ed. Gail Jefferson (Oxford: Blackwell, 1992).

8. Harvey Sacks, "Notes on Methodology," in *Structures of Social Action: Studies in Conversation Analysis*, ed. J. Maxwell Atkinson and John Heritage (Cambridge: Cambridge University Press, 1984) 26.

9. Harvey Sacks, "Everyone Has to Lie," in *Sociocultural Dimensions of Language Use*, ed. Mary Sanches and Ben G. Blount (New York: Academic, 1975) 57-80.

What also needs to be addressed, however, is the difference between oral versus written accounts. A full understanding of dialogue is basically dependent upon a shared understanding of the world. When conversants come from the same culture and social class, their everyday speech is generally filled with shorthand expressions allowing them to speak somewhat disjointedly, with certain words (uh, oh, ah, you know) merely serving as connectors, without specific meaning or significance to the conversation. They may also employ abbreviated expressions or nicknames for persons, places, or events, and there is a level of familiarity when speaking about these things that leave cognitive gaps for persons not a part of that culture. The basic lack of linguistic or cognitive coherence caused by the omissions in what is spoken becomes cognitive opportunities or minefields as the reader attempts to fill in the blanks. If readers do so without analyzing context and researching the linguistic characteristics of that culture's speech patterns, then it is likely they will impose their own schema on what they read, interpreting without understanding and drawing invalid conclusions.[10]

While a skilled writer can reproduce dialects as well as everyday dialogue by mimicking oral pronunciation, this is generally awkward to read out loud and does not have the impact of an impromptu conversation. As a result, a careful study of the context of a written narrative and embedded dialogue is necessary for the storyteller to approximate tone, inflection, use of pauses and gestures, and to express meaning. It will be in the management of these details and the efficient use of linguistic strategies that the author most effectively draws the reader into the story.[11]

More formal addresses are easier to study and reproduce since they do conform to standard use of vocabulary, grammar, and structure. The task of reproducing them in writing (= reported speech) will still lack the benefit of hearing the orator's particular styles of inflection or emotional peaks, witnessing the use of physical gestures, or noting the speaker's accent during an oral address. Therefore, to make the written account more realistic the writer must supply rhetorical cues to the audience that signal when these conversational elements are present.[12] Then, to make clear

10. Guy Cook, *Discourse and Literature* (Oxford: Oxford University Press, 1994) 34-36.

11. Deborah Tannen, *Talking Voices* (Cambridge: Cambridge University Press, 1989) 154-55.

12. See the discussion of the differences in oral and written dialogue in Khosrow

what the reactions are to this speech, similar cues need to be provided to simulate the speech and emotions of the audience.[13] As a result, in the examination of biblical narrative with embedded dialogue special attention will have to be given to apparent structures of speech and any narrative cues inserted for the benefit of the reader. In addition, a careful analysis of embedded dialogue must include the gathering of as much contextual data as possible in order to understand and analyze the story more fully.

Levels of Conversation Analysis

Current practice among conversation analysts operates on several levels, examining speech patterns, word usage, as well as the results of speech on social interaction. Conversation analysis:

- Looks for **patterns of speech in social interaction** that provide evidence of practices of conduct. The assumption is made that a recurrent practice triggers or elicits a particular response or social action based on familiarity with that practice. For example, beginning a conversation with an interrogative expression (Hebrew *mî*, or *mâ*, or *'ahâ* = oh? or what?) or a question solicits a response based on what has been asked.
- Examines the **normal sequence of actions** during social interaction, watching for how competently the participants recognize the proper next step, engage in turn-taking, and take into account previous statements or shared contexts.
- Determines how **competently people adhere to the standardized organization** of speech patterns with both their shared understanding of the rules of social interaction and their awareness of their rights within the range of possible practices.[14] When the rules are broken it is necessary to determine whether this was intentional or simply an example of a verbal faux pas.

Jahandarie, *Spoken and Written Discourse: A Multi-disciplinary Perspective* (Stamford: Ablex, 1999) 131-33.

13. Tannen, *Talking Voices*, 172, points to an inseparability of emotion and cognition in understanding dialogue, whether spoken or written.

14. See Drew and Heritage, "Introduction," xxiv-xxv.

Moses and Jethro (Exodus 18:13-27)

To illustrate these points, let us look briefly at the dialogue between Moses and his father-in-law Jethro in Exod 18:13-27. This pericope parallels an earlier story of shared governance found in Num 11:16-30, and both deal with the reorganization of judicial procedures.[15] The dialogue begins when Jethro witnesses how Moses is trying to mediate all of the disputes among the people. Recognizing this as an inefficient use of Moses' time and energy, Jethro will first try to break Moses' single-minded assumption that he is responsible for all leadership tasks. Then, taking on the role of sage and elder he will recommend a series of steps, outlining a new judicial protocol, that will lift some of the self-imposed burden from Moses' shoulders and share it among 70 men appointed for the task of hearing minor disputes (18:19-23).

Jethro initiates their interaction by stepping forward and asking his son-in-law, "What is this *(mâ-haddābār hazzeh 'ăšer)* that you are doing for the people? Why do you sit alone, while all the people stand around you from morning until evening?" (18:14). In this social context, Jethro's remarks are not simply a request for information. They are a methodical conversational strategy designed to accomplish change.[16] He is invoking the authority of a sage, intentionally employing a form of cutting irony to draw Moses' attention to an unsatisfactory procedure and asking him to stop and think about his actions. His use of words is also significant since they take on the tone of a near insult: "What do you think you are doing to the people!"[17] Of course, the effectiveness of Jethro's questions is dependent upon Moses' recognition of Jethro's communicative intentions.[18]

---

15. Stephen L. Cook, "The Tradition of Mosaic Judges: Past Approaches and New Directions," in *On the Way to Nineveh,* ed. Cook and S. C. Winter (Atlanta: Scholars, 1999) 291-95, details the parallels between these two texts, noting that the Numbers passage predates the account in Exodus and that the former is primarily concerned with the "sacralization" of the judiciary.

16. See the discussion of Harvey Sacks's "wild possibility" that "utterances may be viewed as objects which speakers use to accomplish particular things in their interactions with others," in Hutchby and Wooffitt, *Conversation Analysis,* 19-21.

17. For similar use of the phrase *mah-zzō't 'āśît,* see Gen 3:13; 12:18; 26:10; and 29:25.

18. For the various rhetorical purposes associated with irony and their effectiveness, see John S. Leggitt and Raymond W. Gibbs, Jr., "Emotional Reactions to Verbal Irony," *Discourse Processes* 29 (2000) 3-4. Ironically, another example of a call to reflective and wise action is found in the admonition that the Levite sends to the Israelites to consider, take counsel, and speak out against the evil done in Gibeah (Judg 19:30).

Note that according to the mutually understood social patterns of this community only Jethro could have questioned Moses in this way. There are three narrative clues in the earlier part of this chapter that help to establish Jethro's authority in this scene and provide him with a high level of recognition and respect: (1) the storyteller's incredibly repetitious use of the title "Moses' father-in-law" *(ḥōtēn mōšeh)*[19] instead of the name Jethro, throughout the chapter (18:1, 2, 5, 6, 7, 8, 12, 14, 15, 17, 24, 27); (2) the storyteller reminds the audience of their social relationship by having Jethro use his kinship title when he alerts Moses of his imminent arrival in the camp (18:6); and (3) Jethro makes a singular statement of faith in Yahweh's power following Moses' recitation of the exodus events (18:10-11)[20] and then officiates over the sacrifice rather than either Moses or Aaron, while these leaders of the Israelites are portrayed as joining Jethro in a covenant meal before Yahweh (18:12).[21]

The pattern of social organization in that ancient, traditional society would require this show of respect and would be a signal that both Jethro and Moses are following established speech and kinship protocols.[22] When Moses responds, however, he basically provides only a description of what Jethro has already seen that day, outlining a threefold procedure: the people come to me to inquire of God, I decide the disputes between persons brought to me, and I teach them God's statutes (18:15-16).

Perhaps in frustration of the fact that Moses does not choose to reveal very much about his own feelings on this matter, Jethro first provides a judgment of his own on what Moses is doing (18:17): it is "not good" *(lō'-ṭôb haddābār 'ăšer 'attâ 'ōśeh)*. Then, matching Moses' threefold speech pattern with a threefold response of his own, the father-in-law tells him, "you will surely wear yourself out . . . the task is too heavy . . . you cannot do it alone" (18:18).

Of particular significance for conversation analysis is the word

---

19. Note that *ḥōtēn*, "father-in-law" appears only in this story in Exodus 18, in the mention of Hobab as Moses' father-in-law in Num 10:29, and in Judg 1:16 and 19:4, 7, 9.

20. Cf. Na'aman's statement in 2 Kgs 5:15.

21. Carol Meyers, *Exodus*. NCambBC (Cambridge: Cambridge University Press, 2005) 137, points to Jethro's role as officiant as credence for the position that there is a definite Midianite influence in the development of Israelite religious practice.

22. For a discussion of this social protocol, see Victor H. Matthews and Don C. Benjamin, *Social World of Ancient Israel, 1250-587 B.C.E.* (Peabody: Hendrickson, 1993) 7-9. Cf. the immediate acquiescence of Ruth to Naomi's suggestions in Ruth 3:1-5.

choice that appears in these opening statements. Jethro's question, Moses' response ("When they have a dispute, they come to me and I decide *[kî-yihyeh lāhem dābār, bā' 'ēlay],*" 18:16), and Jethro's rejoinder, spoken in a tone of disapproval ("What you are doing is not good [lit., 'too heavy for you'; *kî-kābēd mimmĕkā haddābār,*" 18:18) all employ the word *dābār,* which in this legal context refers to Moses' action as well as the people's disputes.[23] The choice of this particular word and the common speech pattern each employs represent a conscious effort on the part of the storyteller to highlight the judicial nature of this scene. It is likely that the repetitious use of a wordplay would have appealed to the ears and the minds of the ancient audience.[24]

Completing the scene is a forceful cry by Jethro to be heard as he shapes a solution to the problem (18:19). He signals his call with the imperative phrase, "Now listen to me" (*'attâ šĕma' bĕqōlî*).[25] Jethro then proceeds to affirm the tasks that Moses has previously laid out for himself: "bringing their cases before God," teaching "them the statutes" of God, and instructing them on "the way they are to go and the things they are to do." The basic psychology of these opening remarks creates a conciliatory tone that may be intended to soften the earlier, more aggressive and cutting statements made to Moses. His authority as the mediator between the people and God is affirmed using Moses' own words.[26]

However, this proves to be only a prelude to Jethro's intended

23. Eugene Carpenter, "Exodus 18: Its Structure, Style, Motifs and Function in the Book of Exodus," in *A Biblical Itinerary: In Search of Method, Form and Content.* JSOTSup 240 (Sheffield: Sheffield Academic, 1997) 99, points out the frequency of the use of the words *mišpāṭ* and *dābār* in this section of the narrative as linguistic cues to the leitmotif of justice that presages the giving of the law in Exodus 20.

24. Edward L. Greenstein, "Jethro's Wit: An Interpretation of Wordplay in Exodus 18," in Cook and Winter, *On the Way to Nineveh,* 160-64.

25. See further discussion of the imperative voice in Samuel A. Meier, *Speaking of Speaking: Marking Direct Discourse in the Hebrew Bible.* VTSup 46 (Leiden: Brill, 1992) 112-18. Other examples of this personal summons to be heard are found in Gen 27:8; Num 16:8; and 1 Sam 26:19.

26. Rosalind Gill, "Discourse Analysis: Practical Implementation," in *Handbook of Qualitative Research Methods for Psychology and the Social Sciences,* ed. John T. E. Richardson (Leicester: British Psychological Society, 1996) 143, differentiates discourse analysis from conversation analysis, noting that the latter is more concerned with the structure and patterning of discourse, while the former tends to "regard social life as being characterized by conflicts" so that it focuses on the assumption that "much discourse is involved in establishing one version of the world in the face of competing versions."

agenda, the appointment of 70 God-fearing, trustworthy elders to assist Moses with the lower-level judicial caseload (18:21-22).[27] He then completes his oration with a threefold claim for the authority of his words of wisdom: (1) assuming that God "so commands you," (2) that Moses will be able to "endure" and thus finish his task as leader, and (3) "all these people will go to their home in peace," completing the covenant promise made to them when they were brought out of Egypt. By categorizing his advice as the wise thing to do and associating it with God's plan, Jethro employs a rhetorical device that discourse analysts refer to as "stake inoculation."[28] This is a strategy or speech pattern designed to prevent the dismissal of a position or claim based on the assumption that it is merely an expression of personal interest.[29] When Moses quietly accepts and acts on Jethro's advice (18:24-25), the father-in-law has completed his narrative role as sage. He, like Jacob's father-in-law Laban (Gen 31:55), departs the scene "to his own country" and is not heard from again.

Frame Analysis

The "frame analysis" model created by Erving Goffman provides a useful methodology for conversation analysis, with particular attention to the examination and interpretation of context. In his dramaturgical description of social interaction, Goffman suggests that it is natural for humans to posit or identify social and physical "frames" as they interact with other persons or objects. These "frames" are mental projections that are shaped by a person's understanding of the world and those things that inhabit or structure it.[30] Cognitively, primary frames consist of idealized impressions, supplied

27. Carpenter, "Exodus 18," 99, emphasizes that Jethro has only provided administrative wisdom, not legal content, since that is God's prerogative and it will be Moses' task to instruct the people on the law.

28. For other admonitions to hear and obey words of wisdom, see Ps 107:43; Prov 1:5; and 12:15.

29. Jonathan Potter, *Representing Reality: Discourse, Rhetoric and Social Construction* (London: Sage, 1996) 125-28.

30. Erving Goffman, *Frame Analysis* (Boston: Northeastern University Press, 1974) 38. Note in his definition of a frame (10-11) that an individual frame is only a part of a larger structure. This implies that the universe, or the all-encompassing "definition of the situation," consists of a succession of frames, each enclosing all others as the structure becomes larger.

by previously learned data, of an immediate situation. In other words, they comprise the context within which all forms of interaction take place.[31]

Conversation analysis and discourse analysis benefit from careful attention to ethnographic, linguistic, and physical context. In fact, without taking into account the background data supplied by the total context the analysis of social interaction would be shallow and prone to misinterpretation, even total misunderstanding.[32] It is critical to study how interacting speakers orient to each other and the context in which they are placed. This provides important clues on how or whether the "turn-taking" of speakers is oriented toward each other's words, their comparative social status, their respective gender, or the audience before which they are speaking.[33] One can therefore conclude that when dialogue is added to the mix of sensory and background information contained within the frame, the character of the discourse, its tone, and the conversational strategies employed will necessarily shift as the interaction between the conversants progresses.

Using Frame Analysis

To put this in simpler terms, let us consider a person who is walking down a busy street. The frame of this scenario could then consist of a range of factors including:

- How the person is dressed
- The person's general bodily appearance, gender, ethnicity, and race
- The pace at which a person is walking
- The character of the weather and the effect it has on the person

31. See Goffman's critique of acontextual studies in *Forms of Talk* (Philadelphia: University of Pennsylvania Press, 1981) 67, and the analysis of Goffman's view in Thomas J. Scheff, "The Structure of Context: Deciphering *Frame Analysis*," *Sociological Theory* 23 (2005) 371-72.

32. Aaron V. Cicourel, "The Interpenetration of Communicative Contexts," in *Rethinking Context,* ed. Alessandro Duranti and Charles Goodwin (Cambridge: Cambridge University Press, 1992) 294, provides a warning to analysts who wish to engage in more than a purely local and mundane study, and notes that "language and other social practices are interdependent."

33. Woffitt, *Conversation Analysis and Discourse Analysis,* 64. See also on turn-taking, Harvey Sacks, Emanuel A. Schlegel, and Gail Jefferson, "A Simplest Systematics for the Organization of Turn-Taking for Conversation," *Language* 50 (1974) 696-735.

- The time of day and the season of the year
- Whether it is a familiar or an unfamiliar street

In addition to the basic physical characteristics of the persons involved in this scene, there is also background information that can be posited about them.[34] This includes their mental stability and cognitive awareness of their surroundings, the range of emotions they are currently experiencing, and their familiarity with standardized social obligations in that particular frame. If one person does choose to engage in conversation with someone he or she encounters in this frame, their basic cognitive abilities and emotions will be expressed in their choice of language and physical gestures.[35]

Physical Context

Once a clear picture has been created of the persons in this scene, it is instructive to turn to the inanimate objects that are also part of the framing of the scene. Here again certain factors may be suggested that shape action and speech as the person approaches the intersection. The scene can be framed in terms of the width of the sidewalk, the speed and number of oncoming cars, the color of the street light or the audible signals supplied for those who may be handicapped, and any other objects, such as a construction site, that may impede or facilitate movement. These objects or conditions all contribute to the basic structure of the primary frame. However, both they and the scenario envisioned here are all temporary. It is unlikely that persons are going to spend the remainder of their lives rooted to this spot. They may stop and have a conversation with persons that they meet here. But the light will change and they will eventually move on to experience new framed settings. The transitory and ever-shifting nature of the frame, therefore, requires a continuous cognitive process that encompasses reevaluation of the makeup of the frame situation in which the observer views these occurrences.

34. John A. Daly, "Personality and Interpersonal Communication," in *Handbook of Interpersonal Communication,* ed. Mark L. Knapp and Daly, 3rd ed. (Thousand Oaks: Sage, 2002) 143-56, discusses "cognitive dispositions" that affect conversation including such things as an authoritarian disposition, loneliness, self-esteem, argumentativeness, and rejection sensitivity.

35. Zoltán Kövecses, *Emotion Concepts* (New York: Springer, 1990) 13-20.

While there will be some differences in the frame every time a person encounters a particular place or person, the primary characteristics of the frame do provide a cognitive foundation from which to begin the evaluative process. Goffman uses the example of the routine servicing of equipment in a casino that becomes so much a part of the background of activity within that frame that the players and the casino workers simply take these activities and the consistent conditions they supply for granted while they continue on with their gaming.[36]

Thus, if there is a basic familiarity with the characteristics of a frame, this provides the comfort level associated with the "ordinary,"[37] a sort of cognitive shorthand that does not require a great deal of thought and within which persons can speak or interact in a nearly unconscious manner based on well-established social expectations. For instance, when a family gathers for a meal in their kitchen or dining room, the multiple repetitions of this activity, the familiarity of the persons present, the inviting smells of the food, the expected begging for scraps by the family pets, and even the sight of the "old familiar" dishes and silverware combine to create a comfortable frame of reference.

Social Interaction

Now, couple the physical character of the frame with any activities associated with interactions between persons in our example of the street encounter, and additional factors arise:

- Whether the person encounters a friend or an enemy
- Whether a person encounters an acquaintance or a stranger
- Whether the person encountered is clothed, male or female, handicapped, young or old, of the same ethnic or racial background
- Whether the persons have time to stop and converse
- Whether the persons possess standard interpersonal skills
- Whether there are preexisting conditions such as heightened emotions that will affect the speech and actions of the person(s)

36. Goffman, *Frame Analysis*, 250.
37. See Harvey Sacks, "On Doing 'Being Ordinary,'" in Atkinson and Heritage, *Structures of Social Action*, 413-29.

With these interactional possibilities in play, a reflective process takes place that may determine whether a friendly greeting is offered, a verbal or physical attack takes place, or whether the decision is made to look away or hurry on without speaking. Every conversational choice is made based on these intuitive and reflective exercises, and the success or failure of their interaction is facilitated or hindered by the degree of competence these persons have in exercising their interpersonal skills.[38]

What follows, whether it be a full-blown discourse, a gesture, or disregard for each other, generally proceeds based on a set of social understandings or obligations. If, as Charles Horton Cooley contended in developing his concept of the "looking-glass self"[39] that "we live in the minds of others," then discourse and all other forms of social interaction are dependent on the reflective skills of each person. Therefore, when misunderstandings or socially inappropriate responses occur (leaving aside the actions of the mentally disturbed), they may be based on a true failure to communicate within the context of the overall social setting.

To illustrate this, Goffman uses the term "key" to refer to a level of "mutual awareness," a cognitive ability that contributes to participants' understanding of a meaningful activity, such as offering to shake hands, as a genuine gesture or one that signifies something else entirely.[40] For instance, when Joab greets his old military rival Amasa, he grabs his friend's "beard with his right hand to kiss him." This was a well-known social gesture of affection in ancient Israelite society. In many cultures this action would be recognized as an intentional disarming of potential hostilities between them because the right hand was ordinarily the one used to hold a weapon.[41] In this case, however, Amasa is fooled into a false sense of mutual awareness and Joab stabs him, presumably with a sword in his left hand (2 Sam 20:8-10).

---

38. Brian H. Spitzberg and William R. Cupach, "Interpersonal Skills," in Knapp and Daly, *Handbook of Interpersonal Communication*, 568-69, provide a selective list of interpersonal skills including active listening, conflict management, mutuality, possessiveness, and topic maintenance. They make it clear that "interpersonal skills are vital to the collective state of social and physical health" (573).

39. *Human Nature and the Social Order* (New York: Scribner's, 1902) 151-53.

40. Goffman, *Frame Analysis*, 43-44.

41. See a similar strategy that plays on misdirection and the general assumption that most persons are right-handed in the story of Ehud's assassination of the Moabite king Eglon (Judg 3:15-22).

When a new setting is encountered, such as a child's first day at school, a larger number of factors will have to be assessed and processed. Individuals in these unfamiliar frames become more self-conscious of their surrounding, and they quickly determine how they can best fit into this new frame or escape it. They are reminded through this process of the necessity to identify, classify, and store this data for later use, should this experience be repeated.

Should there be a sudden or unexpected disruption in what is considered to be the idealized or expected setting, the frame is broken and the level of mutual understanding no longer provides a shared view of events. A whole new set of reference points is created requiring a swift mental exercise to cope cognitively with the changes that are being experienced. The easy flow of conversation on old familiar topics now may shift to express alarm, curiosity, or a call to action. Of course, one possible response will be based on the forces of social inertia that try to bring the frame back into its idealized former self. If that does not prove possible, then a new frame or perhaps a whole new set of frames associated with a crisis or the breakup of the "ordinary" will be the result.

Narrative and Frame

As a narrative tool, the disruption of the frame, or frame-breaking, functions as one of the primary vehicles for dramatic effect. To an extent it is facilitated by an assumption on the part of the author and the audiences that certain qualities associated with the physical setting of a story are well understood and that activity within a particular setting is determined by its characteristics. Additionally, it is assumed that speech patterns are formalized based on where in space a dialogue or a pronouncement occurs. The fluidity of social framing, however, indicates that activity and speech are not always so formally restricted and that the basic variability in human interaction allows the cognitive qualities of space to be shifted and adapted based on the desires of a speaker, just as the speaker's words are often shaped by spatial parameters.

For example, when Jeroboam dedicates his new royal shrine at Bethel, he engages in a liturgical performance (including the burning of incense) that is so familiar that his audience could practically go through the motions in their sleep. But the king and his assembled audience are rudely awakened when the unnamed prophet from Judah disrupts the proceedings by completely ignoring the king and instead directing his condemnation to the altar (1 Kgs 13:2). Suddenly the frame that had been fashioned for this occasion, with its carefully orchestrated offerings and ritual pronouncements, takes on a sinister and other-worldly character. With a prophetic voice raised to reject the sanctity of the king's shrine, the power relationships are called into question. Therefore King Jeroboam, who is in the process of dedicating the shrine and its altar before the people, is required to respond aggressively if he wishes to snap the frame and his authority back into its proper shape (13:4).[42]

Turning once again to Goffman's model, he uses the term "front" for the "expressive equipment . . . employed by the individual during his performances." This includes the setting or scenery, including the "personal front" that comprises "insignia of office or rank; clothing; sex, age, and racial characteristics; size and looks; posture; speech patterns; facial expressions; bodily gestures," some of which are "mobile or transitory, such as facial expression" and can fluctuate during the course of a dialogue.[43] Playing on these qualities associated with "front" or context is the potential that comes with exploring the dimensions of intentional manipulation of space by a performer or by conversationalists. Clearly, it is when the basic comfort level and social understanding of space, participants, and all things contributing to the setting are challenged by the storyteller that drama and charged dialogue occur.

Frame-busting in the Story of David and Michal

There are situations in which consensus-building occurs and general agreement is affirmed by the positive or at least passively-acceptant behavior of others.[44] If someone attempts to disrupt the level of mutual under-

---

42. See Jerome T. Walsh, "The Contexts of 1 Kings xiii," *VT* 39 (1989) 357-58.

43. Erving Goffman, *The Presentation of Self in Everyday Life* (Garden City: Doubleday Anchor, 1959) 22-24.

44. See a basic survey of the early literature on consensus building in Thomas J. Scheff, "Toward a Sociological Model of Consensus," *American Sociological Review* 32 (1967) 32-46. Particularly interesting is the finding that "if no one in a community agrees with a view, but everyone thinks that everyone else does, the effect on behavior is sometimes the same as if everyone actually agreed" (33).

standing that serves as the foundation of a consensus belief — frame-busting — this provides for both a good story and an opportunity for a storyteller to affirm further why the general consensus is the correct attitude to hold. A case in point is the story of David's entrance into Jerusalem with the ark of the covenant (2 Sam 6:1-23). The ark had remained in storage for many years and had not been used during the reign of Saul. In this story David seizes the opportunity to transport and install this important sacred object in his new capital at Jerusalem, thereby transforming the city into both a political and religious center for the Israelites.[45]

For our purposes, the heart of the story begins as David and the ark approach the gates of Jerusalem. At this point David removes his garments and joins in the dancing with the other celebrants as they pass through the gate (2 Sam 6:14, 20).[46] There is a range of possibile meanings attached to David's decision to remove his robes of office. Stripped down to very minimal attire, a linen ephod typically worn by priests,[47] he may be indicating at least a temporary role as priest-king leading the joyous celebration welcoming Yahweh into the city.[48] This would set a precedent for royal participation in ritual drama and enthusiastic worship.[49] It is also possible he is doing penance for his failure to follow proper procedures in transporting of the ark from its storage place in Kiriath-jearim, which had already caused the death of Uzzah, one of the men assigned to walk beside the cart (6:3-9).[50]

45. P. Kyle McCarter, "The Ritual Dedication of the City of David in 2 Samuel 6," in *The Word of the Lord Shall Go Forth,* ed. Carol L. Meyers and M. O'Connor (Winona Lake: Eisenbrauns, 1983) 275-76, compares David's ceremony to that of other ancient Near Eastern monarchs and draws the conclusion that it was performed "in the hope of securing the blessing of the national god for himself and his people in a new seat of government."

46. Although dancers are usually described as young women (Miriam and her women in Exod 15:20-21; the daughter of Jephthah in Judg 11:34; the women who celebrate Saul and David's exploits in 1 Sam 18:7), that does not preclude the possibility of male celebrants as well.

47. The Hebrew term is 'ēpôd bād, also found in 1 Sam 2:18 in reference to priestly attire; cf. 1 Sam 22:18.

48. David P. Wright, "Music and Dance in 2 Samuel 6," *JBL* 121 (2001) 201, suggests that the absence of the priestly family of Abinadab in the procession approaching Jerusalem is an indication of David's taking over the priestly role in this ceremonial entrance. That argument is strengthened by David's offering "burnt offerings and offerings of well-being" before the tent housing the ark in Jerusalem (2 Sam 6:17).

49. The Psalms contain numerous instances in which the people are encouraged to raise their voices to the Lord and make a joyful noise (Pss 66:1; 95:1; 98:4, 6; 100:1).

50. See Victor H. Matthews, *Old Testament Turning Points* (Grand Rapids: Baker, 2005) 89-95, for a more extensive discussion of this story.

Regardless of David's potential motive here, it is clear that as a newly-appointed monarch over the tribes of Israel he needed to build a firm consensus in favor of his rule and establish a positive frame for his entrance into the city. He needed to create an impression that he represented a positive future for the people and that his actions should therefore not be challenged. David's very physical demonstration of his delight in entering Jerusalem with the ark is like a modern politician who chooses to leave his armored car, step out into the street in full view of his fellow citizens, and march hand-in-hand with his wife to his swearing-in ceremony. This gesture of egalitarianism visually positions him as the common citizen's social equal "before the Lord." As a result, David's celebratory dance before the ark provides evidence of a "leveling" of authority, a reshaping of the frame to a shape more accommodating to his royal ambitions. David's joining the revelers who welcome the ark and Yahweh into the city makes him the true "people's choice."[51]

The context of this scene is also reminiscent of the episode in which David first came to prominence: his triumph over the Philistine champion Goliath in single combat. On that occasion David had refused to wear Saul's protective clothing/armor (1 Sam 17:38-39). In doing this, he gained a greater freedom of movement that would have been hampered by heavy and ill-fitting armor. He could then dance about while his heavily-armored opponent was reduced to voicing taunting challenges when he could not come to grips with David (1 Sam. 17:43-49).[52] David's decision to fight without the normal protective garments allows him to demonstrate that he is not just "Saul's man."[53] Instead, when he wins an improbable victory, he could be seen as "God's man," a person who enjoys the favor of the divine warrior in much the same way that Moses and Joshua had.[54] Thus

---

51. Cf. the dancers in Jer 31:10-14, who celebrate the restoration of the nation and of Zion as fertility returns to the land and its bounty is once again shared with all.

52. For a discussion of the redactional development of this story and in particular the nature of Goliath's weapons and armor, see Azzan Yadin, "Goliath's Armor and Israelite Collective Memory," *VT* 54 (2004) 375-77.

53. Ora H. Prouser, "Suited to the Throne: The Symbolic Use of Clothing in the David and Saul Narratives," *JSOT* 71 (1996) 31, 34-35, points to David's escaping the need for Saul's approval of his claim to the throne, and then notes a theme in the narrative in which David "accumulates clothing while Saul abuses, destroys or loses clothing."

54. Cf. the equally improbable military victories over the Amalekites (Exod 17:8-13) and the city of Jericho (Josh 6:1-25).

David's choice of attire in both this episode and in his entrance into Jerusalem could be a conscious attempt to set a political tone for his reign, playing off of background material. It also marks him as a figure willing to be vulnerable before the people and before God.

The manner in which the scene is contextualized and then reconstructed is suggestive of a recursive model of mutual awareness.[55] Advocates of recursive frame analysis use the word "recursive" to "describe the way talk unfolds upon itself as we attempt to make sense of conversations: Context and text are in turn contextualized by other contexts and text."[56] In this instance, events are not dependent upon speeches or conversations, but on a series of steps taken by David and the reactions to these steps by the people that provide several enfolding levels of awareness and acceptance (2 Sam. 6:14-19).

Again, the particular importance of the political context in this narrative must be stressed. David is attempting to create a show of authority, but his ultimate success is based entirely on the reaction of his target audience: "Do they actually get his meaning?" David is dealing here with a volatile situation, in which the motivation of the people to coordinate their actions is not well established. He must shape a consensus if he hopes to succeed. The recursive nature of the developing scene is therefore found in the emergent collective consensus of the people. When they exhibit a shared understanding of David's actions, their external response (celebration, covenant meal, and peaceful return to their homes) becomes a reflection of their mutual awareness of his authority.[57]

Thus when David uses the sound of the horns to mark the approach of the royal procession, the populace signals its first level of mutual awareness by turning out to welcome the king and the ark in much the same way

---

55. Scheff, "The Structure of Context," 376. Scheff points to Emile Durkheim's idea, in *Elementary Forms of the Religious Life* (New York: Free Press, [1915] 1965), of the "collective consciousness" as a way for a community to express an "unspoken, taken-for granted agreement" with particular situations.

56. Ronald Chenail, "Recursive Frame Analysis," *Qualitative Report* 2/2 (1995) 34, notes that "the form or shape of a conversation comes from this arrangement of the parts of the conversation: Words are woven together to create contexts and then these frames are configured to create a shape or contour to the conversation. RFA then becomes a way to 'figure out talk.'" In this case it is also a way to figure out staged performance.

57. This follows the principles of the "general theory of coordination," as defined by Scheff, "Toward a Sociological Model of Consensus," 35.

David's Actions to Shape Consensus	Recursive Mutual Awareness by People
Girded in a linen ephod, David dances as the ark is brought into Jerusalem at the sounding of trumpets.	"All the house of Israel" joins in the celebratory welcome of the king and the ark to Jerusalem. (6:14-15)
David places the ark within the tent, officiates over sacrifices, blesses the people, (6:17-18)	The people are present to witness the sacrifice and receive a blessing.
David distributes food following the sacrifice (6:19a)	Both men and women receive a cake of bread, a portion of meat, and a cake of raisins, and then quietly return home. (6:19b)

they would have welcomed a military victory.[58] In doing so, they have a further opportunity to affirm their mutual understanding of David's actions and to demonstrate their loyalty to him and to Yahweh. Furthermore, by participating in a covenant meal, accepting the royal distribution of "a cake of bread, a portion of meat, and a cake of raisins" (the three sustaining crops of Israel's economy), they once again acknowledge David's new executive role as their patron[59] and as the distributor of God's bounty.[60] Finally, when the proceedings have been completed "all the people went back to their homes," a final expression of mutual awareness of the political situation and their place within this newly-constituted society.

The people's actions, as outlined by the storyteller, are an indication of the way they were mentally reading this scene, each person taking

58. See Wright, "Music and Dance in 2 Samuel 6," 210-11, for a discussion of the use of horns here as a signaling device rather than just a part of the orchestra that played on this occasion.

59. Cf. David's position as distributor to the people with his gifts of spoil to the elders of Judah prior to his becoming king (1 Sam 30:26-31). David's efforts in both instances are acknowledged and the accepting of his gifts forms a mutual understanding of his position as patron.

60. See the depiction of the righteous person who distributes freely of his substance to the poor (Ps 112:9).

stock of what he or she perceives is the level of acceptance tendered toward David by the majority and joining in the celebration after determining that this is the correct thing to do.[61] But while the mutual awareness of David's position as king seems to be universal among the people, the storyteller makes a point of noting that Michal, Saul's daughter and David's first wife, views these events in a very different light. To make the reader aware of her mounting emotions as she views the scene from her window, the narrator cleverly injects a significant aside (a form of third-order positioning) while describing how the other spectators join in the revelry (2 Sam 6:16). What appears here is a familiar "mind-as-body" metaphor for her consuming anger:[62] "she despised him in her heart" *(wattibez lô bĕlibbāh)*.[63] Unlike the rest of the city, she alone chooses to remain in the palace throughout the celebration. This defiant decision sets the stage for a dynastic and a verbal confrontation.

The narrative context for the postcelebration scene includes several important items. At the time that the marriage was arranged between David and Michal, the text states explicitly that she "loved David" (1 Sam 18:20, 28). This passionately-expressed, emotional attachment of a woman for a man is not voiced in this way anywhere else in the biblical narrative.[64] After David's falling out with Saul, Michal helps David escape, their marriage is annulled, David is outlawed by Saul, and Michal is given in marriage to Palti ben Laish (1 Sam 25:44).[65] Then, following Saul's death, when

61. Goffman, *The Presentation of Self in Everyday Life*, 53, in speaking about the main obligation in social interaction, points to the necessity to "render our behavior understandably relevant to what the other can come to perceive is going on." David has clearly accomplished this and in so doing has created a strong sentiment that will protect and support his later actions toward Michal. The presumption can also be made that the enthusiasm of the people in this story would be infectious and convincing to those who hear or read it.

62. See the discussion of positioning theory and the three orders of positioning in Chapter 4. Michal clearly does not share the mutual awareness ascribed to by the rest of the people. On the physiological and metaphorical expressions of anger, see George Lakoff, *Women, Fire, and Dangerous Things* (Chicago: University of Chicago Press, 1987) 380-96.

63. For additional examples of the use of this metaphor, see David's thinking process "in his heart" that will lead him to seek employment with the Philistines (1 Sam 27:1) and Eliphaz's advice to Job to consider carefully God's instruction "in your heart" so that he will repent (Job 22:22).

64. See the discussion of Michal's transformation from woman in love to woman filled with hate in J. Cheryl Exum, *Fragmented Women* (Valley Forge: Trinity Press International, 1993) 43.

65. Robert Alter, *The Art of Biblical Narrative* (New York: Basic Books, 1981) 119-21,

Abner offers to join David's political camp, David orders him to return Michal to his household despite that fact that she has been married for several years to another man (2 Sam 3:13-16). By this time, she has simply become a political pawn, a person attached by blood to Saul's house and therefore a valuable item for David to collect as he works to obtain a broad consensus for his rise to power over the tribes.[66]

The politically-expedient, forced displacement of Michal has shamed her and in turn has transformed her love for David, now perhaps only a distant memory, into a new and very present passion — hatred.[67] The narrator then adds a further dimension to her rising anger by referring to her as Michal "the daughter of Saul," not as the "wife of David" (2 Sam 6:20). This focuses her subsequent verbal attack on David in terms of her natural loyalty to her father's royal dynasty, however tenuous its current position might be. All of these contextual factors (an emotionally-charged frame) provide the tinder that is ignited by the spark of David's public actions during his entrance into Jerusalem.[68]

The fireworks begin when David is about to enter his own house. He had publicly bestowed a blessing on the people after completing his sacrificial duties (2 Sam 6:18). Now mirroring that position as "father of the nation," he goes to his household to exercise his position there as "father," intending to announce his return with a blessing on its members. However, instead of passively accepting David as her overlord and husband, Michal steps out of the ordinary routine expected of her and "came out to meet David" (v. 20).[69] Her anger and indignation spew out as she publicly sepa-

---

highlights the one-sided nature of the love affair, since only Michal is ever said to love David and David consistently uses her without demonstrating real affection.

66. Katharine Doob Sakenfeld, *Just Wives? Stories of Power and Survival in the Old Testament and Today* (Louisville: Westminster/John Knox, 2003) 79-81.

67. See the discussion of the "costs of passionate love" to mental health and the resulting violent or vituperative transformation that may take place when that love is shattered in Elaine Hatfield and Richard L. Rapson, "Love and Attachment Processes," in *Handbook of Emotions,* ed. Michael Lewis and Jeannette M. Haviland-Jones, 2nd ed. (New York: Guilford, 2000) 658-59. Helen B. Lewis, *Shame and Guilt in Neurosis* (New York: International Universities Press, 1971) 82-91, points to a psychological loop effect in which shame is usually followed by anger.

68. See the discussion of several marital displacements that occur in the David narrative in John Kessler, "Sexuality and Politics: The Motif of the Displaced Husband in the Books of Samuel," *CBQ* 62 (2000) 409-23.

69. Sacks, "On Doing 'Being Ordinary,'" 415, defines being ordinary as spending time

rates herself from him and his political position.[70] Paralleling David's own "entrance" into the city, Michal attempts to usurp his authority at the entrance to his house. This must have been a shock to David, as it would be to the storyteller's audience. Michal has set aside the normal standards of social decorum and has chosen to violate the established social routines for public interaction as understood in a traditional society.[71] She is violating standardized "turn-taking" rules for discourse that in ancient Israel would reserve the right in any public situation for the head of the household to speak first.[72]

The confrontation between these two characters displays Michal's assessment of what she considers to be David's socially inappropriate behavior and functions in the narrative as an attempt to seek vengeance and perhaps as a call for a restoration of the rights of the Saulides.[73] In so doing, she attempts to shame him with this piece of very stinging speech:

How the king of Israel honored himself today, uncovering himself today before the eyes of his servants' maids, as any vulgar fellow might shamelessly uncover himself! (2 Sam 6:20)

Michal's opening salvo directly targets David for public ridicule using a drippingly sarcastic statement, "how the king of Israel honored himself to-

---

"in usual ways, having usual thoughts, usual interests," but Michal has chosen to step out of this role. She refuses to be social scenery and instead steps forward in an extraordinary manner.

70. Alter, *The Art of Biblical Narrative*, 124, emphasizes this public gesture that was intended to provide Michal with an audience for her accusations.

71. Asma Afsaruddin, "Introduction: The Hermeneutics of Gendered Space and Discourse," in *Hermeneutics and Honor: Negotiating Female "Public" Space in Islamic/ate Societies* (Cambridge, MA: Harvard University Press, 1999) 9, makes it clear that in traditional, contemporary Islamic societies "sexual impropriety may imply not only illicit sexual relations but violation of an elaborate code that prescribes circumspect and decorous social relations between the sexes." Michal has clearly crossed the line in terms of decorous social relations.

72. See Erving Goffman, *Relations in Public: Microstudies of the Public Order* (New York: Basic Books, 1971) 34-38, for a discussion of social protocols on turn-taking and use of public space.

73. Her confrontational speech is comparable to Jezebel's taunting of Jehu in 2 Kgs 9:30-31. Both women are unsuccessfully defending a failed dynasty. Note that this ploy is one identified by psychologists as possibly resulting from the cognitive appraisal of a situation and is expressed in heightened emotions and survival strategies. On this, see Leggitt and Gibbs, "Emotional Reactions to Verbal Irony," 3.

day."[74] Not only is she engaging in a hostile form of address and venting her anger, but she is also implying that David, the former shepherd boy, has no right to the kingship.[75] In framing her statement in this way, the storyteller artfully uses Michal's voice as an attempted challenge to his political legitimacy from one of the few remaining members of the now defunct Saulide household. Once again, it is the social impression created for the reader of an ironic insult as much as for David that is being presented here.[76]

Michal then sharpens her statement by asserting that **her father's** (my emphasis reflecting a superior tone of voice) royal administration would never have engaged in such vulgar, undignified cavorting before the lowliest of its subjects.[77] In this sense, and for this reason, she has apparently made the decision to reverse the tradition that women, once they become part of their husband's household, must uphold its honor.[78] This social understanding does not automatically silence Michal. It would certainly be within her rights as David's wife to champion honorable behavior by the king's household. However, these words, especially ones that are designed to damage her husband, do not have to be voiced in a public forum.

Choosing instead to champion the honor of her father's house, she is actually challenging David's right to rule in much the same way that Jezebel publicly confronts the usurper Jehu. As he enters the gates of Samaria after defeating Joram's army, Jezebel calls him a "Zimri" (an unfaithful, murderous servant; 2 Kgs 9:30-31), hoping to rally support for another failed royal house.

---

74. Christopher J. Lee and Albert N. Katz, "The Differential Role of Ridicule in Sarcasm and Irony," *Metaphor and Symbol* 13 (1998) 9-10, provide a study that demonstrates that sarcasm is a directed form of address designed to express anger or hostility while irony is less specific in its aim.

75. Adin Steinsaltz, *Biblical Images: Men and Women of the Book* (New York: Basic Books, 1984) 149-50, calls this a "clash between two cultures," framing Saul's attitudes and manner as modest and noble in contrast to David's earthiness and lack of common decency.

76. Penny M. Pexman and Kara M. Olineck, "Does Sarcasm Always Sting? Investigating the Impact of Ironic Insults and Ironic Compliments," *Discourse Processes* 33 (2002) 214-15, demonstrate through their case studies that participants considered ironic insults to be "more mocking and more sarcastic than direct insults" because of the social impression they create.

77. See David J. A. Clines, "Michal Observed: An Introduction to Reading Her Story," in *Telling Queen Michal's Story: An Experiment in Comparative Interpretation,* ed. Clines and Tamara Cohn Eskenazi. JSOTSup 119 (Sheffield: JSOT, 1991) 59-60.

78. See Victor H. Matthews, "Female Voices: Upholding the Honor of the Household," *BTB* 24 (1994) 8-15. Cf. Gen 2:24; 24:54-58; 31:19, 33-35; 1 Sam 19:11-17.

Female Advice Voiced in Private

The pattern of intimate or private speech between husband and wife in the biblical narrative most often is conducted in their chambers without witnesses or without sharing these thoughts publicly with others. Wives in this way can exercise some influence over their husbands while allowing for men to continue being the public voice of the household.[1]

> **Gen 21:9-10**: Sarah calls on Abraham to "cast out this slave woman with her son" to protect the inheritance rights of Isaac.
>
> **Gen 27:46**: Rebekah uses her influence to convince Isaac to send Jacob to seek a wife in Paddan-aram. Her argument in the privacy of their tent is, "I am weary of my life because of the Hittite women" that Esau had married (see Gen 26:34-35).
>
> **Gen 38:24-26**: Rather than denounce him publicly as she was being taken out to be burned, Tamar sends Judah a private word about the father of her child, saving him from embarrassment and causing him to acknowledge, "she is more in the right than I."
>
> **2 Sam 13:11-17**: In the privacy of Amnon's chamber, when he attempts to rape her and then states he will abandon her, Tamar argues unsuccessfully against such a "vile" thing.

1. Lila Abu-Lughod, "The Romance of Resistance: Tracing Transformation of Power Through Bedouin Women," *American Ethnologist* 17 (1990) 47-48, notes that among bedouin women "power relations take many forms," including forms of resistance, although this resistance occurs within the gender-related constraints of their culture.

Like Jezebel in a later period whose rhetorical bluff backfires on her, Michal fails to gauge the level of mutual understanding in this situation. David has clearly won the hearts of the people by his actions, and his higher level of understanding of that sentiment transcends Michal's verbal ploy and allows him to maintain control of the conversation very easily.[79] David deflects her attempt to shame him and bust his newly-shaped frame,

79. Scheff, "The Structure of Context," 375, uses the example of competing spies to show that the one who is able to interpret the various levels of mutual understanding when obtaining information or questioning data sources is ultimately going to be the more successful.

and he refuses to acknowledge that her claims have any validity.[80] Like
Jehu, who bypasses any stigma of shame attached to the label Jezebel verbally cast at him (2 Kgs 9:32-33), David now employs his own form of
ironic speech that will strip Michal of her pride and demonstrate to all that
she is incorrect in her assessment and is being socially offensive:[81]

> I will make myself yet more contemptible than this, and I will be
> abased in my own eyes; but by the maids of whom you have spoken, by
> them I shall be held in honor." (2 Sam 6:22)

Employing overstatement to ridicule sarcastically her charges against
him, David states that his acts have been performed before God, "who
chose me in place of your father" (2 Sam 6:21).[82] Therefore, under the protection and with the guidance of the deity, he will be the judge of any vul-
garity on his part. He throws Michal's own words back at her, playing on her
complaint that he had exposed himself before the "eyes" (lĕʿênê) of maidser-
vants, and instead saying that any judgment of his performance will be "in
his eyes" (bĕʿênāy).[83] Instead of seeking the type of honor Michal is espous-
ing, he will be content with abasing himself in order to obtain the more
cherished honor given to him by the lowest members of his society.[84]

---

80. Thomas J. Scheff and Suzanne M. Retzinger, *Emotions and Violence: Shame and
Rage in Destructive Conflicts* (Lexington, MA: Lexington, 1991) 125-26, discuss this facing-off
process that generally ends with pride for one party and shame for the other, depending on
who is able to stand up to sarcasm, labeling, and abuse and maintain both their composure
and their sense of identity.

81. Leggitt and Gibbs, "Emotional Reactions to Verbal Irony," 21. David's remarks fit
into a form of disparagement that consists of humor at the expense of others who have made
mistakes or have broken social custom.

82. P. Kyle McCarter, *II Samuel*. AB 9 (Garden City: Doubleday, 1984) 185-87, posits a
better reading of "Blessed be God!" as David's opening remark here despite the fact that the
MT reads *lipnê yhwh*, "before the Lord." If he is correct, that would be an effective rejoinder
and summons to listen to his argument. See Exod 18:10; Ruth 4:14; and 1 Kgs 1:48 for other
examples of the exclamatory phrase.

83. The use of reversal to deflect insult also appears in David's response to the taunt
by the Jebusites that "even the blind and the lame will turn you back." David had charged his
warriors to attack the city to strike down the Jebusites, whom he characterizes collectively as
"the lame and the blind" (2 Sam 5:6-8).

84. Cf. the insertion of the story of the two prostitutes who come to Solomon for
judgment as the first of several tales designed to support the image of the "wise king" (1 Kgs
3:16-28). Note that his decision caused "all Israel" to stand in awe of their ruler.

Having unsuccessfully attempted to bust the political frame that David has created, even though she has attempted to call upon the social values attached to a previous administration's frame, Michal is left to live in her shame.[85] The remainder of her life will be spent as perpetually barren, a pariah member of the harem (2 Sam 6:23). In this way, the storyteller upholds the principle that her failure to demonstrate her loyalty to her husband and uphold his honor is the social price for her disaffection. Plus, the political book is now closed on the Saulide dynasty, since there will be no child born to David and Michal.[86]

A Social Triangle: Nabal, David, and Abigail

Another example of frame-busting occurs in the story of Abigail, her husband Nabal, and David (1 Sam 25:2-42). The contextual frame for this narrative is expressed in the political reality that Saul is a king under prophetic sentence of ultimate demise (1 Sam 15:28-29) and is spending considerable time and political capital pursuing the outlawed David.[87] In the meantime, David is forced to probe the loyalties of the wealthy and influential as he tries to establish a political network throughout the country and bust Saul's political frame. His maneuvering involves providing "protection" and other favors as a means of obtaining the supplies necessary to support his band of followers.[88] When this strategy is used to solicit sup-

---

85. Thomas J. Scheff, "Shame and Conformity: The Deference-Emotion System," *American Sociological Review* 53 (1988) 401, describes "shame markers" that are associated with the diminishing of self-esteem and with feeling foolish, stupid, or incompetent. While the biblical account does not provide a detailed psychological follow-up to Michal's condition, the ancient audience would have recognized her barrenness as a true marker of shame in their society.

86. Lillian R. Klein, "Michal, the Barren Wife," in *Samuel and Kings,* ed. Athalya Brenner. A Feminist Companion to the Bible, 2nd ser. 7 (Sheffield: Sheffield Academic, 2000) 44-45, adds a further dimension to Michal's barrenness by suggesting that it is caused by her failure to renounce foreign gods in favor of the one God David had so ecstatically welcomed into Jerusalem.

87. Barbara Green, "Enacting Imaginatively the Unthinkable: 1 Samuel 25 and the Story of Saul," *BibInt* 11 (2003) 4-5, outlines the way the editor of this material has used 1 Samuel 24 and 26 to sandwich the narrative in ch. 25. The theme expressed in these chapters is the "changing of the royal guard" that will lead up to the death of Saul and the rise of David in his place.

88. Baruch Halpern, *David's Secret Demons: Messiah, Murderer, Traitor, King.* BIW (Grand Rapids: Wm. B. Eerdmans, 2001) 22.

Interlocking Frames

A complex story such as that contained in the episodes of David's rise to the kingship consists of interlocking narrative frames. The outermost consists of the political agenda of the editor(s) who have reworked this material into a consistent and fairly tight story. Within this primary frame are smaller contexts or settings that serve as keys to the action, signals to the audience of what is really going on in a scene.[1] Thus in the case of 1 Samuel 25, there are the following contextual frames to consider:

1. The primary narrative frame is the "Apology of David," which justifies his eventual rise to become king (1 Samuel 16 — 2 Samuel 6).
2. The narrative theme of David's refusal to harm Saul, the "Lord's anointed" king, directly or physically while his rival's political frame is intact (1 Samuel 24–26, 29).
3. The narrative theme of wise and foolish choices: (a) whether to recognize David's claims to the throne and (b) whether to hold to a foolish decision or succumb to a wise argument.
4. The social frame that identifies the male as the head of a household and the person with the primary responsibility for upholding its honor and preserving it from harm.

1. Goffman, *Frame Analysis*, 44-46.

plies from a rich landowner named Nabal, what follows is a series of charged verbal exchanges that are dependent on the various narrative frames that define the character of this story and the characters in it.

A number of sociolinguistic keys add contextual validity to the contest between David and Nabal. First is the linguistic artistry attached to the names of the two principal characters: Nabal, meaning "foolish" or "senseless," and Abigail, referred to with the phrase "very insightful" or "clever" *(ṭôbat-śekel)*.[89] Such a disparate pair immediately indicates to the audience that this is a wisdom story. In addition, the significant use of the

89. On these names see James Barr, "The Symbolism of Names in the Old Testament," *British Journal of Religious Literature* 52 (1969) 11-29.

word *śekel* pairs Abigail with David, since its verbal form, meaning "to prosper," is used for David's growing successes (*maśkîl mĕʾōd;* 1 Sam 18:14, 15, 30).[90]

Another narrative key is provided by the notation that David's request falls on a feast day following the sheepshearing (1 Sam 25:8). This social key implants in the audience two cognitively-shared expectations: (1) generosity, if not an outright invitation to share Nabal's hospitality, and (2) an Israelite tradition that ties the sheepshearing to a time for both trickery and the vindication of wrongs.[91] Ordinarily, a host would seize the opportunity to offer hospitality since it is a social strategy designed to garner honor for his household.[92] It would be a socially-advantageous as well as a simple matter during a feast day to draw fellow Judeans into the general festivities without disrupting the usual flow of life or the political balance.

Interestingly, the storyteller frames this scene with the chief celebrant, Nabal, forced to expand beyond his natural role as local elder and rich landowner and squarely into the political arena. Instead of enjoying his dinner as the "great man" among his clients, he is thrust into a position of having to make a swift decision in response to David's friendly greeting and importuning words. What further disrupts the normal frame in which clients search for aid or reward from a patron face-to-face is the curious fact that this scene is constructed of a series of information reports using indirect speech.[93] Thus David learns about Nabal's sheepshearing activity in a report from his men (25:4); David's message to Nabal is delivered by unnamed followers (25:5-9), and Nabal's reply is similarly conveyed indirectly through these messengers (25:10-12).

Keeping in mind that language use is more than mundane inter-

<hr>

90. Ellen van Wolde, "A Leader Led by a Lady: David and Abigail in I Samuel 25," *ZAW* 114 (2002) 356.

91. Jeffrey C. Geoghegan, "Israelite Sheepshearing and David's Rise to Power," *Bib* 87 (2006) 60-61.

92. See T. Raymond Hobbs, "Hospitality in the First Testament and the 'Teleological Fallacy," *JSOT* 95 (2001) 7, which points to the political strategy at work here and cites Clifford Geertz, "Thick Description: Toward an Interpretative Theory of Culture," in *The Interpretation of Culture* (New York: Basic Books, 1973) 3-30, in reference to the significance of items contributing to "thick culture" when analyzing the social landscape.

93. See the discussion of indirect speech in this passage in Cynthia L. Miller, *The Representation of Speech in Biblical Hebrew Narrative.* HSS 55 (Atlanta: Scholars, 1996) 254-55.

change and is "best viewed as a pragmatic behavior . . . an attempt to accomplish particular goals,"[94] David's message to Nabal functions as an unveiled political strategy. Demonstrating his intent, it contains a threefold greeting: "Peace be to you, and peace be to your house, and peace be to all that you have" (25:6). This inclusive statement is appropriate for a hospitality situation (cf. Judg 19:20),[95] but also has underlying implication that the peace between them could possibly be for more than just the period of the feast day and even suggests the advantages of a long-term political alliance between their houses.

With a verbal hand outstretched in greeting, David's message goes on to recite the service his men have done for Nabal, reminds his potential host it is a feast day, and asks for "whatever you have at hand" to repay this kindness to "your son David."[96] His request potentially places Nabal in a bind, since failure to comply positively could cause him to lose face and be dishonored. Despite having David humble himself, using client terminology, "your son" (ûlĕbinĕkā lĕdāwid), the storyteller constructs for the audience an impression that Nabal takes advantage of the fact that David is not actually there in person. This is accomplished by having Nabal demonstrate that he is worthy of his name when he foolishly both rejects the request for reciprocity and blatantly insults David, referring to him as a "masterless" outlaw and calling into question his name and his lineage: "Who is David? Who is the son of Jesse?" (25:10-11). His claim to ignorance of David's origins provides Nabal with a form of plausible deniability should anyone ask why he has refused to obey the usual social formalities of hospitality.[97] His false or misleading statement allows him to save face and maintain his support for the existing political frame represented by Saul.[98] In essence, Nabal positions himself as the king's surrogate in this

94. Ben R. Slugoski and William Turnbull, "Cruel to Be Kind and Kind to Be Cruel: Sarcasm, Banter and Social Relations," *Journal of Language and Social Psychology* 7 (1988) 101.

95. See the hospitality protocol outlined in Victor H. Matthews, "Hospitality and Hostility in Genesis 19 and Judges 19," *BTB* 22 (1992) 3-11.

96. Van Wolde, "A Leader Led by a Lady," 358, argues that David's use of language contradicts the interpretation that he is making a threat or is engaged in extortion. I would agree to the extent that he is using language to create an impression for Nabal and the audience of peaceful intentions and is only relying on the expectation of generosity implicit in a reciprocal exchange of services.

97. Hobbs, "Hospitality in the First Testament," 26-27.

98. Slugoski and Turnbull, "Cruel to Be Kind and Kind to Be Cruel," 105-6.

situation, upholding a law-and-order stance and refusing to submit to the demands of outlaws.[99]

Having so effectively insulted David, Nabal has unwittingly placed his property and his people in danger. David's honor is now at stake, and the would-be king cannot allow the political frame that he is attempting to construct to be broken by a "fool." He therefore dispassionately orders his men to "strap on your swords," with the clear intent of utterly destroying Nabal's entire household. Given the subsidiary narrative frame in which David has previously sworn not to harm the "Lord's anointed" (1 Sam. 24:6), this oath threatening extreme violence against Saul's surrogate endangers the character of that political frame. It will therefore be the wise and clever Abigail's task both to violate one social frame (speak for her husband as representative of the household) and to restore the integrity of this narrative frame — by ultimately eliciting a promise from David not to harm Nabal's household.[100]

In order to accomplish these tasks, however, Abigail will have to bust several socially-recognized contextual frames. Having heard the affirmation of David's service to Nabal's "young men" (25:14-17), she is presented with the dilemma of what can be done in the face of a master "so ill-natured that no one can speak to him" (25:17).[101] If Abigail is to save her household's honor from the rash actions of her foolish husband, she must move swiftly and courageously.[102] Her decisive actions, which will include frame-busting, are depicted linguistically with a series of *wayyiqtol* forms in vv. 18-19.[103] They are patterned after the negotiation strategy employed by Jacob when he returned to Canaan (Gen 32:3-21), sending messengers

---

99. Green, "Enacting Imaginatively the Unthinkable," 12, sees David's use of the term "your son" and Nabal's reaction as part of the storyteller's attempt to use this narrative to illustrate further the antagonism between David and Saul.

100. On this motif of female's replacing males in honor-bound situations, see Matthews, "Female Voices," 8-15.

101. Note the parallel here between Abigail's dilemma and the life-or-death situation presented to Esther by Mordechai (Esth 4:1-17). The label given to Nabal, "ill-natured" *(ben-bĕliyaʿal)*, is repeated in Abigail's assessment of her husband in v. 25. Used elsewhere it refers to the basest lawbreakers who ignore tradition and are a danger to social order (see Judg 19:22).

102. See the treatment of Abigail's role in restoring Nabal's honor in Marjorie O'Rourke Boyle, "The Law of the Heart: The Death of a Fool (1 Samuel 25)," *JBL* 120 (2001) 401-27. Hobbs, "Hospitality in the First Testament," 27, also makes this point.

103. Van Wolde, "A Leader Led by a Lady," 360.

who will bring gifts to David before Abigail herself arrives in his camp.[104] Heightening the tension of her appearance before David, the storyteller re-kindles the anger and raw emotion expressed in v. 13. Injected here, as a reminder to the audience, is David's clearance of guilt, that Nabal had "re-turned evil for good," including David's oath to strip Nabal of all that he has denied David (25:21-22).[105] In the midst of such a volatile situation, Abigail's voice and actions stand out as the epitome of political pragma-tism and reason. Her appeal to David includes the following elements:

(1) Unlike her husband, Abigail goes out to meet David face-to-face, makes obeisance to David, and begs him to ignore the "ill-natured" Nabal's foolish words. After all, fools should not be taken seriously and others should not be forced to pay for their ill-conceived actions (Prov 26:4; Sir 27:27). She then absolves herself as the true spokesper-son for the household by saying she was not present when David's messengers had come (25:23-25).

(2) Abigail then reverses their social positions: she becomes the supplicant-client and David becomes the patron. Within this frame she calls on him to place the guilt for what has happened on her head alone (cf. similar statements in 1 Sam 25:24 and 2 Sam 14:9). Her strategy is to deflect the target of his anger away from the household and allow a pause for reflection on his course of action in his new po-sition as patron.[106]

(3) Choosing to disregard the militant character of David's camp, Abi-gail opens her remarks by expressing her relief that Yahweh has "re-strained you from bloodguilt," an action sure to cause grave political repercussions to David (25:26).[107] She further defuses David's previ-

104. See Victor H. Matthews, "The Unwanted Gift: Implications of Obligatory Gift Giving in Ancient Israel," in *The Social World of the Hebrew Bible*, ed. Ronald Simkins and Stephen Cook. Semeia 87 (Atlanta: SBL, 1999) 96-99.

105. David's vow employs a familiar linguistic structure, "God do so to ____ and more also" that also appears in 1 Sam. 3:17; 20:13 and 1 Kgs. 20:10.

106. Tikva Frymer-Kensky, *In the Wake of the Goddesses: Women, Culture, and the Biblical Transformation of Pagan Myth* (New York: Free Press, 1992) 260, n. 91, suggests that this relieves David from breaking his oath, but that requires prior knowledge by Abigail of the oath. The oath seems to serve only as an editorial aside for the benefit of the audience and as part of the rhetorical strategy of this narrative.

107. Van Wolde, "A Leader Led by a Lady," 362, points to Abigail's repeated use of the

ously expressed desire to take revenge by equating David's enemies with those fools who would wish to harm her husband's household. This very skilled rhetorical use of mock irony places David in the same position that Nabal had found himself, having to save face before his assembled followers.[108] However, she hints that David will surely make the right rather than the expedient choice.

(4) By asserting her right as "mother" of the household to distribute food,[109] Abigail fulfills her household's obligation to the protocol of hospitality and gives tribute to God's rightful ruler while predicting God's providential care of David's person against his enemies and the establishment of a "sure house" for him (25:27-28).[110]

(5) Abigail once again assures David that when he becomes *nāgîd* he will be relieved that he had not been guilty of shedding blood "without cause" (25:30-31; cf. Jer 26:15). Playing out the performance of a loyal client, her use of *nāgîd* is designed to flatter him by drawing on its semantic meaning of "someone who is (taken from behind or from amidst his people and is) placed 'before' . . . the people as a divinely-ordained ruler."[111] In that position ("before the eyes of Yahweh"), she assures him, he will always recognize the proper course of action, weighing immediate gratification against true justice.[112]

(6) Abigail's final plea, "remember your servant" (25:31), is reminiscent of the treaty language used in the Rahab narrative (Josh 2:9-13). It places her and her entire household in David's hands and, as David had before (1 Sam 25:8), makes the request for reciprocity for services rendered.

---

deictic sign *wĕ'attâ*, "and now," as an indication that events have already happened or are in place due to God's intervention.

108. The summary of the clinical experiences found in Slugoski and Turnbull, "Cruel to Be Kind and Kind to Be Cruel," 116-18, indicates how "speakers exploit inter-relations to manage others' impressions of the nature of their relationship."

109. See this right expressed in "A Sufferer and a Soul in Egypt," in Victor H. Matthews and Don C. Benjamin, *Old Testament Parallels*, 3rd ed. (Mahwah: Paulist, 2006) 226. See also T. Raymond Hobbs, "Man, Woman, and Hospitality — 2 Kings 4:8-36," *BTB* 23 (1993) 95.

110. Again Abigail uses the opening phrase *wĕ'attâ* to draw attention to something that has already occurred, the arrival of her offering of food for David's men.

111. See van Wolde, "A Leader Led by a Lady," 365-72, for an extended discussion of Abigail's use of metaphorical language to emphasize David's future rise, with the help of Yahweh, to the position of *nāgîd*, "prince," over Israel.

112. Frymer-Kensky, *In the Wake of the Goddesses*, 134.

In the face of this wisdom argument, David, unless he wants to be "a Nabal," can only give her a positive response. He acknowledges and thanks her for her wise advice and makes a covenant with her by accepting her tribute payment and then giving her a benediction, "Go up to your house in peace," that matches the offering of peaceful relations that he had originally proffered to Nabal (25:35). In this way, the various interlocking frames that had served as a complex setting for this drama are either affirmed, transformed, repudiated, or repaired:

1. The political frame that David and the storyteller have created is upheld for the future ruler of Israel.
2. Saul's political frame is busted, both by David's success and by the death of Nabal, apparently as divine retribution (25:37-38).
3. The basic pattern of the social frame that Abigail busted when she assumed the role of spokesperson for the household is repaired when David marries this wise widow and makes her a part of his household (25:39-42). Upon being presented with his offer of marriage, she repeats her bowed obeisance, speaks for the last time proclaiming that she is his obedient servant, one so totally submissive that she is willing to "wash the feet of the servants of my lord" (25:41).[113] She then immediately sets out to join her new husband. At that point she falls silent, resuming the position of behind-the-scenes supporter of the male head of household.

Conclusions

The examination of these biblical narratives within the context of conversation analysis and frame analysis demonstrates the potential usefulness of these methodologies. Careful attention to social, linguistic, and political frames within a story provides interesting results that go far beyond what can be obtained from a superficial reading. In particular, conversation analysis, discourse analysis, and frame analysis contribute to a constructionist approach to the determination of social identities, power relation-

---

113. It is interesting to note that washing the feet of guests is a normal part of the hospitality protocol (cf. Gen 18:4), and this reference may serve as yet one final indication of Abigail's fulfilling the role of host that her husband had failed to perform.

ships, and rhetorical interaction.[114] What is required for these approaches to become more acceptable to mainstream biblical studies, however, is a broadening of perspective beyond the literary realm and a willingness to explore the findings and theories developed by the disciplines in the social sciences. In the end, any text containing dialogue has the potential to glean insights into the social world that it reflects rhetorically.[115]

114. For an examination of social constructionism as an approach to studying the processes "by which human abilities, experiences, commonsense and scientific knowledge are both produced in, and reproduce, human communities," see Shotter and Gergen, "A Prologue to Constructing the Social," 1-19.

115. Jonathan Potter, "Discourse Analysis and Constructionist Approaches: Theoretical Background," in Richardson, *Handbook of Qualitative Research Methods for Psychology and the Social Sciences*, 155.

CHAPTER FOUR

Dialogue as a Social Kaleidoscope: Using Positioning Theory

Conversation creates and re-creates a people's social world. The basic components that comprise personal identity, status, and power are continually being defined and redefined in every dialogue. Conversation, both verbal and in combination with gesture and body language, is in fact the primary social act. Dialogue, including that found in embedded discourse in storytelling, is the basis for social interaction on all levels, facilitating simple exchange of ideas, providing a medium within which business is conducted, legal principles are upheld, and emotions are expressed. It involves the institutionalized use of language and gestures and is dependent on the formality or informality of the discourse and the topic.[1]

It is generally the case that individuals speak in a certain manner because they believe that is the natural or proper manner in which to converse given who they are, who their interlocutor or audience is, and the present circumstances in which they are speaking. While that is appropriate in most cases, if the manner of discourse is overly dramatized or made either sinister or unrealistically lighthearted, it can contribute to intentional or unintentional misunderstandings that could lead to conflict or incorrect or unwise actions by the participants. It is in the positioning that constantly occurs during conversation that impressions are formed, actions initiated, and identities are shaped or transformed.

1. Bronwyn Davies and Rom Harré, "Positioning and Personhood," in *Positioning Theory: Moral Contexts of Intentional Action,* ed. Harré and Luk van Langenhove (Oxford: Blackwell, 1999) 34.

For example, one of the most common topics that occur in discourse is reference to social icons (school, courtroom, President of the United States). While these references can be conscious or unconscious, simply bringing them up, naming or describing them provides them with power and social recognition. We also position ourselves by including particular icons in our speech and set in motion mental and physical steps by our words, inflection, and gesture. For instance, if we stand up in a public forum and recite the Pledge of Allegiance to the Flag, we draw attention to a national icon (the flag), we orally renew a pledge of loyalty to the principles embodied in that icon, and we accompany our words with the significant and socially recognizable gesture of placing our right hand over our heart. In addition, given the opportunity to explain its meaning to someone not familiar with the pledge, we engage in "rhetorical redescription" by creating and telling its story.

In a similar way, we tell stories about ourselves and our family that help to define our identity and position us within our society. In fact, most family or social gatherings include reference to "family stories" or the remembered versions of events by both young and old. When we include icons and archetypal images (hero, sage, adventurer, or warrior) in our stories or our analysis of events, we provide the intellectual and social underpinning for these cherished social images.[2]

The analysis of discourse, oral or embedded in narrative, demonstrates that it can be either structured or free-floating, but it is not always predictable. In public discourse, as in a debate, positions are explained, defended, or altered based on counterarguments or even the threat of physical or material harm. Initially, some may choose to position themselves so that they are attuned to or in opposition with established positions. Then, during the course of the dialogue, they may change their positions as they are convinced by or disagree with statements that are being made. The fluidity of chosen positions and positioning add tension that may result in heightened emotions, such as anger or fear, and be expressed with descriptive statements indicating their present emotional state: "I have a lump in my throat," "I am wound up or on edge,"[3] or they may simply be seen as a form of recreational verbal sparring for those who enjoy rhetorical contests.

2. For a further description of this process, see Rom Harré, "Images of the World and Societal Icons," in *Determinants and Controls of Scientific Development,* ed. Karin D. Knorr, Hermann Strasser, and Hans G. Zilian (Dordrecht: Reidel, 1975) 257-83.

3. See a discussion of the language of emotion in Zoltán Kövecses, *Emotion Concepts* (New York: Springer, 1990) 6-11.

Contributing to this process is the manner in which the participants "act out" their positions (professor, lawyer, or mother) so that the combined weight of their arguments and social status may cause others to accept or validate their position. For instance, a judge, arrayed in his legal robes, sitting at his raised desk in the midst of a courtroom is generally able to magnify the weight of his pronouncements by acting the part. Of course, anyone can portray themselves in a particular position, but unless their audience accepts them in that position, they are unlikely to be an effective or authoritative speaker.[4]

Public opinion also is easily molded or influenced by shifting circumstances or personal interests. Thus, a stated position on some issue may have to be altered to fit changing circumstances. This can be a problem for political leaders. If they choose to reposition themselves, allowing their take on an issue to evolve, they can be perceived as indecisive or someone who "flip-flops" and therefore cannot be trusted.[5] Recognizing the dangers of being caught in a verbal gaff, it is quite common for public officials to engage in a proactive strategy, positioning others by labeling them as wrong, incompetent, or misinformed or as right, competent, or knowledgeable.[6] By employing a "name-calling" strategy, sufficient misdirection or latitude can be created so that if one positioning strategy fails another may be tried.[7] Naturally, when one appears to be succeeding it will be prolonged or expanded upon to insure success.[8]

---

4. Bruce Lincoln, *Authority: Construction and Corrosion* (Chicago: University of Chicago Press, 1994) 4-5.

5. Meg Greenfield, "Political Flip-Flops," *Newsweek* 114/18 (30 October 1989) 88, asks the question, when "the national political scene is awash in these conversions, confusions and inconsistencies. Are we supposed to be glad or vindictive when someone comes over to our side, welcoming or suspicious?" These are precisely the cognitive confusions that occur during the course of conversations or in public debate.

6. The literature also demonstrates that those who engage in deviant behavior and their victims are labeled and have to work to overcome or cope with these socially-recognized identifiers. See an overview in J. Scott Kenney, "Victims of Crime and Labeling Theory: A Parallel Process?" *Deviant Behavior* 23 (2002) 235-65.

7. The fact that the participants may not always have time to shift to another strategy is demonstrated by Jezebel's failed attempt to label Jehu as a Zimri (= traitor) because his riposte brought men to cast her down from her vantage point into the street to her death (2 Kgs 9:30-37).

8. See the discussion of labeling theory in Victor H. Matthews and Don C. Benjamin, *Social World of Ancient Israel* (Peabody: Hendrickson, 1993) 142-46.

What becomes clear is that during social interaction, just as the slow turning of a kaleidoscope shifts the image created by interlocking pieces of glass, conversational circumstances evolve. As a result, the engaged characters jockey for positions of power or move to place themselves in the most favorable or advantageous position possible. With this in mind, it is necessary to remember that when analyzing characters involved in either a staged or impromptu dialogue, whether it is in a live situation or in a written narrative, the normal mental process is to label or position each participant in the scene. It is typical to refer to these labels as character roles, but that does not always do justice to the potential for social fluidity. Furthermore, the degree of verbal dancing in any dialogue requires continuous re-evaluation of the position of each character at any given moment in order to track how they relate to each other from moment to moment.

Positioning Theory

In order to address the fluid nature of personal identity and the shifting power relationships that are evident in discourse, positioning theory attempts to replace the fairly rigid social category of "role" with the more flexible designation of "position." It recognizes the existence of the ever-changing kaleidoscope of possible positions within the social realm and in space.[9] This concept is an extension of marketing practices in which companies and their products are "positioned" to create a brand recognition that encompasses theme, name, identity, and aesthetic values in order to increase desirability, visibility, and consumer loyalty.[10] In essence, a dialogue is created through packaging, advertising verbiage, and product recognition between producer and consumer in which the producer attempts to create a market niche, positioning its product so that it "speaks" persuasively to the consumer.[11]

In psychological case studies, positioning theory's intent is to examine the varying skills of individuals as well as the ethics of manipulating

9. Luk van Langenhove and Rom Harré, "Introducing Positioning Theory," in Harré and van Langenhove, *Positioning Theory*, 14.

10. For recent trends in marketing, see Iain Ellwood, *The Essential Brand Book,* 2nd ed. (London: Kogan Page, 2002) 121-46.

11. Alice M. Tybout and Tim Calkins, eds., *Kellogg on Branding* (Hoboken: Wiley, 2005) 11-26.

others. Practitioners have identified three modes of positioning theory (see inset) that include the following aspects of positioning: (1) the mental or physical capacity to position oneself and/or others, (2) a basic willingness to self-position or to be positioned by others, and (3) the power to employ positioning techniques.[12] This third aspect is the one most fraught with moral implications, since those who have the power to position others may do so for personal gain or glory or for altruistic or perceived "greatest good" purposes.[13]

As both clinical analysts and literary critics have discovered, a multiplicity of factors shape and drive the conversational flow. For example, during the course of a conversation, persons may take oral positions on issues based at least in part on their own physical (gender, age, health condition) and social (veteran's status, profession, candidate for office) attributes.[14] As a result, the reaction of a person with a disability when faced with the offer, "Let me get the door for you," may be quiet acceptance or a quick and angry riposte, "I am not helpless!" The first statement is termed first-order positioning, in which one person makes the decision to position another based on a reasoned or superficial judgment of his or her condition. The negative response by the disabled person is in the form of a second-order positioning statement. It rejects the attempt at forced positioning and offers an alternative view of her relationship and the circumstances.

It is possible, of course, for individuals or a storyteller to create an identity for themselves or for characters in a narrative. Then, during the course of dialogue, they can speak from the position of a particular social group, gender, age, class, or political party, even though this may be an intentionally false or fanciful position.[15] Variability of physical condition or

12. David Howie, "Preparing for Positive Positioning," in Harré and van Langenhove, *Positioning Theory,* 53-56, describes these three aspects of positioning as part of the development of a symbiotic relationship between caseworker and subjects with inadequate social skills.

13. See the discussion of whether the drive for power or to manipulate others is inherent in human psychology or simply a means to self-gratification in Dennis H. Wrong, *Power: Its Forms, Bases, and Uses* (New Brunswick: Transaction, 1995) 218-27.

14. Wendy Hollway, "Gender Difference and the Production of Subjectivity," in *Changing the Subject: Psychology, Social Regulation and Subjectivity,* ed. Julian Henriques, *et al.* (London: Methuen, 1984) 236, points out how discourse makes it possible to take positions and to use them as a means of establishing a relationship with another person.

15. Rebecca L. Jones, "'Older People' Talking As If They Are Not Older People: Positioning Theory as an Explanation," *Journal of Aging Studies* 20 (2006) 81.

Modes of Positioning

(Based on van Langenhove and Harré, "Introducing Positioning Theory," 20-23)

First-order positioning: A reflexive process in which persons locate or define themselves and others by implying moral right to command or request and by using social categories and story to justify their statements.

Second-order positioning: An accountative process that occurs when first-order positioning is questioned and negotiations begin between participants, thus extending the conversation.

Third-order positioning: An accountative process that occurs when one person speaks to another about something said by a third person and statements are made to position that third person by one or both of the other two.

---

stance may also play a part in determining relative position. For example, an unnamed prophet disguises himself with a bloody bandage in order to address King Ahab as if he were a common soldier. Then, once the king has inadvertently condemned himself for the crime described in their dialogue, the bandage is removed, the prophet's identity is revealed, and their proper social relationship is restored (1 Kgs 20:38-42).[16]

Similarly, a handicapped or an obviously diseased person or one who is stooped, supine, sitting or standing may choose to communicate his position in these physical terms as a way to illicit sympathy or aid or to take control over a scene (first-order positioning). His condition also contributes to his current power relationship with others regardless of their actual status or social category. Thus Na'aman, the leprous Syrian military commander, seeks a cure for his affliction by using his political connections, wealth, and the authority associated with a man accompanied by an entourage (2 Kgs 5:4-9). However, he is reduced to the position of a supplicant

16. See Burke O. Long, *1 Kings*. FOTL 9 (Grand Rapids: Wm. B. Eerdmans, 1984) 221-22, and the similar use of juridical parable by Nathan when addressing David's adultery with Bathsheba (2 Sam 12:1-15).

with no choice but to follow the indirectly communicated instructions of the prophet Elisha if he truly wishes to be cured (5:10-15).[17]

While there are distinct differences between a live scene in which participants speak and act in real time and the description of characters in a scene contained in a written drama, it seems patent that the decisions made by live participants and the author/recorder of a written account may be analyzed in similar ways. Characters in a story are positioned by the storyteller to fulfill particular and socially-recognizable roles, and their positions are voiced in embedded dialogue. In fact, there are familiar metaphors, plots, and characters that everyone in a particular culture world knows and to which they can easily relate.[18]

It becomes the task of the audience or reader to recognize strategic positioning by the storyteller, since characters in a drama only play the parts assigned to them by the author. Even in historical accounts of events that include embedded dialogue, it cannot be assumed that the recorder of these events is without prejudice or even has full knowledge of what actually happened.[19] Therefore, within a live or created conversation, careful attention needs to be given to the setting, body posture of the participants, and any socially significant props that are present. Each of these items provides charged meaning to what is said. Once these factors have been analyzed, it is possible to gain greater insight into the cognitive nuances of the words they speak that trigger action, heighten the emotional and physical situation, and produce reactions by the other participants in the conversation.[20] As characters interact, their words are understood within the context of their social position, identity, and location within the story and are further illustrated or magnified by socially recognized acts or gestures.

---

17. Note here the use of second-order positioning by the prophet, who chooses to negate the importance of Naʿaman's connections and wealth by speaking through his servant Gehazi and later by refusing to accept any payment for the cure (2 Kgs 5:16).

18. Davies and Harré, "Positioning and Personhood," 41-42, describe the use of the "dramaturgical model" in social psychology that allows subjects to choose subject positions for themselves as part of therapy sessions.

19. See the discussion of the semiotics of history in Victor H. Matthews, *Studying the Ancient Israelites* (Grand Rapids: Baker, 2007) 162-64.

20. Van Langenhove and Harré, "Introducing Positioning Theory," 17.

Modes of Positioning in the Heroic Tales in Daniel 1, 3, 6

In order to demonstrate the use of the three modes of positioning (see inset) within embedded dialogue, we will briefly examine the heroic tales contained in the book of Daniel. These narratives each employ a "court tale of contest" motif,[21] demonstrating the Israelites' heroic character, courage, and commitment to their Jewish identity when they refuse to be assimilated into the dominant Mesopotamian culture.[22] When confronted with situations in which they would be required to obligate themselves to foreign powers or give up their faith and their religious values, they consistently proclaim that they are willing to leave their fate up to Yahweh. In this way, they engage in second-order positioning and propel the narrative's agenda by demonstrating the power of the divine patron of the Jews.

DANIEL 1

1st-order Positioning	2nd-order Positioning	3rd-order Positioning
King commands training, education, diet for Israelites (vv. 3-5)	Daniel and friends tell palace master they will be defiled (v. 8)	Storyteller to audience: Yahweh interceded with guard (v. 9)
Daniel requests a 10-day test (vv. 11-13)		Palace master tells Daniel he fears the king's wrath if he does not obey (v. 10)
Guard agrees and withdraws royal rations (vv. 14-16)		Storyteller to audience: four men very wise (v. 17)
		Storyteller to audience: impressed king appoints the Israelites to high positions (vv. 18-20)

21. See W. Lee Humphreys, "A Life-Style for Diaspora: A Study of the Tales of Esther and Daniel," *JBL* 92 (1973) 211-23.

22. On this practice of training elite members of a conquered people as bureaucrats, see Donald J. Wiseman, *Nebuchadnezzar and Babylon*. Schweich Lectures 1983 (Oxford: Oxford University Press, 1985) 81.

DANIEL 3

1st-order Positioning	2nd-order Positioning	3rd-order Positioning
King orders all people on signal to bow down to idol (vv. 1-7)		Chaldeans tell king three Jews did not comply (vv. 8-12)
King interrogates, warns them (vv. 13-15)	Three Jews refuse, express faith in Yahweh to protect them (vv. 16-18)	King tells counselors of miraculous survival (vv. 24-25)
King orders three Jews to emerge from furnace; they comply (v. 26)		
King decrees no blasphemy against Jews' patron deity (v. 29)		

DANIEL 6

1st-order Positioning	2nd-order Positioning	3rd-order Positioning
King responds to his counselors' call for a 30-day decree to worship only him (vv. 6-9)		Storyteller to audience: Daniel deliberately prays to Yahweh (v. 10)
Counselors twice remind king a decree cannot be revoked and accuse Daniel (vv. 12-13, 15)	King delays condemning Daniel (v. 14)	
King commands Daniel be brought to lions' den (v. 16a)	King expresses hope Daniel's patron deity will intercede (v. 16b)	
King asks if Daniel has received divine protection; Daniel says he has (vv. 20-22)		Storyteller to audience: King fasted all night, unable to sleep (v. 18)
King commands execution of counselors, decrees people "tremble and fear" Daniel's God (vv. 24-27)		

In Daniel 1 the storyteller structures the dialogue within the narrative around a patron-client theme. Nebuchadnezzar, in the mode of a generous power broker with the moral right as conqueror, engages in a form of magnanimous gift-giving with the expressed intention of transforming the sons of his enemies into his loyal servants. This process includes placing the chosen young men into the custody of one of the king's eunuchs *(rab sārîs)* for directed and intensive instruction in all of the necessary scribal and administrative skills.[23] Then, in the embedded dialogue, second-order positioning is employed when they refuse the king's gift, a daily ration of food and wine from the royal table. The grounds for this refusal, concern that it would "defile" them, may be a Hellenistic-era defense of the Jewish dietary laws or simply a rhetorical means of refusing full client status.[24] Voicing no objection to a formal education or even the imposition of Babylonian names, Daniel and his three friends now take a stand expressing their unwillingness to accept this "rich food" *(patbag)* from the king's table.

Their strong desire to avoid defilement is signaled in the text by the use of a "focusing device," the common Hebrew phrase "and he set" *(wayyāśem).* The use of this phrase helps to demonstrate that, except in the most mundane and inoffensive of situations, the success of second-order positioning is dependent on effectively conveying the impression of either genuine outrage or a deep-felt conviction that prevents compliance with a first-order positioning statement. Thus, Daniel's response is designed to indicate that he and his fellows have weighed this matter in their hearts *(wayyāśem dānîyē'l 'al-libbô),* and they are unable to accept the king's food (1:8).[25] Note how the author expresses this deep emotion by

23. On whether this official or Daniel and his friends were eunuchs, see the discussion in John J. Collins, *Daniel.* Hermeneia (Minneapolis: Fortress, 1993) 134-36. Cf. how Esther and other young women are put into the custody of one of the king's eunuchs and ordered to undergo a 12-month cosmetic transformation before being presented to the king (Esth 2:8-12).

24. See W. Sibley Towner, "Daniel 1 in the Context of the Canon," in *Canon, Theology, and Old Testament Interpretation,* ed. Gene M. Tucker, David L. Petersen, and Robert R. Wilson (Philadelphia: Fortress, 1988) 289-93, for extended discussion of legal and textual arguments for and against an interpretation based on the dietary regulations. See Joyce G. Baldwin, *Daniel.* TOTC (Downers Grove: InterVarsity, 1978) 82-83, for the argument that their demur is based on the desire to be free of obligation to the king.

25. Bill T. Arnold, "Word Play and Characterization in Daniel 1," in *Puns and Pundits: Word Play in the Hebrew Bible and Ancient Near Eastern Literature,* ed. Scott B. Noegel (Bethesda: CDL, 2000) 232-41.

employing a "mind-as-body" metaphor that uses a combination of the preposition "in" *('al)* plus "heart" *(lēb)* to indicate the inclusive nature of the thinking process.[26]

In order to push the narrative forward, Daniel offers an alternative suggestion that provides a clinical test based on a much different diet. It also plays upon the assumption that Yahweh will favor these faithful servants with good health and sharp minds. The third-order positioning statements by the storyteller are in the form of narrative asides addressed to the audience and are designed to make sure they understand the nature of the contest and the true power figure in this story.

A similar court-contest story is found in the tale of the "fiery furnace" in Daniel 3. First-order positioning occurs in 3:1-7 when King Nebuchadnezzar identifies himself as the supreme leader of his people and claims the moral right to command them. He demonstrates his power to position them forcefully by creating a huge golden statue and then ordering all of his subjects, on pain of death, to bow down and worship the image when a fanfare is sounded by the king's orchestra. His assumption of supreme power seems to be justified when his subjects dutifully respond on cue. However, and unexpectedly for him, second-order positioning occurs when the three Israelites (Shadrach, Meshach, and Abednego) fail to comply with the royal command. In an attempt to regain his preeminent position and force their compliance, the full decree, in all its redundant detail, is reiterated. The rote repetition of these details may in fact be a further use of second-order positioning by the storyteller, poking fun at a very pompous king (3:13-15).[27]

Instead of submitting to his command, the three Israelites propose a test to determine whether they should put their trust in Nebuchadnezzar's gods or in their divine patron Yahweh (3:16-18).[28] In this way they deny the king's moral right to command them when they find that command to be unjust or contrary to their beliefs. Third-order positioning then occurs in

---

26. George Lakoff, *Women, Fire, and Dangerous Things* (Chicago: University of Chicago Press, 1987) 439.

27. Hector I. Avalos, "The Comedic Function of the Enumerations of Officials and Instruments in Daniel 3," *CBQ* 53 (1991) 580-88.

28. This proposal is quite common in the biblical narrative and is part of the contest-between-gods theme. For a prime example, see the second-order positioning statement by Gideon's father when ordered by the people of his village to turn his son over to them for execution. Joash tells them to let Baal "defend his [own] cause . . . if he is a god" (Judg 6:30-31).

this narrative when an astonished Nebuchadnezzar speaks to his advisors about the miraculous survival of the three Israelites and remarks that they are not only unhurt, but are accompanied by a previously unseen fourth figure, who has "the appearance of a god" (3:24-25).[29] At that point the story line returns to first-order positioning when the king calls on the Israelites to come out of the furnace and they obey without question (3:26). Then positioning himself once again as the one who commands while others are expected to obey, Nebuchadnezzar decrees that anyone who blasphemes "the God of Shadrach, Meshach, and Abednego" will be executed (3:29). This use of first-order positioning also forms an inclusio with the king's first command.

The final example of this contest and deliverance motif occurs in Daniel 6 as part of the story of the "Lions' Den."[30] In this case, it is Darius the Mede who is manipulated by his counselors into issuing a decree that he cannot rescind. Rather than waiting for Daniel to run afoul of a royal command, these jealous officials plot to remove Daniel from the court and use the king as their unwitting instrument of destruction.[31] When Daniel is caught in the act of praying to Yahweh, he is denounced and, although he attempts to delay the inevitable, the sympathetic and grief-stricken king finally has to have Daniel arrested and thrown into a den of lions (6:16a).

This is an interesting example of forced self-positioning of the king. The counselors take advantage of an apparently weak or easily-flattered ruler and call on the authority of state institutions to force him to comply.[32] Although it is his decree that sets events in motion, the king is the one who wishes, using second-order positioning, to avoid or prevent the legal consequences (6:14, 16b). The storyteller even supplies a third-order positioning aside to the audience remarking on how the king "spent the night fasting" and unable to sleep (6:18). It is only when the assemblage returns in the

29. Terry L. Brensinger, "Compliance, Dissonance and Amazement in Daniel 3," *EvJ* 20 (2002) 7-19.

30. See Karel van der Toorn, "In the Lions' Den: The Babylonian Background of a Biblical Motif," *CBQ* 60 (1998) 627-29, for extrabiblical examples of the vindicated courtier and the use of a lions' den as the mode of execution.

31. See the discussion of Daniel's position within Darius's administration in Danna Nolan Fewell, *Circle of Sovereignty: A Story of Stories in Daniel 1-6*. JSOTSup 72 (Sheffield: Almond, 1988) 143-45.

32. See van Langenhove and Harré, "Introducing Positioning Theory," 26-27, for further examples of the use of forced self-positioning.

morning that Darius at last assumes the role of supreme ruler and frees himself of his false counselors. Using first-order positioning, he calls on Daniel to demonstrate that his divine patron has protected him from the lions and vindicated him of the charges against him. Darius, in a nice piece of irony, then orders the counselors to be thrown to the hungry beasts (6:20-24). As in the case of the other examples, the story then ends with Daniel returning to the good graces of the king and Darius proclaiming a warning to his people that they should "tremble and fear before the God of Daniel" (6:25-26). In this way, the cause and effect of the events in the story and the language employed by the author create the desired emotions by the characters and possibly the audience.[33] Furthermore, the force dynamics that ordinarily would be centered on Darius as the one force-exerting entity are repositioned and transferred to Daniel's divine patron.[34]

Of course, the narrative in Daniel, like any other unfolding narrative, requires authors or storytellers either to have a shared knowledge of the world of their characters or to create consciously a believable world for the narrative. This is accomplished by utilizing inference procedures.[35] Inference requires a pragmatic approach to narrative and embedded dialogue in which the author who wishes to create a sense of reality must fill in enough detail to demonstrate a practical knowledge and basic believability in the world in which the story is set. When the author shares in or is a member of the society portrayed in the story, an emic shorthand takes place that assumes a basic knowledge by the audience of the schemata, basic norms, of that culture and place.[36] In those instances when an author must create a setting entirely out of learned or fabricated data, inferences are less subtle and more attention is given to detail so that the audience is

---

33. For a discussion of language as a means of eliciting specific emotions and framing them in terms of metaphors, see Zoltán Kövecses, *Language, Mind, and Culture* (Oxford: Oxford University Press, 2006) 214-19.

34. Leonard Talmy, "Force Dynamics in Language and Cognition," *Cognitive Science* 12 (1988) 53.

35. For a fuller discussion of inferencing procedures, see Dan Sperber and Deirdre Wilson, *Relevance: Communication and Cognition* (Cambridge, MA: Harvard University Press, 1986).

36. Guy Cook, *Discourse and Literature* (Oxford: Oxford University Press, 1994) 11-12, employs schema theory to explain the narrative gaps in a story that are left by a storyteller who has a shared knowledge of the setting of the story. It is only when authors cannot assume that their audience shares their worldview that additional details must be added to flesh out statements that require further explanation.

clued in about what is occurring in the story. Then, in both types of story-telling, as part of the staging of the narrative a conscious decision is made to position the characters in stances of weakness or power. Naturally, these assigned positions can shift many times during the unfolding of the story.

Step-by-Step Positioning in 1 Kings 22

Careful analysis of the scenes described in 1 Kings 22 will illustrate further the use of positioning theory in embedded dialogue. What becomes immediately clear is that the storyteller has artfully positioned the characters throughout the narrative in an effort to set up a series of dialogues between kings, as well as a discussion of prophetic pronouncements and the confrontations between kings and prophets. During the course of the narrative all three modes of positioning as described above occur, and this takes place in the midst of the shifting landscape of the dialogue.

The story begins after a three-year period of peace between rival minor powers, Israel and Aram (Syria). The arrival of King Jehoshaphat of Judah in Ahab's court in Samaria provides a political catalyst or narrative trigger for resumption of strategic positioning along their borders by the rival nations. The nature of the power relationship between the kings of Israel and Judah is made explicit by a series of indications in the text that effectively position the king of Judah as the client of his neighboring sovereign.

(1) The narrative makes clear that Jehoshaphat "came down to the king of Israel" (22:2). This is meant both physically, since Jerusalem is located at a higher elevation in the central hill country than Samaria, and politically, indicating that Jehoshaphat is Ahab's vassal, not his equal, and he must therefore come to Samaria.[37]

(2) Jehoshaphat's appearance at this point, possibly for a scheduled diplomatic visit to renew his loyalty oath to Ahab, gives Ahab the opportunity to position himself as the dominant political leader in the room.[38] He will use his preeminent position to question and cajole

37. Cf. how the elders of Israel came to David in Hebron to request that he become their king (2 Sam 5:1-3). In essence they place themselves in a subsidiary position by making the journey rather than summoning to them a prospective candidate for the kingship.

38. See the discussion of the Omride "golden age" and the ascendancy of Israel over Ju-

his ally. The king of Israel, speaking in a ruminating tone and in a rhetorical, didactic manner to his "servants" (*ʿăbādāyw*) that presumably include his vassal Jehoshaphat, says, "Do you know that Ramoth-gilead belongs to us?" He then puts out the challenging statement, "yet we are doing nothing to take it out of the hand of the king of Aram" (22:3-4a). Although Ahab's statement is not a direct command to his ally, it is an example of first-order positioning in which the king of Israel is claiming the moral right to call for action and to draw his allies into the fray. He would not have framed the question without knowing the answer he would receive, nor would this be a "trial balloon" since he has already made up his mind to go to war.[39]

(3) Faced with a public situation in which he cannot equivocate, Jehoshaphat displays his awareness of current political events and that his loyalty is being tested by this question. His quick and forceful reply before the royal court is one that would be expected of a trusted ally: "I am as you are; my people are your people, my horses are your horses" (22:4b).

Once the decision has been made to go to war, the storyteller sets aside the mundane matters of gathering troops, equipment, and intelligence as apparently unimportant. The assumption is that the audience can mentally picture that process and therefore the drama moves on with a new narrative focus being created for the audience. Ultimately, this will lead to a dual contest between Ahab and Micaiah and between Micaiah and the 400 prophets.[40] First, however, is an interesting reversal of positions by the kings. It is Jehoshaphat who now steps forward with the first-order positioning request that Ahab "inquire first for the word of the Lord" (22:5).

Jehoshaphat's request falls within the range of the proper procedures that ordinarily are required prior to any military endeavor, since every Israelite military commander wishes to elicit the aid of the Divine Warrior Yahweh. The fact that Jehoshaphat makes the suggestion instead of Ahab

---

dah during this period of the 9th century B.C.E. in J. Maxwell Miller and John H. Hays, *A History of Ancient Israel and Judah,* 2nd ed. (Louisville: Westminster/John Knox, 2006) 300-13.

39. R. W. L. Moberly, "To Speak for God: The Story of Micaiah ben Imlah," *Anvil* 14 (1997) 244.

40. Mordechai Cogan, *1 Kings.* AB 10 (New York: Doubleday, 2001) 496-97.

reverses their respective positions as the dominant voice in this conversation. Jehoshaphat's request also could be part of the storyteller's intentional positioning of him as a "good king."[41] The impression given here stands in stark contrast to the very judgmental assessment of Ahab's reign as the king who "did evil in the sight of the Lord more than all who were before him" (16:30).

This time it is Ahab who quickly responds without hesitation to a royal request and gathers up about 400 prophets to determine God's will for their expedition. There is no mention of how he does this, and presumably it did not involve combing the kingdom for these men. There is, however, an apparent shift in tradition here since all previous examples in which Israelite forces sought out divination involve priests, not prophets (cf. 1 Sam 14:37; 23:2).[42] In any case, it seems likely that these men were part of Ahab's royal court,[43] and this could explain their enthusiastic and unanimous response to his query about the upcoming struggle: "Go up; for the Lord will give it [Ramoth-gilead] into the hand of the king" (22:6).

What is interesting here is that Jehoshaphat, who had been so quick to acquiesce to Ahab's call for war with Syria, now freely questions the reliability of the unqualified message delivered by the king's court prophets. In this way, he repositions himself at this point as the dominant voice in the pre-war preparations. His demur also functions as a rhetorical form of resistance in a situation where he cannot officially argue against the plan espoused by his ally. Even though Jehoshaphat has put up a public display of loyalty and complete agreement with Ahab's planned campaign, he may have been concerned with breaking the truce between the nations and the likelihood that he could not fully rely on Israel in a military setting.[44] Thus

---

41. See his glowing regnal note in 1 Kgs 22:41-50 in comparison to the horrendous assessment provided for nearly every other king of Israel and Judah except David and Josiah.

42. Note that prophets are involved in bringing the word of Yahweh to Israelite leaders and kings prior to battle. Thus Deborah summons Barak and exhorts him to "go, take position at Mount Tabor" because the Lord has determined to give Jabin and Sisera "into his hand" (Judg 4:6-7), and the unnamed "man of God" comes unasked to Ahab and tells him that God will give the forces of Ben-hadad into his hand so "you shall know that I am the Lord" (1 Kgs 20:28). On the difference between divinatory requests for priests and prophets, see Burke O. Long, "The Effect of Divination upon Israelite Literature," *JBL* 92 (1973) 489-97.

43. See the reference by Micaiah to "your prophets" in 22:23.

44. This possible concern is fully demonstrated when Ahab disguises himself prior to the battle and leaves Jehoshaphat as the prime target of the enemy forces on the field (22:29-33).

this delaying tactic, a form of passive resistance using established protocols, might at least slow down Ahab's rush to war.[45] On another level, it also serves the purposes of the storyteller by pre-positioning the upcoming scene highlighted by the confrontation between Micaiah and Ahab's 400 prophets.[46]

Of course, it is possible that Jehoshaphat is expressing simple caution in a potentially dangerous situation, but his reluctance to trust Ahab's prophets also indicates that some matters between allies can be questioned while others cannot. Jehoshaphat dares not demonstrate any reluctance to join his more powerful ally in matters involving political or military efforts. However, his request that an independent prophetic voice be consulted rather than reliance on the word of men possibly in the king's employ is one that Ahab apparently cannot challenge.[47]

The circumstance in which Ahab found himself may be comparable to the dilemma he faced in dealing with his stubborn neighbor Naboth. Ahab is stymied when his subject refuses to sell him his vineyard based on the argument that it is a matter of covenantal priority that Naboth keep the land in trust for his descendants (1 Kgs 21:2-4). Second-order positioning is certainly at work in this case. It includes the deflection of the king's attempt to use moral authority to position his neighbor and thus gain the land. When Naboth cites an irrefutable, moral argument based on the covenantal rights of his household,[48] his moral authority transcends that of the king. In the same way, Jehoshaphat's rhetorical tactic of requesting yet another prophetic response to their question cannot be ignored or dismissed by Ahab because it would have been considered a moral, honorable request.

Thus, even though he grumbles over the delay and the added step

45. Lila Abu-Lughod, "The Romance of Resistance: Tracing Transformations of Power Through Bedouin Women," *American Ethnologist* 17 (1990) 41-42.

46. The obvious parallel between this confrontation of a single prophet and a force of about 400 others and Elijah's contest with the 450 prophets of Baal in 1 Kgs 18:17-40 continues the underdog theme of the Elijah cycle and eventually magnifies their recognition as true prophets.

47. This is reminiscent of the confrontation between Amaziah, the priest of Bethel, and the prophet Amos over who has the right to speak in the "king's sanctuary" (Amos 7:12-17).

48. As Alexander Rofé, "The Vineyard of Naboth: The Origin and Message of the Story," *VT* 38 (1988) 90, points out, Naboth's argument is not based on law, but tradition as spelled out in Num 36:7-8. However, since tradition binds a community based on shared expectation and understanding of what is honorable behavior, if Naboth had agreed he would have shamed his household and lost status in his community.

imposed on him by his ally (another, although milder, form of second-order positioning), Ahab finds it necessary to arrange for a messenger to bring the prophet Micaiah ben Imlah to court. It could be argued that since the king had to send for the prophet he was admitting the need to draw on "outside" help and this would weaken his position. However, there is precedent in the story of Balaam (Numbers 22-24) that demonstrates that kings did recognize they had limitations in divining the will of the gods and needed to employ prophets and priests to perform this task. Therefore, summoning Micaiah would fall within the normal powers of the king and would not lessen his standing a great deal.

If that be the case, it is truly ironic how great an effort Ahab employs to set the stage for his eventual confrontation with the prophet. The entire show is pre-positioned in the minds of the audience and the participants by King Ahab's harsh third-order positioning statement that he hates Micaiah because "he never prophesies anything favorable about me, but only disaster" (22:8a). It is an indication of a long-standing enmity between Ahab and the prophet and functions in this case as a third-order warning to his ally and to the audience of a charged scene to come.

Ahab's strategy is to attempt to pre-position Jehoshaphat's attitude toward Micaiah by labeling the prophet as a troublemaker.[49] Because the phrase *(kî lō'-yitnabbē' 'ālay ṭôb kî 'im-rā')* is repeated later in the story (v. 18), it serves as a narrative connector. The repetition of the significant word *ra'* ("bad") provides an interactional reminder to Jehoshaphat and to the audience of the latent tension present in any meetings between this prophet and the kings.[50] It also adds to the charged background in his heated confrontation with Ahab's prophets.[51] What is made very clear here is that their positions toward each other are not only well known but are unlikely to change. Even Jehoshaphat's cautionary plea (again a mild form of second-order positioning) that he should "not say such a thing" is useless and merely reiterates the storyteller's positioning of his characters in the stereotypical counterstances of the fool and the wise king.[52]

---

49. Cf. a similar attempt by Ahab to label the prophet Elijah as the "troubler of Israel" (1 Kgs 18:17).

50. Deborah Tannen, *Talking Voices: Repetition, Dialogue, and Imagery in Conversational Discourse* (Cambridge: Cambridge University Press, 1989) 51.

51. Long, *1 Kings*, 235. Cf. a similarly displayed, antagonistic relationship between Elijah and Ahab recorded in 1 Kgs 18:17.

52. Matthews and Benjamin, *Social World of Ancient Israel, 1250-587 B.C.E.*, 142-45. For

As we await the prophet's arrival, positioning strategies are taking place on two levels. First, the storyteller is taking advantage of the audience's shared knowledge of the physical attributes of the gate area of Samaria and of the symbolism attached to royal vestments and thrones. This set of created circumstances is designed to highlight the confrontation between king and prophet. There is also a sense here that the author wishes to position the audience to believe in the power relationships as they are first portrayed: dominant monarchs vs. subordinate and submissive prophet. Once that has been established it will be possible to increase the level of surprise, irony, and even comedy that ensues during the scene.

Matching this at the character level are the efforts of one or both of the kings to manipulate the scene consciously by positioning themselves and all associated props of power in such a way as to magnify the manifest sense of authority implicit in their meeting and, of course, to intimidate the prophet Micaiah. Actually, everything in the scene is pre-positioned since this is obviously not a spontaneous demonstration. What the kings apparently hope to accomplish is to enforce on their potential opponent, one who has been a troublesome prophetic voice in the past, a defined position and script.[53] The key verse is 22:10: "The king of Israel and King Jehoshaphat of Judah were sitting on their thrones, arrayed in their robes, at the threshing floor at the entrance of the gate of Samaria; and all the prophets were prophesying before them." Taken together, these various elements of place and person combine to create one of the most powerful scenes in the biblical narrative. With two royal persons displayed in their robes of office, seated on their thrones that have been strategically positioned at the gate of the capital city, and drawing on the authority of that place's original position as a threshing floor,[54] what more could be done to awe and intimidate anyone in the audience?

The question arises why the kings went to the trouble of staging such a grand spectacle. They could just as easily have interviewed the prophet in

---

other examples of this dichotomy of personality type in Wisdom literature, see Psalm 1; Prov 10:8; and Eccl 10:2.

53. Van Langenhove and Harré, "Introducing Positioning Theory," 17, note that "the social force of an action and the position of the actor and interactors mutually determine one another."

54. See Moshe Anbar, "'L'aire à l'entré de la porte de Samarie' (1 R. XXII 10)," *VT* 50 (2000) 121-23, for a discussion of the arguments over whether the *gōren* should be translated "threshing floor" or simply an "open space."

Positioning Elements of Power

Two kings: Persons of power and authority doubling their overt sovereignty by joining forces in this scene

Thrones: Special and restricted furnishings moved for this occasion out of the throne room of the palace to a place associated with the legal and economic affairs of the city[1]

Royal robes: Rich vestments indicating power status and separating individuals from those wearing ordinary clothing[2]

Threshing floor: A facility associated with agricultural production, as well as legal and business transactions in the village culture (see Ruth 3)

City gate: A significant spot in urban settings where legal and business transactions are conducted, associated with the defense of the city (see Gen 19:1)

Samaria: Capital city of the kingdom of Israel and thus the political nexus for administrative pronouncement and display

400 court prophets: Spokespersons for God employed by King Ahab dancing in a frenzy and even employing props (ox horns that represent the deity's strength and virility)

1. See John C. H. Laughlin, "The Remarkable Discoveries at Tel Dan," *BAR* 7/5 (1981) 22-24, for photographs and description of the official's platform discovered in the Iron Age gate at Tel Dan.
2. On the importance attached to vestments and investiture of power through clothing, see Victor H. Matthews, "The Anthropology of Clothing in the Joseph Narrative," *JSOT* 65 (1995) 25-36.

private or in the palace rather than in a public place associated with law (Josh 20:4) and business transactions (Gen 19:1). However, it is possible that the very public nature of going to war, so often associated with the city gate (see Josh 8:29; Judg 9:35; 2 Sam 10:8), demanded a public display in a place that had emerged as integral to the public sphere and represented the survival of the city/nation.[55] Therefore the takeover of public space, the

55. Jürgen Habermas, *The Structural Transformation of the Public Sphere* (Cambridge, MA: MIT Press, 2001) 2-5, discusses the emergence of public space as a recognizable domain and as a bridge between civil society and the state.

gate area, by the kings for this purpose is a further demonstration of their power to commandeer or reposition any suitable or symbolic place for their own aims. In this way the position of the public sphere of commerce, demonstrated ordinarily by the mundane activities in the gate conducted by merchants and the city elders, is usurped by the political desires of the government.[56]

As they await the arrival of Micaiah, a sort of "grand pause" takes place in the narrative that is filled by the continued performance of the 400 court prophets, now given a face and an ever more strident voice by the appearance of the prophet Zedekiah ben Chenaanah.[57] Zedekiah's dramatic use of "horns of iron" (22:11) to simulate Yahweh's intention to gore the enemy and thus bring Ahab a victory over the Arameans would have been an entertaining public spectacle for both the kings and the audience in the gate area. However, this seems more appropriate for a prophet of Baal than for one speaking in the name of Yahweh.[58] Given the obvious parallels between this episode and Elijah's confrontation with the 450 prophets of Baal on Mount Carmel (1 Kgs 18:20-29), the storyteller may well be injecting a not so subtle indication to the audience that these prophets may also serve more gods than just Yahweh. There is also the likelihood that prophetic paraphernalia from the neighboring cultures in Canaan and Syria could have been adopted for use by prophets in Ahab's court.[59]

It is into this remarkable tableau, swollen by the rising tide of optimistic prophetic utterance at Samaria's gate, that Micaiah and his guide now step. But before the next sequence actually commences, the king's messenger inappropriately attempts to manipulate the prophet by giving him a verbal warning that Micaiah's position is subsidiary to these more acceptable

56. This practice is demonstrated today every time the public streets are blocked off to facilitate the movement of the motorcade of political leaders or by the imposition of zoning laws by a city council. See Neil Smith and Setha Low, "Introduction: The Imperative of Public Space," in *The Politics of Public Space*, ed. Low and Smith (New York: Routledge, 2006) 5, 12-13.

57. Burke O. Long, "The Form and Significance of 1 Kings 22:1-38," in *Isaac Leo Seeligmann Volume: Essays on the Bible and the Ancient World*, ed. Alexander Rofé and Yair Zakovitch (Jerusalem: Rubinstein, 1983) 3:202-3.

58. Othmar Keel and Christoph Uehlinger, *Gods, Goddesses, and Images of God in Ancient Israel* (Minneapolis: Fortress, 1998) 76, describes a late Ramesside-era scarab found in Grave 120 at Lachish depicting Baal-Seth sporting bull's horns.

59. Paul Eugène Dion, "The Horned Prophet (1 Kings xxii 11)," *VT* 49 (1999) 260, describes a 9th-century Luwian text that mentions a horned hat or mask worn by a spokesman for the god Tarhunza, the storm-god of Aleppo.

prophets. As they enter the scene, the king's man stiffly enjoins Micaiah to stick to the proper storyline. He is instructed to "speak favorably,"[60] just as "the words of the prophets with one accord are favorable to the king" (22:13).[61] To make such a statement to a prophet ignores the societal position he holds. It diminishes him as a person and, by extension, his membership in the profession.[62] As such it is a challenge to the legitimacy of Micaiah and is an attempt to strip him of his identity as a prophet. This rhetorical gambit requires an immediate response or it will be confirmed through default by the king's man and by those who witness Micaiah's submission to loss of self.[63]

In this verbal joust, however, Micaiah stands his ground, refusing to be labeled or to be positioned forcefully. He rather officiously recites the standard prophetic disclaimer, "whatever the Lord says to me, that I will speak" (22:14).[64] In this way the prophet escapes the trap of being fixed into a predetermined pattern of behavior and maintains his own determination to respond to the discursive situation on his own terms as a free participant. His decision is an argument that an individual's identity, while it can be shaped by events and the tone of a conversation, remains an open question until he becomes a participant in the discourse.[65] This scene also

60. Note the forceful use of the Hebrew word *ṭôb*, "good," as a rhetorical contrast and counterpoint to Ahab's expectation that all he will hear from this prophet is *ra'*, "bad."

61. Moshe Weinfeld, "Ancient Near Eastern Patterns in Prophetic Literature," *VT* 27 (1977) 184-85, points to a parallel between the Mari letter ARM X 4:37-39 and 1 Kgs 22:13. In both instances the report is that the prophets have not been forced to speak, but they prophesy "with one voice." He suggests that it was normal procedure to separate the prophets to test whether they would answer with the same prophecy. This may well be the case, and Ahab is simply following proper protocol. However, I would suggest that the messenger is doing more than reporting that fact and is actually trying to put pressure on Micaiah to follow suit in voicing the same message.

62. Van Langenhove and Harré, "Introducing Positioning Theory," 26-27, refer to this practice as "forced self-positioning" and indicate that "when an institution [in this case represented by the king's messenger] has the power to make moral judgments about persons and about their behavior, it will ask people to account for what they are doing (or not doing)."

63. See a constructionist application of positioning theory as it relates to the maintenance and assertion of self-identity by persons with Alzheimer's disease in Stephen Sabat and Rom Harré, "Positioning and the Recovery of Social Identity," in Harré and van Langenhove, *Positioning Theory*, 93-98.

64. See the similar disclaimer repeatedly used by Balaam in Num 22:38; 23:12, 26; 24:13.

65. Davies and Harré, "Positioning and Personhood," 35.

allows the storyteller to reiterate the classic position that a true prophet is one who speaks the word of Yahweh and whose statements are subsequently proven to be true (Deut 18:18-22). We will learn just how ironic that position is when Micaiah asserts in 22:23 that God had "put a lying spirit in the mouth" of the 400 prophets.[66]

Turning now to the wider scene before us, Ahab once again takes the lead. Jehoshaphat, who had requested this oracle of divine intentions, takes no part in the remainder of this positioned scene. He has been shuffled aside by the narrator, and all focus is now placed on the verbal sparring between Ahab and Micaiah. Note the ritualized manner in which Ahab asks Micaiah exactly the same divinatory question that he had posed to the 400 prophets (22:6, 15a). Repetition in this case is necessary to maintain proper rhetorical protocol when consulting prophets, and it has a "referential and tying function" linking the two scenes and their discourse.[67] Perhaps more importantly in this case, it allows Ahab to maintain control "over the floor" and show his audience that he is positioned as the person in charge, the dynamic force in this situation.[68]

The spark that will set off this powder keg of heightened emotions is the prophet's initial response that exactly mimics that of the 400 prophets (22:15b) and does not seem to conform to Micaiah's own assertion that he will speak only God's word. The fact that Micaiah echoes the prophetic speech of the king's prophets fits into a rhetorical pattern of repetition employed here by the storyteller. It matches and complements Ahab's question and sets the audience up for the next heated exchange.[69]

Micaiah's response might be interpreted as his acquiescence to the messenger's demand and as evidence that he indeed has been intimidated by the kings' show of power. However, it seems more likely that his echoing of the massed prophets' cry, "Go up and triumph!" is actually a sarcastic taunt or an assertion on his part that the king really did not want to hear

66. One could argue that a difference is made here between "word" and "spirit." However, the source of both is Yahweh, and that is not disputed.

67. M. A. K. Halliday and Ruqaiya Hasan, *Cohesion in English* (London: Longman, 1976).

68. Tannen, *Talking Voices,* 48-52, describes the four functions of repetition as production, comprehension, connection, and interaction. It is this fourth quality that is employed here in Ahab's rhetorical strategy.

69. Meir Sternberg, *The Poetics of Biblical Narrative* (Bloomington: Indiana University Press, 1985) 411.

any other message.[70] The façade of power created by Ahab must be shattered if Micaiah is to assume his authoritative position as the one who speaks God's word. To do this he engages in a rhetorical strategy that is designed to illicit a heated response from Ahab that will weaken the king's command over the scene and trap him into demanding to hear the "true words" of Yahweh.[71] Micaiah, now in full control of events, has positioned himself to speak a prophecy that contradicts that of the 400 court prophets, and it then will be up to the king to decide how to react.

There is almost a comic tone to Ahab's exasperated assumption of taking the "moral high ground" in this matter.[72] His command that Micaiah swear always to "tell me nothing but the truth in the name of the Lord" (22:16) sets Ahab up for a fall from his moral pinnacle. Caught in the web of a rhetorical master, the king cannot avoid the inevitable. In fact, Ahab has been trapped from the beginning of this drama by his own publicly-expressed ambitions, his attempts to position himself as the dominant character in this social drama, and now by his repeated consultation of the prophets.[73] Plus, when he agreed to have Micaiah brought to his court, his horde of court prophets became superfluous in their assumed position as sole spokespersons for God, and they were forced into the background by Micaiah's solo voice of true authority.

Micaiah's Oracles

Freed to speak candidly, Micaiah takes advantage of his astute positioning strategy and steps forward to place himself physically and professionally into the spotlight. First, he distinguishes himself from the court prophets, by describing a vision of doom. In a horrific oracle that graphically depicts the result of this ill-fated expedition, he sees "all Israel scattered on the

70. Moberly, "To Speak for God," 246. As Amos will later lament, "they abhor the one who speaks the truth" (Amos 5:10).

71. Keith Bodner, "The Locutions of 1 Kings 22:28: A New Proposal," *JBL* 122 (2003) 537.

72. R. W. L. Moberly, "Does God Lie to His Prophets? The Story of Micaiah ben Imlah as a Test Case," *HTR* 96 (2003) 7, points to the irony of a king who does not want to hear an unfavorable message but fears to trust completely the assurances of his court "toadies."

73. Cf. how David is trapped by his own words when he condemns the "rich man" of Nathan's parable of the ewe lamb (2 Sam 12:1-9).

mountains, like sheep that have no shepherd."[74] Masterless men, who have no recourse and no leader, are forced to return to their homes without the expected prizes of war (22:17).[75] To be sure, this confirms Ahab's worst fears as he repeats his earlier assessment of Micaiah's gloomy prophetic repertoire and nervously jokes in an aside to Jehoshaphat: See! I told you so! (22:18).

The crux of the matter, however, is whether the king can back down from his publicly proclaimed, militant position.[76] In fact, there is precedent for discontinuing an untenable plan due to the pragmatics of their political and military position (see Baasha's forced withdrawal from Ramah in 1 Kgs 15:16-21). However, in this case the expedition has not yet begun and Ahab is in danger of losing face before his court and the people. That is not a position into which he or any other politician would gladly place himself.[77] Still, he cannot say that he has not been warned. If he chooses to act without taking Micaiah's vision into account, this is a blatant rejection of the traditional intercessory position of the prophet. God's warning can only be ignored at one's peril.[78]

Since Micaiah cannot assume that he has convinced the king, despite his clear warning against the proposed attack on Aram, he details a second vision that intentionally parallels the scene at the gate of Samaria and once again provides an example of intentional repetition in this story (22:19). The court scene that Ahab had so carefully orchestrated is now trans-

---

74. A. Graeme Auld, "Prophets Shared — But Recycled," in *The Future of the Deuteronomistic History,* ed. Thomas Römer (Leuven: Leuven University Press, 2000) 24, points out that the use of the phrase "all Israel" (see 2 Sam 8:15 and 1 Kgs 11:42) is an indication of the alliance between Israel and Judah and a warning to both kings.

75. Cf. the similar prophetic image in Ezek 34:5-6 in which the people/sheep are scattered on the mountains because of the neglect and unfaithful management of the flock/nation.

76. Cf. Jeremiah's threefold injunction to the people, to King Zedekiah, and to priests during the siege of Jerusalem to accept the yoke of Babylonian rule and "not listen to the words of your prophets" who predict the return of the exiles and the sacred vessels (Jer 27:9-17).

77. Moberly, "Does God Lie to His Prophets?" 4, correctly notes that Ahab had already resolved to carry out his expedition against Aram and that his original question in 22:3 was merely a leading query designed to command support from the members of his court. This therefore becomes the social dynamic of the story and the crux upon which each character or group speaks in turn.

78. See a fuller discussion of this prophetic position in Moberly, "Does God Lie to His Prophets?" 8. Cf. Ezekiel's prophetic warning that those who fail to heed God's warning cannot blame anyone but themselves for their subsequent death (Ezek 33:1-4).

formed into the Divine Assembly with Yahweh enthroned at its head.[79] In this way Micaiah effectively sets aside earthly powers and human justice and replaces them with the majesty of the divine realm. The position that true authority rests in the person of the king and his administration is discounted and replaced with an alternative view of governance. A wise king, and one who cannot easily be fooled/deceived *(patteh)*, will recognize this true authority and will not succumb to false words *(šeqer)*,[80] embodied here as the "lying spirit" that deceives the prophets into telling him only what he wants to hear.[81] As Jeremiah repeatedly warns the kings of Judah, it is the minority voice with the courage to prophecy disaster when all others promise peace that should be perceived as the true voice of God (Jer 6:14; 8:11; 28:9).

In Micaiah's vision of Yahweh surrounded by the Divine Assembly (1 Kgs 22:19), the divine entourage serves a militant purpose as the "Host of Heaven," the army with which the Divine Warrior will rout Israel's enemies and in this scene sits in a position of subordination to the High God who commands them.[82] This scene provides a reversed (AB/BA) juxtaposition to the power situation between Ahab and Jehoshaphat. In this case, rather than follow the pattern of Jehoshaphat who immediately responds in the affirmative when his overlord proposes action, the Divine Assembly apparently debates God's call for a volunteer to "entice Ahab" into a foolhardy and fatal expedition. In this way, they display second-order positioning, delaying an affirmative response to the deity's call. At last a single spirit responds "I will entice him" (22:21).[83]

It is clear that Micaiah's second vision also is aimed at solidifying his

79. Cf. the scene in Job 1:6 and 2:1. Similar depictions of a divine assembly of the gods are found in the Babylonian creation epic, *Enuma Elish* VI 60-80 (*ANET*, 69), and in the Ugaritic epic of Baal and Anath II AB v: 20-50 (*ANET*, 133).

80. The prototypical figure of the "wise king" is Solomon as he is portrayed in 1 Kgs 3:5-28 and 4:29-34. Standard admonitions to a ruler to be wise are found in Ps 2:10 and Prov 20:26, while the failings of the fool are categorized in Ps 94:8-11.

81. Moberly, "Does God Lie to His Prophets?" 10, argues persuasively for this psychological ploy. I would add that the admonition that Ahab not be enticed by the lying spirit — in other words, not be a fool in this matter — fit nicely into traditional wisdom speech such as Tamar's arguments that Amnon not act like a "scoundrel" by raping her (2 Sam 13:11-13).

82. See Keel and Uehlinger, *Gods, Goddesses, and Images of God in Ancient Israel*, 347, for discussion of this attribute of the Divine Assembly.

83. Cf. the similar situation in which the prophet Isaiah first demurs when called to speak, but once he has been purified he steps forward to say "Here am I; send me" (Isa 6:5-8).

Jehoshaphat	Divine Assembly
Responds affirmatively to Ahab's call to arms against Aram = first-order positioning	Debates God's call for one to "entice Ahab" to his death (22:20) = second-order positioning
Demurs twice asking Ahab to "inquire for the word of the Lord" (22:5) and then to consult yet another prophet (22:7) = second-order positioning	A spirit steps forward to fulfill God's call for one to entice Ahab (22:21) = first-order positioning

own position at the expense of Ahab's court prophets. However, these men have been extremely embarrassed by Micaiah's contradiction of their promise of a military victory. In addition, his prediction of the death of King Ahab (22:19-23) challenges their legitimacy as true prophets. Now their leader attempts to reassert their authority by literally striking back. Zedekiah slaps Micaiah and publicly denounces him as a false prophet (22:24).[84] This violent gesture serves as an unspoken but socially-understood statement of first-order positioning. In effect, Zedekiah's physical act combines two forms of a nonverbal discourse, the insult and the retort, defensive measures designed to reassert the self-worth of the king's prophets and to impose once again their primacy as spokespersons for Yahweh at their opponent's expense.[85] Rather than resorting to an exchange of blows, Micaiah simply rebukes Zedekiah. His retort, remarkably, does not include a curse, and this may be because the 400 court prophets had been duped into a false prophecy by God's strategic positioning of Ahab.[86]

What results is a situation that is fraught with cognitive dissonance. Unable to discern which prophet is telling the truth, Ahab attempts to re-

---

84. James Luther Mays, *Micah.* OTL (Philadelphia: Westminster, 1976) 115. See the model of patience defined in Lam 3:25-30 as the person who waits on God and even "gives one's cheek to the smiter" (v. 30).

85. See R. S. Perinbanayagam, *Discursive Acts* (New York: Aldine de Gruyter, 1991) 120-23.

86. Cf. the harsh confrontation between Jeremiah and Hananiah that results in Jeremiah's denunciation of this false prophet and a curse predicting his death within a year (Jer 28:13-17).

Violence as a Form of Positioning

Both first-order and second-order positioning can be expressed through violent acts. A blow can be struck to position an opponent forcefully or to express insult and outrage.

Job 16:10 — Job's third-order lament describes how his adversaries "gaped" at him and struck him "insolently on the cheek." Such aggressive behavior could only occur if the adversaries sensed his weakness and felt the moral right and personal ability to position their target as one deserving public scorn and physical punishment.[1]

Ps 3:7 — The Psalmist acknowledges the powerful position of Yahweh, confirming that his divine patron has the ability to "strike all my enemies on the cheek." This is a third-order positioning statement.

Jer 20:2 — Following Jeremiah's execration ritual in Jerusalem's Potsherd Gate, a high-ranking priest, Pashhur, strikes the prophet on the cheek and puts him in the stocks as a forceful first-order statement rejecting the prophecy and publicly humiliating the prophet.

1. Cf. the treatment of the king by his enemies in Mic 5:1.

store his control over events by imprisoning Micaiah and placing him on short rations (22:26-27). It is ironic that Ahab uses a speech formula (22:27) very similar to that employed by Micaiah in 22:19: "Thus says the king" *(kōh 'āmar hammelek)* and "hear the word of the Lord" *(lākēn šĕmaʿ dĕbaryhwh)*. Both are command forms implying the authority to speak and carry with them the expectation that they will be heard and obeyed. Once again, the audience is presented with the dichotomy of power: human vs. divine. And once again Ahab is presented with the option to act like a fool or a wise king. The imprisonment of Micaiah, like that of Jeremiah (Jer 37:11-21), provides a temporary solution by removing an embarrassing voice from the public sphere. However, Micaiah's final vocal salvo, spoken to the king and all the people, must have remained with Ahab as he prepared to go to war: "If you return in peace, the Lord has not spoken by me" (22:28).

Uncertain and fearful of making a mistake, Ahab disguises himself, consciously repositioning himself, before going into battle (22:30), but this simply allows the enemy to focus on Jehoshaphat as the obvious military commander (22:31-33). When his army is forced to withdraw, Ahab's forces must have been scattered "like sheep on the mountains" (22:17), and his death comes in the form of a chance arrow that penetrates his armor (22:34). Although there is no mention of Micaiah's ultimate fate, he is vindicated and his position as a true prophet is certified by these events.[87]

---

87. Cf. the statement of certification by the widow of Zarephath, who proclaims "Now I know that you are a man of God, and that the word of the Lord in your mouth is truth" (1 Kgs 17:24).

CHAPTER FIVE

Spatiality and Context

With the discussion of frame analysis and conversation analysis as background, we turn now to the physical and perceived qualities of particular space that provide both opportunity for and restraints on speech. Space, in fact, comprises both physical location and a set of cognitive associations that have become attached to that specific location.[1] However, to understand truly the significance attached to space, it is necessary to delve deeper for the cultural meanings, keeping in mind that the culture of the ancient Israelites may not have had a concept of space equivalent to our own.[2] Still, it is possible to examine the reflective process that is attached to particular or defined space and to the social interaction that occurs within it. This in turn will help to illumine the cognitive qualities of narrative and dialogue.

The process of examining the social dynamics of interaction within defined space begins with recognition of the social context attached to that space. Physical space is usually divided between public and private spaces. The primary difference between them is the restriction on access. Within the public sphere are open, unrestricted areas associated with commercial and other activities that require free access. In private space the rules of access are more restricted since it functions as the private domain of house-

1. Dawn Freshwater, "The Poetics of Space: Researching the Concept of Spatiality through Relationality," *Psychodynamic Practice* 11 (2005) 178.
2. Hilda Kuper, "The Language of Sites in the Politics of Space," in *The Anthropology of Space and Place: Locating Culture*, ed. Setha M. Low and Denise Lawrence-Zúñiga (Malden: Blackwell, 2003) 247.

holds or of the elites in society such as the king.[3] Some locales (fields, vine-yards, buildings) are privately owned and are tied to the pattern of inheritance recognized in that society. This makes their use for conversation subject to the permission or invitation of the owner. Others (city and temple gates, threshing floors, public squares) are set aside for particular civic or religious purposes and are therefore open to either impromptu or formal interaction. Some of these ostensibly public domains, such as thresholds or gates, by their nature or by accepted association are considered to be liminal and are perpetually identified as transitionary space. All of these spaces, however, can be transformed at least temporarily by events and by the imaginative capacities of persons who live, work, and dream within them.

Modern geographers recognize that space consists of various facets, both real and imagined, and they conveniently label them in three distinct categories:

Firstspace = The "real" or physical world

Secondspace = The imagined world or imagined representations of spatiality

Thirdspace = A "multiplicity of real and imagined places" combining the social aspects of both to create a new synthesis called "lived space"[4]

The multilocality of place can be easily illustrated by the varied properties of the place name Zion. In Ps 137:1-7, the poet speaks of the city of Jerusalem and the temple on Mount Zion as a physical place (= Firstspace) where people live and which has been attacked by its enemies. Since that place has been transformed by war and the destructive activities of the armies, the writer now can only extol the remembered virtues of this sacred place associated with the presence and worship of Yahweh. Such

3. Neil Smith and Setha Low, "Introduction: The Imperative of Public Space," in *The Politics of Public Space*, ed. Low and Smith (New York: Routledge, 2006) 3-4.

4. Edward W. Soja, *Thirdspace: Journeys to Los Angeles and Other Real-and-Imagined Places* (Cambridge, MA: Blackwell, 1996) 6. See also this tripartite division of space into the physical, mental, and social in Henri Lefebvre, *The Production of Space* (Oxford: Blackwell, 1991) 11. Kuper, "The Language of Sites," 258, adds to this analysis by defining the term site as "a particular piece of social space, a place socially and ideologically demarcated and separated from other places."

idealized memories commonly held by dislocated persons provide an awareness of the known and familiar that has been physically transformed into the unfamiliar.[5] However, the place and its cognitive image are so precious to these individuals that an oath is taken never to forget them or to consider any other place to be so perfect and full of joy (137:6), creating an image that transcends the physical, mundane, and humanly tarnished characteristics of that place (= Secondspace).[6] This memory of a perfect place and the fond desire to return to its environs, much like the desire/hope for return to Eden,[7] create a combined geographic image made up of both imagined and real qualities that will eventually become once again "lived space," but now having acquired a more complex cognitive character (= Thirdspace).[8]

In this way, Zion is not only a physical location with a specific place name where humans live and work, but it is also a hoped-for sanctuary of relief from the social dislocation of the exile in Mesopotamia (Isa 52:1-2; 62:1-4).[9] When the descendants of these original exiles return to Jerusalem they begin to rebuild its walls and the temple that will carry with them the imagined qualities of that place. Although the reality for the returnees may be somewhat disappointing, they will still express their identity as a righteous remnant in terms of a newly-reordered social existence centered on

5. Margaret C. Rodman, "Empowering Place: Multilocality and Multivocality," in Low and Lawrence-Zúñiga, *The Anthropology of Space and Place,* 212. This could help explain how Zion could be "seen" as an idealized, restored image in later prophetic literature, even though its familiar dimensions no longer exist (see Zech 14:8).

6. Shimon Bar-Efrat, "Love of Zion: A Literary Interpretation of Psalm 137," in *Tehillah le-Moshe,* ed. Mordechai Cogan, Barry L. Eichler, and Jeffrey H. Tigay (Winona Lake: Eisenbrauns, 1997) 4-5, describes the polar opposites in the mind of the psalmist of Babylon and Zion that transcend the reality that the exiles may have obtained a measure of comfort and security in the exilic communities because of the enduring memory of Zion's sacred qualities.

7. Victor H. Matthews, *Old Testament Turning Points* (Grand Rapids: Baker, 2005) 32-35.

8. See the summary of critical geography and the theoretical base for Thirdspace in Jon L. Berquist, "Critical Spatiality and the Construction of the Ancient World," in *"Imagining" Biblical Worlds,* ed. David M. Gunn and Paula M. McNutt. JSOTSup 359 (London: Sheffield Academic, 2002) 18-21.

9. See the similar cognitive transformation of the Valley of Achor from its physical reality, a place that once was cursed by the execution and burial of Achan, who violated the rules of *ḥērem* (Josh 7:20-26), and becomes the symbol for restoration and hope in Hos 2:15 and Isa 65:10.

Jerusalem and Zion and on their responsibility as a group to restore the temple (Hag 2:1-9; Zech 8:1-8).[10]

Reuse and Reordering of Space

Among the conclusions that can be drawn about space is that "places are not inert containers. They are politicized, culturally relative, historically specific, local and multiple constructions."[11] As a result, a large part of the reflexive process that provides social context to defined space is discovering that significant events that have previously occurred in a place permanently mark it as authoritative. They give place a new or expanded identity that remains in place as long as the culture continues to voice a memory of these events. For instance, landmarks like Deborah's palm tree (Judg 4:5), a battle site,[12] or the place where a national assembly occurs (Shechem in Josh 24:1) become traditional locations for subsequent events of a similar nature. Of course, some battlefields, like the plains before the city of Megiddo, were reused many times because of their topography and strategic importance (2 Kgs 23:29-30; 2 Chr 35:22).[13] The places where sacred acts were performed or the sites of divine manifestation (theophany) subsequently became sacred space and are often the site of temples. Sometimes sacred and political events were combined, adding even greater significance to place.

When a geographic location has not yet been tied to previous events, the reflexive process that will add it to the public consciousness is depen-

10. John Kessler, "Persia's Loyal Yahwists: Power Identity and Ethnicity in Achaemenid Yehud," in *Judah and the Judeans in the Persian Period,* ed. Oded Lipschits and Manfred Oeming (Winona Lake: Eisenbrauns, 2006) 108-9. See also in this same volume, Jon L. Berquist, "Constructions of Identity in Postcolonial Yehud," 57-59.

11. Rodman, "Empowering Place," 205.

12. Compare the story of Jehu's victory over Joram and Ahaziah in the Valley of Jezreel (2 Kgs 9:14-27) with the reuse of the knowledge of this victory as a divine threat against Jehu's descendants in Hos 1:4-5. Note the play on the word "bow" *(qešet),* a weapon Jehu used to kill the kings of Israel (2 Kgs 9:24) and the symbol for the rulers of Jehu's dynasty that God intends to break (Hos 1:5).

13. The Egyptian pharaoh Tuthmosis III brags in his annals inscribed at the temple city of Karnak that "the capture of Megiddo is equal to the capture of a thousand cities!"; Victor H. Matthews and Don C. Benjamin, *Old Testament Parallels,* 3rd ed. (Mahwah: Paulist, 2006) 145.

Location	Initial Event	Subsequent Event
Threshing Floor of Araunah (Ornan the Jebusite)	David experiences theophany, purchases site, makes sacrifice (2 Sam 24:18-25)	Solomon constructs Jerusalem temple on this site, also called Mount Moriah (1 Chr 21:28–22:1; 2 Chr 3:1)
Cave of Machpelah (Hebron)	Abraham purchases burial cave (Gen 23:7-20); reused by family (Gen 25:9; 50:13) in later generations	Tying authority of ancestors to Hebron, David uses this city as his political headquarters (2 Sam 2:1)
Gilgal (west of Jordan River)	Site of Israelite camp after crossing Jordan (Josh 4:19-20) under Joshua's leadership; place where the allotment of territory took place after the conquest (Josh 15–19)	Becomes cultic center in Samuel's time (1 Sam 7:16); site where Saul's kingship is recognized (1 Sam 11:14)
Bethel	Abraham builds an altar and worships Yahweh while Jacob experiences a theophany at this site (Gen 12:8; 28:10-17)	Jeroboam creates one of his royal shrines at Bethel, playing on its sacred history (1 Kgs 12:30-33)

dent upon the intuitive powers of those who enter or view it. For example, an experienced military commander, with a wealth of experience as a tactician and a vast knowledge base upon which to make spatial judgments, has a peculiarity superior ability to measure the attributes of a potential battle ground.[14] In the process of his deliberations, he creates a cognitive map of its topographic features by employing his own well-developed spatial understanding to that place or similar places. In turn, its strategic value to him and to his opponent is inhabited by their cognitive mapping of its characteristics, including possible emplacements for their forces and hazards to be avoided or used as natural defenses. Ex post facto evidence of this process is found in battle accounts in which the formation of troops

14. William G. Chase and Michelene T. H. Chi, "Cognitive Skill: Implications for Spatial Skill in Large-Scale Environments," in *Cognition, Social Behavior, and the Environment,* ed. John H. Harvey (Hillsdale, NJ: Lawrence Erlbaum, 1981) 131.

and the tactics employed are based on an examination of the ground where fighting will take place (see Josh 8:4-23; Judg 20:19-43).

Reuse of Significant Space in Isaiah

The spatial context of an event[15] often adds symbolic meaning or strategic significance to a story and its recorded direct speech and embedded dialogue. Two incidents recorded in the book of Isaiah (paralleled in 2 Kgs 18:17-35) provide excellent examples of how space contributes to the importance of what is said by tying it to where it is being said. In these cases, social identity, political crisis, and theodicy are all part of the ongoing narrative. Both stories center on the geographic identifier: "at the end of the conduit of the upper pool on the highway to the Fuller's Field" (Isa 7:3 and 36:2). This significant open area, approximately "0.5 km (ca. 1/4 mile) S of Jerusalem near the junction of the Hinnom and the Kidron Valleys," contains surplus water from the Gihon Spring and from En-rogel that provides a welcome resource needed for fullers to clean and process wool.[16]

Faced with the threat of another invasion by the kings of Israel and Syria (Isa 7:1-2), King Ahaz of Judah went out to inspect the city's defenses and inventory the resources that could be called on during a siege. It is during Ahaz's tour that Isaiah confronts him and offers him a choice (Isa 7:3-9). The storyteller orchestrates this scene by prefacing it with God's direct speech to the prophet, giving him instructions on where to find the king and what to tell him about the coming events.[17] The symbolic value attached to this place, however, transcends its commercial value and points directly to the potential for the survival of the city during the ap-

15. Kuper, "The Language of Sites," 252, provides a useful definition of event "as a series of interactions between people interested and involved in a particular issue" regardless of whether their interests are similar or divergent.

16. Dale C. Liid, "Fuller's Field," *ABD*, 2:859. See an extensive discussion of the possible locations for the Fuller's Field in T. Raymond Hobbs, *2 Kings*. WBC 13 (Waco: Word, 1985) 260-62. He tends to favor a site to the northwest of the city, but acknowledges that topographic, archaeological, and textual evidence cannot combine to confirm the exact location.

17. See the discussion of the literary structure and the "embedded domain" of this pericope in Archibald L. H. M. van Wieringen, *The Implied Reader in Isaiah 6-12*. Biblical Interpretation 34 (Leiden: Brill, 1998) 61-67.

proaching threat. While gauging the military potential of any area near the city walls and insuring a continuous water source are essential in the light of the inflated population of a besieged city, this reality is then juxtaposed with the symbolic name of the prophet's son, Shear-jashub,[18] and the prophet's message that the hope of the city lies not in physical resources but in the willingness of God as the divine warrior to protect the nation from harm. Ahaz needs only to "be quiet" and his fears will evaporate (7:4). It will be Ahaz's inability to think beyond the political realities that confront him and to appreciate the symbolic value of the site of this prophetic confrontation that will then lead to a less glorious fate for the nation embodied in the Immanuel prophecy (7:13-17).

The second passage in Isaiah that centers on the Fuller's Field records a later threat in 701 B.C.E. when the Assyrian army camped outside the walls of Jerusalem (Isa 36:2).[19] Once again the significance of its physical location and its qualities as a natural resource for the besieged population comes into play. Here too, the storyteller records direct speech as the Assyrian ambassador, the Rabshakeh, addresses King Hezekiah's advisors in a voice loud enough for all those standing on the wall to hear and in their own language. This scene, like that in Isaiah 7, centers on the fate of the city, but in this case, with the Assyrians literally camped on their doorstep, it is even more in question. Therefore it is not surprising that the Rabshakeh is depicted as speaking on a site that is the physical and symbolic nexus point representing two possible futures. His reasoned arguments, taunts, and not-so-veiled threats include an artful use of theodicy in which the Assyrian makes the case that Yahweh has sent this army here because Hezekiah has failed to maintain proper worship and devotion to ritual practice (Isa 36:4-10).[20]

---

18. See the argument for translating the child's name as "A remnant shall return" in John Day, "Shear-Jashub (Isaiah vii 3) and 'the Remnant of Wrath' (Psalm lxxvi 11)," *VT* 31 (1981) 76-78. He makes the point that the remnant will be the survivors of the Syrian army that stagger back to their land after being repulsed by the power of the God of Judah.

19. For a discussion of the chronological and historical issues of reconstructing the Assyrian siege of Jerusalem, see Bob Becking, "Chronology: A Skeleton Without Flesh? Sennacherib's Campaign as a Case-Study," in *"Like a Bird in a Cage": The Invasion of Sennacherib in 701 BCE,* ed. Lester L. Grabbe. JSOTSup 363 (London: Sheffield Academic, 2003) 46-72; and in the same volume, Walter Mayer, "Sennacherib's Campaign of 701 BCE: The Assyrian View," 168-200.

20. See a discussion of ironic reversal in this narrative as Sennacherib moves from total power to no power and Hezekiah moves from "total impotence to total effectiveness," in

The question is, however, whether the compiler of the accounts found in Isaiah 36 and 2 Kings 18 is speaking of an actual location or is simply reusing the site as a metaphorical place of cosmic conflict and confrontation. Thus the actual Fuller's Field has Firstspace reality and must have been a recognizable and well-known site in Isaiah's time. There is a social memory attached to this place associated with both the mundane activities of working-class individuals and the Isaiah-Ahaz incident. As such, to locate another event or story in this same space draws upon those memories as part of the spatial context of these later episodes.[21] In that sense, therefore, the site also has Secondspace qualities, imagined as a source of needed water, a place of business activity, and a potential battleground (both physical and cosmic) before the walls of Jerusalem for its inhabitants. Plus, as a metaphor, it may represent the life of the city, keyed to concepts of hope, victory, and freedom from oppression, or it may represent Assyria and the choice to fall into vassalage or to trust in Yahweh's protection.[22] Finally, as Thirdspace, the site embodies both the lived activities of workers in an important industry and the image of a strategic point that in name and quality, if not in reality, may be reused in the unfolding story of the nation. In that sense, the social landscape as conceived or described, whether physical or metaphorical, adds authority to the recorded speech of the characters in the scene.[23]

Danna Nolan Fewell, "Sennacherib's Defeat: Words at War in 2 Kgs 18:13–19:37," *JSOT* 34 (1986) 81-83. The Rabshakeh's argument parallels the claims of divine support found in the Persian king Cyrus's cylinder inscription; Matthews and Benjamin, *Old Testament Parallels,* 208.

21. For a more modern example that discusses the implications of reusing or overlaying space that has emotional value and significant cultural memories, see Jonathan I. Leib, "Separate Times, Shared Spaces: Arthur Ashe, Monument Avenue and the Politics of Richmond, Virginia's Symbolic Landscape," *Cultural Geographies* 9 (2002) 286-312.

22. For this latter metaphorical value, see Dominic Rudman, "Is the Rabshakeh also Among the Prophets? A Rhetorical Study of 2 Kings xviii 17-35," *VT* 50 (2000) 102-3. He goes on to posit whether the use of the upper pool in 2 Kings 18 is intended to remind the audience of Isaiah's "earlier" prophecy and thus demonstrate the Rabshakeh's role as a prophet, albeit a false one.

23. See a further discussion of the affective aspect of landscape in Denis E. Cosgrove, *Social Formation and Symbolic Landscape* (Madison: University of Wisconsin Press, 1998) 16-27.

Space and Behavior

Viewing or describing space is one important factor in determining context, but another is the determination of how space shapes behavior and in turn what cognitive factors are involved in spatial behavior. One source of data that is fairly easy to obtain is based on the physical realities of space and the patterns of activity or the formations commonly developed by participants within the space they occupy. For instance, the physical limitation placed on movement or the size of a group (e.g., the weight limits posted in an elevator) is one such physical parameter. Another is simply measuring the amount of time spent in a particular space and using technology to track entrance and exit as well as travel patterns within a defined space.[24] However, these approaches do not take into account the shifting goal-directiveness of human participants or the range of probabilities based on human decision-making within or across space.[25]

It is also necessary to keep in mind how the spatial frame of reference that includes physical objects and also influences identity and status changes as a person shifts from one type of space to another.[26] For instance, the cognitive frame of reference for a person of high status, such as a university president, shifts or is veiled when that person moves from the president's office to a place, such as a church, where he or she is merely a participant and not the focus of authority and attention. Similarly, this will occur when the move is from space where a person is among equals to space where that person becomes a supplicant or a client, or from space that only certain persons may enter to space that may be occupied by any-

24. See on the use of GIS and other tracking technologies, Noam Shoval and Michal Isaacson, "Application of Tracking Technologies to the Study of Pedestrian Spatial Behavior," *The Professional Geographer* 58 (2006) 172-83.

25. See the discussion of the development of a process-oriented behavioral approach to geography in Reginald G. Golledge and Robert J. Stimson, *Spatial Behavior: A Geographic Perspective* (New York: Guilford, 1997) 4-7.

26. In speaking of frames of reference, Stephen C. Levinson, *Space in Language and Cognition: Explorations in Cognitive Diversity* (Cambridge: Cambridge University Press, 2003) 24-25, chooses to use "coordinate systems" rather than having to deal with the ambiguities caused by multiple frames of reference. Irvin Rock, "Comment on Asch and Witkin's 'Studies in Space Orientation II,'" *Journal of Experimental Psychology: General* 121 (1992) 404, provides a Gestaltist definition of "frame of reference (or framework)," identifying it as a "unit or organization of units that collectively serve to identify a coordinate system with respect to which certain properties of objects, including the phenomenal self, are gauged."

> **Equations of Spatiality**
>
> Space + Persons with access to that space = Accepted social actions within that space
>
> Concentric zones established within a larger space demarking selective admission areas = Determination of access to each zone[1]
>
> Space + Activities that occur in that space = Domestic, economic, and political connotations of that space
>
> Shift in personal status and identity = Shift in spatial frame of reference
>
> 1. Tim Richardson and Ole B. Jensen, "Linking Discourse and Space: Towards a Cultural Sociology of Space in Analysing Spatial Policy Discourses," *Urban Studies* 40 (2003) 7, make the point that "many spaces may co-exist within the same physical space."

one. In each case, the status and identity of that person is transformed as their spatial frame of reference changes.

Awareness of the shift in the spatial frame of reference and its effect on status or on patterns of behavior makes it more likely that persons will be most comfortable and effective when operating within space that they control. For instance, a doctor, when seeing patients in a medical clinic, moves freely from exam room to exam room based on his credentials, his familiarity to the nursing staff, and his own awareness of his position. In the process the physician tends to follow a well-beaten path that is seldom interrupted except for emergencies or personal needs. Once the examination begins, unless there is a personal relationship between the physician and the patient, the doctor primarily addresses the patient's specific symptoms, takes little time to chat about any extraneous matters since there is a financial urgency to see as many patients as possible, and moves on quickly to the next examination room. This verbal script, which may include some use of silence or minimal expressions of encouragement to the patient, is repeated throughout the work day, accompanied by a prescribed set of physical diagnostic acts that are shaped by the character of that space and by the constraints of a medical practice in a clinical setting.[27]

27. Hilde Eide, V. Vicenç Quera, Peter Graugaard, and Arnstein Finset, "Physician-

The positioning of the participants in this minidrama also is con-strained by the size of the room, the requirements to lie down for the ex-amination, and the authoritative manner and perfunctory speech patterns of the doctor when addressing the patient. Few patients in fact are able to overcome a basic apprehension associated with medical treatment and the physician's aura of authority to initiate any topic beyond the immediate concerns of their health condition.[28] Should the doctor have to perform a similar set of diagnostic acts outside the clinic, the level of authority and personal comfort may well be diminished given the uncertainty associated with unfamiliar space.

Turning back to the social situation in ancient Israel, a wife work-ing in her own house is situated within a very familiar, culturally-designated space associated with ordinary life experiences. Because this dwelling consists of many coexisting or concentric spaces, its walls serve as an outer container separating this space from the void outside its con-fines. Its rooms function separately as utilitarian space (for storage or cottage industries), as communal space (for meals and storytelling), and as private space (sleeping areas, house shrines, and taboo areas).[29] Within this "lived space," some social activities are shared by the entire family while other domestic activities may become associated with par-ticular persons or are gender-specific.[30] Conversation, associated with the participants' cognitive frame of reference, will therefore vary within these rooms based on whether the participants consist of all males, all fe-males, or a mixed group, are engaged in various forms of work, are en-

patient Dialogue Surrounding Patients' Expression of Concern: Applying Sequence Analysis to RIAS," *Social Science and Medicine* 59 (2004) 145-55, includes some breaks in normal speech patterns in oncology exams due to the heightened anxiety levels of patients in this setting and the openings provided by the physician to solicit questions and responses from the patients.

28. For recent studies of patient-physician dialogue, see Kathleen J. Roberts and Paul Volberding, "Adherence Communication: A Qualitative Analysis of Physician-Patient Dia-logue," *AIDS* 13 (1999) 1771-78.

29. See the description of activities in ancient households based on "household ar-chaeology" in James W. Hardin, "Understanding Domestic Space: An Example from Iron Age Halif," *NEA* 67 (2004) 73-83.

30. Vincent Berdoulay, "Place, Meaning, and Discourse in French Language Geogra-phy," in *The Power of Place*, ed. John A. Agnew and James S. Duncan (Boston: Unwin Hyman, 1989) 130, considers "lived space" to include activity areas and social space and the cultural values attached to both.

joying an entertaining moment together, or are having a serious discussion affecting the welfare of the household. In fact, "a place comes explicitly into being in the discourse of its inhabitants, and particularly the rhetoric it promotes."[31]

Any deviation in social pattern or speech within this familiar setting will generally result from unexpected or extraordinary intrusions into the ordinary events that comprise the majority of their existence. The story of the Shunammite woman in 2 Kgs 4:8-37 provides a series of episodes that fluctuate between the ordinary and the extraordinary. The narrative begins when a wealthy woman prevails upon her husband to provide hospitality and shelter to the itinerant prophet Elisha whenever he visited their village (4:8-10). The story goes into remarkable detail to describe the furnishings of the prophet's room (bed, table, chair, and lamp; 4:10) providing an extension of the offer of hospitality and an encompassing sense of domestic peace for the prophet when he is in residence.[32] In the face of such kindness, Elisha expresses the wish to reciprocate by rewarding the couple, and it is at that point that the conversation shifts away from the mundane or the polite exchanges expected within the domestic setting.

What follows is a very curious discourse in which the Shunammite woman alone is called to the prophet's roof chamber, ordinarily a social gaff, but in this episode that tends to transcend normal gender roles it is a further acknowledgement that this "wealthy woman" (*'iššâ gĕdôlâ*) is his true benefactor (2 Kgs 4:12). While she stands mutely, perhaps just out of immediate earshot or simply ignored by the prophet, Elisha discusses her possible needs with his servant Gehazi. When the offer is then made to speak a word on her behalf to the king or to a military commander, she responds simply, "I live among my own people" (4:13). She apparently has no desire to break the continuity of her existence by bringing her person or her property to the attention of social elites and power brokers. After deliberating with Gehazi a second time and learning that the couple is childless, the woman is called to the door once again and Elisha speaks using the formal language of an annunciation, promising that she will conceive

31. Berdoulay, "Place, Meaning, and Discourse," 135.

32. Yairah Amit, "A Prophet Tested: Elisha, the Great Woman of Shunem, and the Story's Double Message," *BibInt* 11 (2003) 284, compares these furnishings to those found in a sanctuary like that at Shiloh. However, I contend that they are intended to create a sense of the "ordinary" necessary when one wishes to rest from the troubles of the road.

and give birth to a son (4:14-16).[33] The woman expresses surprise, a common reaction to an annunciation,[34] but then the story resumes, returning to its domestic character until another break in routine occurs when the child has a seizure and apparently dies (4:18-21). That in turn leads to the woman's breaking routine and social norms by riding off alone to find the prophet in order to confront him with her loss (4:22-28).

The bereft mother's emotional distress is signaled by her determined clasping of the prophet's feet and her reproachful words, "Did I ask my lord for a son?" (4:28). In this way, she breaks up the indirect pattern of speech that Elisha has previously used. She bypasses Gehazi and speaks directly to the prophet. Her passion and refusal to leave the prophet (4:30)[35] drive the narrative to its conclusion when the child is revived, the prophet passes a test of character and ability, and normalcy is restored.[36] The narrative signal that brings this episode to its proper conclusion is the repetition of Elisha's command to Gehazi: "call the Shunammite woman" (*qěrā' laš-šûnammît hazzō't*; 4:12 and 36).[37] Her son is restored to her, and after bowing in respect to the prophet for keeping his word she departs, presumably drawing her life and the audience's perception of it back into its domestic mold.

---

33. Fokkelien van Dijk-Hemmes, "The Great Woman of Shunem and the Man of God," in *A Feminist Companion to Samuel and Kings,* ed. Athalya Brenner (Sheffield: Sheffield Academic, 1994) 226-27, remarks on the curious lack of perception on Elisha's part, not realizing the couple are childless and apparently only capable of reacting within a patriarchal framework to the "need" for her to have a child.

34. See Sarah's sarcastic and amused reaction to the annunciation spoken to Abraham in Gen 18:9-15.

35. Here is another narrative irony embedded into the story. She speaks almost exactly the same vow, "As the Lord lives, and as you yourself live, I will not leave without you" (2 Kgs 4:30), that Elisha uses several times in his exchange with Elijah (2:2, 4, 6): *ḥay-yhwh wĕḥēy-napšĕkā 'im-'e'ezbekkā.*

36. Amit, "A Prophet Tested," 281, sees the primacy theme in this story to be "testing and reprobation" for Elisha.

37. See the discussion of speech and narrative patterns in this story in Burke O. Long, "Framing Repetitions in Biblical Historiography," *JBL* 106 (1987) 390-91. He makes the point that repetitive patterns help the storyteller frame the relationship between protagonist and antagonist in the narrative.

Spatial Patterning

When at least two people are gathered together they create a spatial pattern (what Adam Kendon[38] terms F-Formations) that is shaped by both the physical domain in which they are interacting and by the placement of their bodies. The physical properties of the setting for their interaction may constrain movement, the number that can be present, the social status or gender of those who can participate, and the type of transaction that can occur here. Contained within that transactional zone is the "internal interactional space" that can be referred to as the "o-space," representing that portion of space which they occupy and which separates them.[39] In essence these interacting persons have created and organized the rules for a temporary space based on the purpose of their meeting, the number present, and its duration. If this o-space is violated, either inadvertently or on purpose, a reaction can be expected ranging from a loss of focus in the discussion, an emotional outburst, a verbal reminder or reprimand, or even physical violence.

F-Formations: Lot in Sodom

A type of social maneuvering takes place in the development of F-Formations. Ordinarily, when an interaction begins individuals will stake out their positions based in part on the size of the space, the noise or other distractions that may be present, and their relative social status. In setting up the formation, there generally are words of greeting that will indicate the status of the individuals and whether they have interacted previously. While their positions within the formation may shift to accommodate gestures or interruptions by outsiders, the participants will try to keep their formation tight enough to allow for full comprehension of what is said.

An example of how this would work in a standard situation is found in Boaz's use of the city gate area of Bethlehem to present a legal issue to the elders of the town. First, as one of the town elders, he places himself in

38. "The F-Formation System: The Spatial Organization of Social Encounter," *Man-Environment Systems* 6 (1976) 291-96.

39. T. Matthew Ciolek and Adam Kendon, "Environment and the Spatial Arrangement of Conversational Encounters," *Sociological Inquiry* 50 (1980) 243.

Social Dynamics of Conversation

Participants engaged in focused conversation tend to station themselves in space based on a number of factors, including internal dynamics and the setting:[1]

1. A gathering is shaped in space based on the physical characteristics of the spatial domain in which they are interacting, including its dimensions, the number of persons present, the amount of extraneous activity, and the noise level.

2. Participants of equal social status or who are both friendly and well acquainted tend to situate themselves closer together, while potential rivals or persons of lesser social status choose or are forced to occupy space in less intimate contact or advantageous positions.

3. Full or partial participation in social interaction is evidenced by how close participants stand or sit to each other without violating personal space. Disinterested parties or lesser participants tend to occupy the fringe of a discussion.

1. See Ciolek and Kendon, "Environment and the Spatial Arrangement," 237-38.

that liminal zone associated with the defense of the people, the conducting of business transactions, and the determination of legal consensus by the elders (Ruth 4:1). By sitting there, Boaz engages in a recognized social gesture that he wishes to conduct business with those entering and leaving the gate. Sitting here in this official capacity, he calls out to the "next of kin" involved in the case and to 10 elders to join him to discuss this matter. Once they are all seated (4:2; a sign of equal status among them), presumably in a circle so all can see and hear the proceeding, the particulars of the case can be discussed and a decision reached (4:3-6). Their o-space would consist of the area which they enclose with their bodies and which facilitates the appearance to all other witnesses that an important deliberation is in progress. With a meeting in progress, this o-space would be perceived by witnesses as an official, although temporary, physical place that carries the social connotation of legal proceeding.

To illustrate how F-Formations do not always follow set social patterns, let us examine two encounters involving Abraham's nephew Lot. In the first (Gen 19:1-2), he, like Boaz, is "sitting in the gateway of Sodom." In this liminal place where citizen, resident alien, and stranger can interact freely, Lot encounters two strangers as they are about to enter the city. Although the text does not explicitly say that Lot recognizes these visitors as angels, he goes to remarkable lengths to show them great deference by (1) rising to his feet, (2) bowing before them with his face to the ground, (3) speaking to them in an imperative form and referring to them as "my lords" *(hinneh nā'-'ădōnay)*, and (4) offering them the hospitality of his house using an abbreviated form of the verbal formula employed by Abraham in Gen 18:3-5 when greeting these same visitors.[40]

In this passage, the storyteller is violating or at least bending the normal sequence associated with the creation of an F-Formation. Lot, a wealthy resident alien in Sodom, has risen socially during his time there to the extent that he now has a place to sit in the gateway of that city. Here he would conduct his business, presumably associated at least in part with the herds he had received from Abraham (Gen 13:5-11), and he would associate with the other established merchants, landowners, and elders of the city. He would, as Prov 31:23 says, be "known in the city gates." As such, it would be remarkable for him to take the initiative over other merchants or to begin any conversation with strangers beyond offering to have them sit down with him. His expectation would be that they would respond to his friendly invitation either if they chose to do business with him or if they wished to make an inquiry. Instead, however, his interaction with these strangers begins with him jumping to his feet and bowing to the ground before them. This grand gesture, an exact parallel with Abraham's actions (Gen 18:2), places him in a social position as their client or a potential host, and it sets a tone that places them on a higher status level than he presently holds.

Furthermore, Lot is not a full citizen of Sodom and, although he could make use of public space, he could not represent himself as someone

---

40. Scott Morschauser, "'Hospitality,' Hostility and Hostages: On the Legal Background to Genesis 19:1-9," *JSOT* 27 (2003) 464-67, makes the case for Lot's placement in the gate in an official capacity with sentrylike duties based on the previous capture of the city as described in Genesis 14. This does not follow the pattern of behavior he evidences here since his concern is for the welfare of the strangers, not the city. Morschauser's assertion (469-70) that Lot offers them a restricted form of hospitality and conditional, even protective custody, does not take into account the parallels with Abraham's statement of hospitality or Lot's apprehension about anyone staying in the public square overnight.

with the right to offer hospitality.[41] That privilege would be reserved for full citizens. Thus his performance violates normal social practice and his use of body language (bowing) goes beyond what would have been expected. In addition, his manner of argumentation becomes increasingly urgent *(wayyipĕṣar-bām mĕ'ōd)*. Calling on them to "turn aside" and spend the night in his house suggests insider knowledge and lets the storyteller subtly indict the citizens of Sodom as inhospitable. Therefore, Lot's inappropriate offer of hospitality, one of the standard forms of address found in everyday life, could be seen as a form of social resistance that will transform Lot's house, like that of Rahab (Josh 2:1-16), into a "space of resistance," a sanctuary from the citizens of Sodom.[42] In both cases, Lot and Rahab are acting in opposition to the normal flow of power in their city by offering strangers a place to stay and placing their own welfare in jeopardy to protect them.[43]

Of course, the agenda of the storyteller is to parallel Lot's and Abraham's actions in greeting these strangers, bowing to the ground, demonstrating honorable behavior, and ultimately obtaining a reward from these divine messengers. In that sense, the normal social protocols are set aside to meet a higher narrative purpose.[44] In the second instance (Gen 19:5-11), the F-Formation occurs at the door of Lot's house within Sodom. Although the threshold, like a city gate, is liminal in character, its proximity to Lot's private dwelling and his family makes it a more intimate setting and one that ordinarily would be tied to polite or formal interaction.[45]

---

41. See the discussion of the protocol of hospitality in Victor H. Matthews, "Hospitality and Hostility in Genesis 19 and Judges 19," *BTB* 22 (1992) 3-11.

42. On resistance space hidden within the midst of "the minutia of the everyday," see James A. Tyner, "Self and Space, Resistance and Discipline: A Foucauldian Reading of George Orwell's *1984*," *Social and Cultural Geography* 5 (2004) 142.

43. See L. Daniel Hawk, "Strange Houseguests: Rahab, Lot, and the Dynamics of Deliverance," in *Reading Between Texts: Intertextuality and the Hebrew Bible*, ed. Danna Nolan Fewell (Louisville: Westminster/John Knox, 1992) 89-91, for a discussion of the literary and dialogic parallels between these two stories. See Gilles Deleuze, *Foucault* (Minneapolis: University of Minnesota Press, 1998) 71, for a discussion of the techniques of resistance as a set of acts or processes that serve to counter the exercise of power.

44. Paul Tonson, "Mercy Without Covenant: A Literary Analysis of Genesis 19," *JSOT* 95 (2001) 99, suggests that this is a narrative device designed to demonstrate that Lot is more hospitable and therefore more honorable than the citizens of Sodom.

45. See the use of the door to a private house as a place of execution in the case of fraud (Deut 22:20-21) and the site where an oath and ritual take place perpetually binding a slave to that household (Deut 15:16-17).

Lot's action in bringing these strangers into the city without consultation with the elders has now brought a massive delegation of its male citizens to his door. When they demand that the two strangers be brought out and made known to them, Lot steps outside and closes the door to his house, effectively barring entrance with his own body. He then engages in a reasoned argument, calling on them not to "act so wickedly" (19:7), and then demonstrates his commitment to maintain his honor as host by offering the crowd his two virgin daughters as hostages in exchange for the strangers' safety (19:8).[46]

The F-Formation in this case consists of the surrounding crowd with Lot as its focal point. Presumably, the packing of the area in front of his door would have compressed the o-space to such a small area that Lot would have felt the growing emotions of these men as they called on him to bring out the strangers so that they may "know" them.[47] He surely felt the sting of their response to his offer when they demand that he "Stand back!" (19:9a); their verbal assault includes an accusation that he is overstepping his rights as a resident alien, one who has come "to sojourn" *(bā'-lāgûr)* there and now presumes to "play the judge!" (19:9b).[48] They then conclude in a rising tide of anger by swearing to "deal worse with you than with them" (19:9c). The formation is then broken as the men rush Lot's house and Lot slams the door in their faces. The potential for violence is blunted only when the angels display their power by blinding the crowd and giving Lot and his family the opportunity to escape (19:10-11).

46. I agree with Morschauser, "'Hospitality,' Hostility and Hostages," 474-82, that the confrontation between Lot and the assembly is not based on their desire for sexual gratification and that Lot's offer of his daughters represents a legal gambit designed to offset any threat his guests may pose for the city.

47. See the anthropological evaluation of possible motives for the actions of the crowd in Ken Stone, "Gender and Homosexuality in Judges 19: Subject — Honour, Object — Shame?" *JSOT* 67 (1995) 94-103. His conclusion that a sexual assault on Lot's guests would effectively dishonor Lot and demonstrate their power over him and his guests is quite plausible if that was their actual intent.

48. Frank A. Spina, "Israelites as *gērîm,* 'Sojourners,' in Social and Historical Context," in *The Word of the Lord Shall Go Forth,* ed. Carol L. Meyers and M. O'Connor (Winona Lake: Eisenbrauns, 1983) 324-25, discusses how *gēr*-status is obtained and notes that the manner in which a *gēr* is treated in the new social setting is entirely up to the traditions and manner of the inhabitants of that place.

Interaction in Sacred Space

The designation of space as sacred, domestic, commercial, or polluted is the direct result of a reflective process. Seen in that way, space becomes an imagined, but not imaginary, concept.[49] Each individual has a mental picture of the characteristics attached to specific places, whether large or small, important or insignificant. For instance, the sanctification of space that transforms it into sacred space in the minds of a community requires recognition through reflection on what has made this a reality. It becomes an imperative linking the believers to the divine both physically and mentally — a sort of "intertextuality between two spaces."[50] Any rituals that they then employ to sketch out publicly the limits of this space are clearly secondary to the original mental process. They are merely socially-accepted boundaries, not an actual limit on space, and are temporally based, since communities in later periods may not choose to recognize in the same way the sacred nature or social designations assigned by previous communities.[51]

What occurs in different types of space, including communication, will be shaped by the current cognitive understanding of that particular space or can take advantage of the associations as part of a strategy of communication. Space in fact plays an essential role in the socialization of children or newly-admitted persons. It functions as part of the development of knowledge and each person's ability to know the world, and it is therefore among the factors that influence or shape communication. Thus spatialization of events, including ritual and everyday activities, implies that location always matters.[52]

Thus for an Israelite priest officiating over ritual performance in the temple in Jerusalem, space is perceived in terms of a set of concentric zones governed by physical barriers and by the social concepts of purity and im-

---

49. Akhil Gupta and James Ferguson, "Beyond 'Culture': Space, Identity, and the Politics of Difference," *Cultural Anthropology* 7 (1992) 11. In their discussion of "remembered space" they touch on cultural memories of place cherished and retold by displaced populations. In this same way, the psalmist pledges to Jerusalem while they are in exile in a foreign land (Ps 137:5-6).

50. Jean-François Lyotard, *The Postmodern Condition: A Report on Knowledge* (Manchester: Manchester University Press, 1984).

51. Barbara Bender, "Time and Landscape," *Current Anthropology* 43 (2002) 103.

52. Rob Shields, "Knowing Space," *Theory, Culture & Society* 23 (2006) 149.

purity.[53] Sacred or pure space is first defined by the walls of the temple, which serve as a sort of envelope demarking the limits of recognized purity. Nested within its confines are progressively more sacred zones hierarchically leading inward to the ultimate holy of holies, or as Mircea Eliade called it, the *axis mundi*.[54] Social status for this all-male priestly community will be determined by how far inward a person can progress toward the inner sanctum and to what sacred duties that person is assigned.[55] Presumably, when engaged in sacrificial or other worship rituals the expectation will be that they refrain from extraneous discussion in order to insure that the ritual is carried out without a variation that could damage its efficacy. However, a large cultic center like the temple is not "monofunctional."[56] Its side chambers would have served as storage areas and offices for the clerical bureaucracy,[57] discourse would have been freer, and the range of topics more expansive and perhaps less sacred in character.

However, the cognitive character of this complex and the status of those who worked or visited this place would still have governed their behavior to the extent that they wished to maintain their social identity or to present themselves as religious professionals. As long as a perception (sensual and cognitive) existed that behavior within the temple remained within comfortably recognized and acceptable structures, then there would be no concerns raised over its sanctity.[58] When that facade is smashed by incorrect or corrupt behavior, the character of the sacred space is also damaged. Thus when Ezekiel's visionary tour of the temple includes the sight of the 70 elders of Judah burning incense to foreign gods within one of the temple chambers (Ezek 8:10-12), the case is begun that will eventually result in Yahweh's abandonment of this place (Ezek 10:1-19).

53. See the summary of current approaches on purity and theories of sacrifice in Jonathan Klawans, *Purity, Sacrifice, and the Temple: Symbolism and Supersessionism in the Study of Ancient Judaism* (Oxford: Oxford University Press, 2006) 17-48.

54. *The Sacred and the Profane* (New York: Harcourt, Brace, 1959) 42-47.

55. See the architectural description of each zone within the Jerusalem temple in Victor Hurowitz, "Inside Solomon's Temple," *BRev* 10/2 (1994) 24-37, 50.

56. Frank S. Frick, "Ritual and Social Regulation in Ancient Israel," in Gunn and McNutt, *'Imagining' Biblical Worlds*, 225-26, employs Roy A. Rappaport's model in *Ritual and Religion in the Making of Humanity* (Cambridge: Cambridge University Press, 1999) to caution against simplistic identification of cultic place and cultic practice.

57. See the discussion below of Baruch's mission to the temple in Jeremiah 36.

58. See Golledge and Stimson, *Spatial Behavior*, 188-90, for varying definitions of perception and cognition within the social sciences.

Jeremiah, the Written Word,
and Linked Zones of Communication

We conclude this examination of spatiality and context by examining a pericope in the light of many of the principles discussed above. The unknown author of the story of Baruch's mission to the temple in Jeremiah 36 uses a spatial strategy to link together a set of significant locations as part of a chain of events and staged dialogue.[59] The social frame within which these events take place is the period of political uncertainty in the early years of Jehoiakim's reign over Judah (609-604 B.C.E.). Although the composition of this particular episode may have a complex history, based on the ideological agendas of the compilers of the book of Jeremiah, it functions within a set of well-known historical events and contains sufficient information on the temple and palace complex to evidence a basic familiarity with these precincts.[60]

The premise that initiates the events of the story is that Jeremiah has been barred from entrance into the temple precincts following the uproar caused by his temple sermon and trial (Jer 26:16-19, 24).[61] Now when Jeremiah is charged to write down "all the words that I have spoken to you against Israel and Judah and all the nations, from the day I spoke to you, from the days of Josiah until today" (36:2), he must find a way to deliver the message once again. It is his responsibility as a prophet to warn the people of "all the disasters that I intend to do to them" (36:3).[62]

---

59. See Jack R. Lundbom, *Jeremiah: A Study in Ancient Hebrew Rhetoric,* 2nd ed. (Winona Lake: Eisenbrauns, 1997) 140-43, for a structural analysis of what he calls the "Jehoiakim Cluster" (Jeremiah 25, 26, 35, 36) and his argument that Jer 36:1-8 is the original story while the remainder of the chapter consists of later addenda by Baruch.

60. Mark Leuchter, *Josiah's Reform and Jeremiah's Scroll.* HBM 6 (Sheffield: Sheffield Phoenix, 2006) 147.

61. See Yair Hoffman, "Aetiology, Redaction and Historicity in Jeremiah xxxvi," *VT* 46 (1996) 183-84, for a discussion of the meaning of the unusual phrase *'ănî 'āṣûr* in Jer 36:5 that the prophet uses to explain why he cannot go to the temple himself. He makes the case that the obscurity of the phrase is another indication on the part of the author that the excuse for Jeremiah's absence is unimportant and that the scroll is of paramount importance.

62. The Hebrew prophets are seldom associated with written documents. Some rare exceptions include Isaiah's "large tablet" (Isa 8:1-2), the scroll that Ezekiel consumes (Ezek 2:9–3:3), and Daniel's book of the righteous (Dan 12:1). However, on at least three occasions, Jeremiah's message is intimately tied to the written word. The first of these comes in Jer 36:4 when the prophet dictates a scroll to his friend Baruch. The second document is Jeremiah's

Given the difficulties or possible dangers associated with Jeremiah carrying out this mission himself, it is not unreasonable that the prophet chose to dictate his message to Baruch in order to preserve his oracles for future reference. The scroll itself may have consisted of previously-voiced prophecies and therefore would serve to reiterate the call to repentance voiced in the temple sermon and as a challenge for the leaders of the nation to bring the people to proper compliance with the covenant.[63] Still, the fact remains that there is no explicit mention of what Jeremiah's dictated scroll did contain, only that Baruch performed this service for the prophet.

In addition, since Baruch is expected only to read the scroll, it will function as a physical prop or surrogate for the prophet[64] and ultimately will serve as the focal point for the subsequent confrontation with King Jehoiakim. Note also that in performing this service for Jeremiah, Baruch elevates the status of the scribal class and gives a primacy to the written word that, at least in this instance, somewhat diminishes or overshadows the person of the prophet and the oral presentation of his words.[65] In that sense, it can be said that the story in Jeremiah 36 functions as an etiology for the legitimacy of the second scroll dictated by Jeremiah to Baruch, transforming it into an "authorized version" of Jeremiah's prophecies that will outlive the person and serve as a continual reminder of the warnings he voiced.[66]

"letter to the exiles" in ch. 29. Since he cannot physically go to the exiles, he sends them his message in the form of a letter — a sort of guide to their present condition and future hope. The third document is found in Jer 32:9-12 and takes the form of the land contract drawn up by the prophet, in multiple copies, to certify his "redemption" of a field. This serves as a deed of sale, duly witnessed like the contract drawn up between Ephron the Hittite and Abraham in Gen 23:16-20 for the cave of Machpelah, noting the exchange of ownership. It also serves as both an inclusio with Abraham's contract and a certification for the future that when the exiles return home they will still retain title to the promised land.

63. Mark Bummitt and Yvonne Sherwood, "The Tenacity of the Word: Using Jeremiah 36 to Attempt to Construct an Appropriate Edifice to the Memory of Robert Carroll," in *Sense and Sensitivity*, ed. Alastair G. Hunter and Phillip R. Davies. JSOTSup 348 (Sheffield: Sheffield Academic, 2002) 5, call this "The Collected Oracles of Jeremiah: The Josiah-Jehoiakim Years."

64. It could be compared to other objects of power associated with a prophet such as Elijah's mantle (2 Kgs 2:8-14), which represented the transference of power to Elisha.

65. Robert P. Carroll, "Manuscripts Don't Burn — Inscribing the Prophetic Tradition: Reflections on Jeremiah 36," in *"Dort ziehen Schiffe dahin . . .,"* ed. Matthias Augustin and Klaus D. Schunck (Frankfurt am Main: Peter Lang, 1996) 31-33.

66. Hoffman, "Aetiology, Redaction and Historicity in Jeremiah xxxvi," 185-86.

When Jeremiah has dictated the scroll and charged Baruch to read it "in the hearing of all the people of Judah," the focus in this episode then turns to the delivery of the written message. The scroll will travel to a series of activity places in the temple and the royal palace that are not otherwise linked together. However, as each serves as a venue for the reading of the scroll and subsequent analysis or reaction to its contents, they will become "chained spaces." The words, these actions, and Jehoiakim's gesture of defiance (36:23) create a "fluid field of meaning" that links the spaces and the various forms of communication together.[67]

Setting One

Jeremiah's original charge to Baruch is to go to the Lord's house on a fast day and read his dictated words "in the hearing of all the people of Judah who come up from their towns" (36:5-6). The scene, tied to a time cue that indicates a substantial crowd will be available, is much like the one in which Jeremiah harangued before the temple the crowd of people who had journeyed from "all the cities of Judah that come to worship in the house of the Lord" (26:2).[68] However, Baruch, a member of the scribal guild, employs a more targeted spatial strategy that creates the first link in the chain of places where the words on the scroll will be heard. He chooses to read Jeremiah's dictated message first "in the hearing of all the people" inside the temple, "in the chamber of Gemariah . . . , which was in the upper court, at the entry of the New Gate" (36:10).[69]

The author employs very explicit language to pinpoint which of the

---

67. Annice I. Barber, "Chaining Spaces," *Journal of Linguistic Anthropology* 15 (2005) 194.

68. J. A. Thompson, *The Book of Jeremiah*. NICOT (Grand Rapids: Wm. B. Eerdmans, 1980) 620, suggests this was a special fast day proclaimed in the face of the national crisis brought on by the Neo-Babylonian victory over the Assyrians at Carchemish in the summer of 605. The imminent change of masters from Egypt to Babylon could certainly serve as the basis for this fast and provides an opportunity for Jeremiah to confront indirectly an already troubled king. Thompson notes (623) that it may have been proclaimed on "the arrival of the Babylonian armies on the Philistine plain" and this would place the reading of the scroll in December 604.

69. Setha M. Low and Denise Lawrence-Zúñiga, "Locating Culture," in *The Anthropology of Space and Place*, 30, contend that spatial tactics are designed to use "space as a strategy and/or technique of power and social control."

many chambers in the temple complex is meant: *bĕliškat gĕmaryāhû ben-šāpān hassōpēr behāṣēr hā'elyôn petaḥ ša'ar bêt-yhwh heḥādāš*. A direct tie is made to the assembly point at the New Gate where Jeremiah's trial was held (26:10) in order to provide an unmistakable frame of reference for the scene and to link Jeremiah's former address to this reading of the scroll. It establishes a spatial domain that includes not only the room itself, but the "ground" or wider domain within which it is located. Thus the temple-palace complex is nested within the larger frame of the upper city and the even larger frame that included the entire environs of Jerusalem as well as the cities and towns from which the people have come on this fast day.

Of course, Gemariah's chamber could not accommodate "all the people," so we have a conflation here or a euphemism. What may be intended in the use of the phrase "all the people" *(kol-hā'ām)* is a reminder to the audience of the events in Jer 26:7-9, 11-12, 16 where there were significant numbers of witnesses to Jeremiah's sermon and his trial.[70] Even though only a fraction of that potential population will be able to witness and hear Baruch's performance, they are included by extension in the events that day.[71]

Situated in an "upper chamber," the office would have been a semipublic place.[72] Baruch could have commanded the attention of the persons immediately below if they were interested; but since the text records no reaction from the crowd, it is possible that either they were not moved by his reading or his efforts were directed primarily to the higher-echelon audience of the priestly community, royal advisers, and perhaps other fairly high-ranking members of the male population who had direct access to this office. The space itself has a character that it derives from those who frequent it. After all, it is called the "office of Gemariah," not a storage room or a public gallery. There would be an expectation that those who enter it would be of a certain social class or status and that the issues raised there would be of substance equal to the gravity of the men who gathered there on a regular basis.

---

70. Cf. the use of this phrase in Jer 29:25 in reference to the audience for the letter of Shemaiah.

71. Levinson, *Space in Language and Cognition*, 65, points to the existence of major spatial domains as well as internal divisions or subdomains that are given greater specificity when described as part of the whole "ground."

72. Thompson, *The Book of Jeremiah*, 625, and Andrew J. Dearman, "My Servants the Scribes: Composition and Context in Jeremiah 36," *JBL* 109 (1990) 405, accept this to be a good vantage point for a public pronouncement.

It is fair to assume that Baruch has been in this office before, has regular access to it, and is comfortable in coming here to read the dictated scroll.[73] If Baruch felt a degree of ownership of this office based on his past familiarity with it and past association with those who frequented it, then he is likely to be more in command of the situation and less shy about carrying out his assigned task. Furthermore, if the author of this story is not really intent on reaching a general audience in this scene, then it is quite likely that he is merely using this semiprivate room as a springboard for the movement of the scroll to increasingly more restricted spaces. The interaction initiated by Baruch will transform, at least temporarily, this familiar office space by generating fierce emotions of apprehension and fear.[74]

Rather than ignore the larger audience, however, it is also clear that the author wishes to present through the crowd's silence a generally negative impression to the words read from the scroll. Andrew J. Dearman rightly judges that the silence of the people functions as a narrative parallel to Jehoiakim's silent destruction of the scroll (36:23).[75] Given the silence of the audience, with only one scribe apparently driven to respond to Jeremiah's words, attention is shifted away from the general population to the smaller group, comprised in part of the scribal community that supports Jeremiah. The author of the story then demonstrates the effectiveness of the scroll *(mĕgillâ)* as the chief protagonist, given Jeremiah's forced absence, as these influential men attempt to get the king, however unsuccessfully, to treat the scroll and the prophecy with more respect.[76]

The close association made here with the influential family of Gemariah son of Shaphan, who have served as priestly advisors to the kings of Judah for several generations, is a further indication of Baruch's or

73. B. Aubrey Fisher and Katherine L. Adams, *Interpersonal Communication: Pragmatics of Human Relationships* (New York: McGraw-Hill, 1994) 107-8, point to the importance attached to "ownership" of the setting of personal interaction.

74. Paige West, James Igoe, and Dan Brockington, "Parks and Peoples: The Social Impact of Protected Areas," *Annual Review of Anthropology* 35 (2006) 252, note that it is through human interaction with the world and places within it that space is altered in terms of "language-using and symbol-making." Thus Baruch's interaction here alters space and how it is described because it will hereafter be associated with this incident.

75. "My Servants the Scribes," 405-7.

76. Hoffman, "Aetiology, Redaction and Historicity in Jeremiah xxxvi," 182, points to the use of *mĕgillâ* 14 times in the narrative as this protagonist moves from being dictated, to being read several times, to its being burnt and then replaced by a newly-dictated scroll.

the author's targeting of strategic space and influential witnesses.[77] Thus the object of this rhetorical exercise is to target men who will recognize the importance of Jeremiah's message and will see the necessity of apprising the king of the prophet's words of warning.

Clearly, Baruch's spatial strategy succeeds. As the messenger for a prophetic figure whose design is to disrupt the current political and religious status quo, he has his designated audience's attention and has received the response he had expected since the men present are quite concerned. The true test of discursive authority is the effect on an audience and that audience's willingness to take some action in response to the message.[78] Since Jeremiah cannot be there in person, his use of Baruch at this point plays on the personal integrity and authority of the scribe and counts on the chilling effect that his words will have when read from the scroll to the proper audience. It may well be that Baruch's message would have been forbidden or cut short by the authorities if he had read it in the public gate area, but even in this semiprivate setting he clearly has upset his audience. When Micaiah reports what he has heard to an impressive group of the king's officials, including Micaiah's father (36:11-15), they quickly take the initiative to have Baruch brought to them and their more intimate chamber for the second reading of the scroll.[79]

Setting Two

At this point, it can be said that the scroll has become a "chained-space artifact" that will link the original setting to each subsequent site.[80] When

---

77. See Shaphan's role in Josiah's government in 2 Kgs 22:3-14.

78. Bruce Lincoln, *Authority: Construction and Corrosion* (Chicago: University of Chicago Press, 1994) 9-10, points to silence as both a sign of respect and an indication of disinterest on the part of an audience. Discursive power is therefore based on "the capacity for producing" the desired effect on the audience (11).

79. Timothy Zick, "Speech and Spatial Tactics," *Texas Law Review* 84 (2005) 583-84, in discussing the First Amendment right to free speech, indicates that legal restrictions have been upheld based on concerns over security and over the emotional effect that speech may have on persons present in a particular setting. He also notes that "social and political movements require disruption and a degree of confrontation with authority in order to be even marginally effective."

80. Barber, "Chaining Spaces," 195. While not all "artifacts" are physical objects, they all represent a conscious awareness of the link between chained spaces.

the scroll is taken to the palace it has moved from one place of authority and generally-defined activity to another where it will be read to a select group of the king's personal advisers. Once again careful attention is given to identify the place: in the "king's house" within "the secretary's chamber" (*bêt-hammelek 'al-liškat hassōpēr;* 36:12).[81] Not only has the scene changed, but so has the audience. At the command of the king's officials spoken by Jehudi ben Nethaniah, Baruch has been brought from a larger setting with a more general audience — whoever happened to be immediately outside and within Gemariah's chamber at the time — to a room designated specifically for the work of the king's advisers and only open to these men.

Ordinarily, one might think that this narrowing of the size of the audience is counterproductive to the success of the message, but in this case it is essential that the message work itself up through the layers of royal authority to the ears of the king. What this suggests is that some speech cannot have its desired effect unless it is heard by the correct audience. For example, I could make a statement regarding the administration of my university, but if I only speak to a group of people who have gathered in a break room for coffee and my words are not repeated beyond that room, then my words are lost. If, however, I make an appointment to speak with my dean about my ideas, and if she feels that they are of sufficient importance to pass them on to a higher level, then my message has begun to follow the same path that Jeremiah's scroll traveled and the dean's office is linked to the provost's office as part of the information stream. Ultimately, we both hope to have an impact, and the more power brokers who hear our words and act on them, the better.

Indicating that the author intends to convey to his audience the growing tension attached to the scroll's movements is the use of *wayĕhî* at the beginning of v. 16. This phrase, translated as an indication of time passing, is in fact a narrative indicator of intensity when it is followed by an infinitive construct *(kĕšāmĕ'ām).*[82] This marks a new segment of the narrative and puts the audience on special notice to recognize the importance of the scroll, Baruch's audience, and the place as contextual keys to this scene.

81. William L. Holladay, *Jeremiah 2.* Hermeneia (Philadelphia: Fortress, 1989) 257, suggests this chamber was set aside for meetings of the king's councilors. Hoffman, "Aetiology, Redaction and Historicity in Jeremiah xxxvi," 182, n. 8, considers the list to be a way of authenticating the scroll and to follow typical onomastic style.

82. Dearman, "My Servants the Scribes," 406.

Note that when queried about the words he is reading by the "alarmed" audience of scribes, Baruch assures them that they had been written down faithfully as Jeremiah had dictated them to him (lit., from "his mouth"; *mippîw*).[83] Once the officials have been assured of the scroll's authenticity, they caution Baruch to find a safe place to hide (36:19), in essence sending Baruch into the background to join Jeremiah and leaving only the scroll to continue the journey to the next space in the chained link.

Setting Three

Completing its journey and introducing a final linked space, the scroll is read by a high-ranking advisor to the king and his officials "in his winter apartment," an area of the palace restricted to a very select group indeed (36:21-22). Presumably, it is a cold December day in the ninth month of the Israelite calendar (36:9), and thus there is a need to hold court in his "winter apartment," one that was better heated and protected from drafts of cold air. Beyond the climatic features of this physical location, its most important quality is that it represents and embodies the very highest levels of the government. At last the scroll has traveled to the heart of Jehoiakim's administration, something that Jeremiah himself could not have done at that point because of his previous, inflammatory public statements. Direct prophetic speech has been suppressed by government action or intimidation, but Jeremiah has found a way to make his voice heard through the scroll. In this way it is clearly demonstrated that "place can be a powerful weapon of social and political control."[84] However, it is in fact the person who most effectively manipulates the use of space during a conversation or public address who is truly powerful and effective.

By traveling up through these concentric circles of power, one signif-

83. Hoffman, "Aetiology, Redaction and Historicity in Jeremiah xxxvi," 184-85, notes that the phrase *mippîw yiqrā' 'ēlay*, "he dictated all these words to me," occurs six times in the narrative and concludes that the repetitive emphasis is designed to reiterate that it is Baruch who wrote this scroll as well as the second one, adding importance once again to the scribal role while authenticating its validity as the words of the prophet. This strikes an interesting parallel with God's empowering Jeremiah's mouth during his call narrative, placing God's own words in his mouth so that he could speak to the people (Jer 1:9; *bĕpîkā*).

84. Zick, "Speech and Spatial Tactics," 581.

icant space at a time, the message has the opportunity to have a greater impact because it is not just reported/summarized for the king. Instead, the scroll is read by an official in its entirety before the king and his official entourage in the very seat of government.[85] Add to this the shared cognitive spatial framework for this setting, and a whole host of real and imagined qualities apply to this space.[86] These shared physical characteristics and cognitive concepts include: palace, audience chamber, royal authority, seat of power, and restricted zone.

There would also be an F-Formation pattern and corresponding o-space created by the persons gathered in this royal audience chamber.[87] Naturally, the king as the highest-status person in the room would be the focus of attention. But the question is, who else is in this chamber besides the king and the advisor who is reading the scroll? The text is not explicit. However, the reference to the king's servants in 36:24-25 demonstrates that they were not alone, and this means that social interaction within this context cannot be a neutral or private affair.[88]

With the king seated beside a brazier, the rest of the assemblage (except Jehudi, who is standing close to the king while he reads the scroll) would be ranged around him. Presumably each person would be placed according to social protocols that would assign all those assembled to a designated space within the room based on their relative status and the desire of the king or his advisors to show preference.[89] Raising the level of anxiety for Jehoiakim is the good possibility that there was a Babylonian ambassador present, who was placed in Jerusalem to monitor Jehoiakim's

85. Cf. Shaphan reading the "book of the law" to Josiah in 2 Kgs 22:10-11.

86. Golledge and Stimson, *Spatial Behavior,* 45-46, point to research that indicates that "in many cases the perceived or *cognized environment* was the most important one in which decision-making processes took place."

87. Ciolek and Kendon, "Environment and the Spatial Arrangement," 239-40, discuss both the formation of the F-Formation and the physical constraints placed on persons based on effective use of field of vision and hearing range.

88. Janet Holmes, Maria Stubbe, and Bernadette Vine, "Constructing Professional Identity: 'Doing Power' in Policy Units," in *Talk, Work and Institutional Order,* ed. Srikant Sarangi and Celia Roberts (Berlin: Mouton de Gruyter, 1999) 354, point out that interaction in formal situations is "seldom neutral in terms of power."

89. Golledge and Stimson, *Spatial Behavior,* 50-54, point to decision-making as a reflection of a form of game theory that is dependent upon the degree of risk the decision-maker wishes to take. The process intends to cover many possible scenarios, with the ultimate goal being the most desirable or advantageous.

political leanings and to report any possible suspicion of rebellion or collaboration with Egypt.[90]

Interestingly, Jehoiakim does not engage in the normal behavior expected of high-status individuals when in the presence of those of lower status.[91] Unlike managers who tend to frame debate or wish to show their power by controlling conversation, Jehoiakim never speaks a word nor does he respond to the entreaties of his servants (36:25).[92] Instead, he engages in a nonverbal rhetorical gesture that reflects the king's power and perhaps his anxiety over this face-threatening communication,[93] which is just as effective as if he has made a brazen speech.[94] As Jehudi unrolls the scroll and reads its contents, Jehoiakim takes his knife and snips off the portion that has been read and tosses each piece into the brazier to be consumed by the fire (36:23). In that way both Jehoiakim and Jeremiah are "speaking" at the same time, with messages that are diametrically opposed to each other. Both are playing to the same audience, but it is in the king's personal and professional space and he therefore has an edge in commanding the scene — especially since Jeremiah is not physically present.

The fact that Jehoiakim is therefore capable, at least temporarily and in this setting, of overpowering Jeremiah's prophecy is found in his intimidated audience's silence and their failure to react with the normal gesture of repentance and mourning that might be expected when hearing such dire warnings (no tearing of their garments; 36:24). In performing this very public act Jehoiakim clearly intends to demonstrate his high status position and to impress those present with his bravado in the face of Jere-

90. See Holladay, *Jeremiah 2,* 256-57, for discussion of the possible historical scenarios centered on the date of the reading of the scroll.

91. See the study on typical reactions of high- and low-status individuals in Ann Leffler, Dair L. Gillespie, and Joseph C. Conaty, "The Effects of Status Differentiation on Nonverbal Behavior," *Social Psychology Quarterly* 45 (1982) 154-55.

92. Deirdre Boden, *The Business of Talk: Organizations in Action* (Cambridge, MA: Polity, 1994) 9-15, points out that talk is central to what organizations are and is a "primary mover in making organizations happen."

93. See Paddy Austin, "Politeness Revisited: The Dark Side," in *New Zealand Ways of Speaking English,* ed. Allan Bell and Janet Holmes (Clevedon: Multilingual Matters, 1990) 279, for a definition of the concept of a "face attack act" as a "communicative act that is injurious to the hearer's positive or negative face."

94. For a general summary of the effects of anxiety, see Richard S. Hallam, "Some Constructionist Observations on 'Anxiety' and Its History," in *Constructing the Social,* ed. Theodore R. Sarbin and John I. Kitsuse (London: Sage, 1994) 139-56.

miah's words of doom for the city of Jerusalem. As such he attempts to maintain the pattern of behavior implicit in his royal audience chamber so that a pattern of power is produced and reproduced whenever he is in place there.[95]

Admittedly, Jehoiakim cannot afford to show weakness or concern over Jeremiah's words. But when he burns the scroll, he actually and ironically enacts the prophecy by physically and publicly rejecting its contents.[96] This imprudent act could be compared to Isa 7:12 and Ahaz's verbal refusal to accept the prophet's proffered "sign" from God. Ahaz had chosen to put his faith in the Assyrians to get him out of his political dilemma. So too Jehoiakim either expects a resurgence of aid from his Egyptian ally or is playing to the Babylonians as one who expects them to protect him. Jehoiakim has his own political agenda and does not intend to be intimidated or swayed by the prophet.

Robert P. Carroll makes clear in his comparison of Jeremiah 26 and 36 that "the written word has *replaced* Jeremiah." He notes that a scroll can be rewritten and preserved, unlike a human, who can be executed and thus have his message cut off for good.[97] Later, when the prophet once again dictates his scroll and predicts the king's inevitable demise, there is the potential for a different result. After all, it is the words of the prophet that are preserved, and Jehoiakim does come to a bad end during the siege of Jerusalem in 597 B.C.E. The shifting effectiveness of each party's rhetoric therefore requires a longer view than just the immediate reaction of the original audience, especially if these professional politicians understand the emptiness that attends many public displays.

Each of these locations represents the establishment of spheres of influence, defined by personal accessibility and proximity to increasingly powerful individuals. Baruch, the scribe, first reads the prophet's message "in the hearing of all the people" inside the temple, "in the chamber of Gemariah . . . , which was in the upper court, at the entry of the New Gate" (36:10). From this public place, which was accessible to a fairly large num-

95. Boden, *The Business of Talk*, 79-80, ties patterning to Erving Goffman's (*Relations in Public* [New York: Basic Books, 1972]) interaction order to "a tangible and consequential place located in real time and space" and argues that it is the task and desire of organizational members to maintain the smooth flow of events and agendas.

96. Cf. Jeremiah's execration ritual in ch. 19; Robert P. Carroll, *Jeremiah*. OTL (Philadelphia: Westminster, 1986) 663.

97. *Jeremiah*, 662.

ber of the male population, the scroll is then taken to the palace and read in a place set aside for a select group of the king's personal advisers, within "the secretary's chamber" (36:11-15).[98] Finally, the scroll is read before the king and his officials "in his winter apartment," an area of the palace restricted to a very select group (36:21-22). Each of these linked locations represents distinctive spheres of influence, defined by personal accessibility and proximity to increasingly powerful individuals. None, however, is immune from Jeremiah's scroll and each is transformed by its words.

Postscript

Following the public destruction of the scroll is a postscript to this episode in 36:27-32. Jeremiah is commanded by God to "take another scroll and write on it all the former words that were in the first scroll" (36:28). While again there is nothing very explicit about what is written on this second scroll, a hint is found in 36:29 referring to Jehoiakim's question: "Why have you written in it that the king of Babylon will certainly come and destroy this land, and will cut off from it human beings and animals?" Of course, this question is not voiced in the scene in which the king destroys the scroll, and this may simply be an ex post facto condemnation of the king's policies.[99] In any case, it is out of context with the throne room scene that depends on the king's silent gesture to generate its power.

According to Christopher R. Seitz, this implies that Jeremiah is advocating at this point (605-604 B.C.E.) — even when the political events are not clear — that Judah should submit to Babylon. Jehoiakim, in turn, is disputing this position, declaring Jeremiah's statement to be "treasonous" (based on Jer 26:1-6).[100] Although Jehoiakim had been placed on the throne by Necho II (609 B.C.E.), the back-and-forth successes and failures of the Egyptians and Babylonians on their borders must have made it difficult for petty rulers like Jehoiakim to make good political

---

98. Holladay, *Jeremiah 2*, 257.

99. See the discussion of the series of condemnations against Jehoiakim tied to the year 605 B.C.E. in John Hill, "The Construction of Time in Jeremiah 25 (MT)," in *Troubling Jeremiah*, ed. A. R. Pete Diamond, Kathleen M. O'Connor, and Louis Stulman. JSOTSup 260 (Sheffield: Sheffield Academic, 1999) 152-55.

100. *Theology in Conflict: Reactions to the Exile in the Book of Jeremiah*. BZAW 16 (Berlin: de Gruyter, 1989) 87.

decisions.[101] Furthermore, the swiftly-moving changes brought on by the battle of Carchemish and the obvious ascendancy of Nebuchadnezzar of Babylon put the situation into such flux that it would not have been wise for Jehoiakim to take a public position that identified him too clearly as the vassal of Egypt or the opponent of Babylon.

Conclusions on Spatial Qualities and Discourse

Summarizing what has been discussed in this chapter and as a way to facilitate further investigations into how space shapes communication, here are a number of questions that one might ask about the biblical narrative and its spatial context:

1. What is the basis upon which specific space becomes defined? Is its use or ownership, physical presence, explicit boundaries, or architecture the basis upon which analysis should be made or are there other factors?
2. How are personal status and identity defined by the space one habitually inhabits or is allowed access to? Does every space contain "nested space" within it?
3. How is space differentiated in the village culture? In the urban culture? Is it based on mundane, utilitarian function or more complex social connotations based on traditional use?
4. What is the cognitive difference between public and private space?
5. When public and private space are combined for communal purposes, is their cognitive transformation always temporary? (See Deut 22:20-21, stoning a nonvirgin bride on her father's doorstep.)
6. Are gender roles a factor in utilization of public and private space?
7. Who is allowed to enter particular space?
8. How do entrance ways function as places for communicative acts?
9. How does individual social and economic status shape communication?
10. How does particular space affect speech patterns, language, and communication?

101. See Nadav Na'aman, "The Deuteronomist and Voluntary Servitude to Foreign Powers," *JSOT* 65 (1995) 37-53.

11. How is space used for coercive purposes? (See 1 Kgs 22:9-12.)

12. How is space used as a communicative prop or backdrop to establish symbolic or metaphorical cognitive links? (See Jeremiah's temple sermon in Jeremiah 7 and 26 and the condemnation of Bethel as the symbol of false worship in 1 Kings 13.)

13. What possibilities exist of unintended consequences that arise from the creation of space or its utilization for purposes other than those of its original creators?

14. Is the space occupied considered to be "sanctuary" or "vulnerable space"?

15. When space is defined as sacred, how are its dimensions determined and access to it guarded or prevented?

Glossary of Technical Terms

Adjacency pairs: A conversation structure that assists with turn-taking and precipitates subsequent speech and/or action. It consists of pairs of utterances that commonly occur together such as: questions and answers, introductions and greetings, statements and acknowledgements, complaints and answers.

Chained spaces: A means of illustrating how activity spaces (spaces in which social interaction takes place) are linked through talk, gesture, and other actions in order to create a framework of everyday activity. Thus a farmer may discuss his plans for plowing a field, go plow the field, and then discuss this activity with other farmers in the city gate at the end of the day, thereby linking all three spaces through conversation and action.

Cognitive linguistics: The study of the mind through language and the study of language as a cognitive function. Cognitive linguistics has two main goals: (1) to study how cognitive mechanisms like memory, categorization, attention, and imagery are used during language behavior; and (2) to develop psychologically-viable models of language that cover broad ranges of linguistic phenomena, including idioms and figurative language. Research in cognitive linguistics is multidisciplinary; evidence is drawn from text analysis, language acquisition, language change, psycholinguistic experimentation, and brain imaging, among other sources.

Constructionist theory: The idea that learners construct knowledge for themselves — each learner individually (and socially) constructs meaning — as he or she learns and in the manner best suited for them to learn and therefore "build" meaning.

Conversational analysis: The systematic analysis of the talk produced in everyday situations of human interaction: talk-in-interaction. It examines both the ordinary conversations that take place constantly between people as well as the occasional extraordinary dialogues that occur spontaneously or as part of staged performances.

Discourse analysis: An approach to studying language's relation to contextual background features. Methods associated with this approach require a thorough study of the use of language forms, syntax, word order, and the context in which words are used in embedded dialogue or the surrounding narrative.

Discourse communities: Those defined groups that share similar thoughts, ideas, and common stories. Ideologically based, the community develops its own distinctive rules for what may be discussed and in what manner.

Discursive authority: The effect that the words, mannerisms, and personality of a speaker have on an audience and that audience's willingness to take some action in response to the message.

Ethnomethodology: The study of the ways in which people make sense of their social world. It is concerned with the methods which people use to establish a reasonable account of what is happening in their social interaction and to provide a structure for the interaction itself. Ethnomethodologists do not assume that people actually share common symbolic meanings. In relation to conversation analysis, they avoid imposing narrative structures on the text and instead focus on the local level of the participants in the dialogue.

F-Formations: When at least two people are gathered together they create a spatial pattern that is shaped by both the physical setting in which they are interacting and by the placement of their bodies in relation to each other and to the confines of the setting.

Frame analysis: Humans posit or identify social and physical "frames" as they interact with other persons or objects. These "frames" are mental projections that are shaped by a person's understanding of the world and those things that inhabit or structure it. "Frames" comprise the context within which all forms of interaction take place.

Gestalt theory: An existential and experiential psychotherapy that focuses on the individual's experience in the present moment. During social interaction, the environmental and social contexts in which things take place generate the means to self-regulate perception. Advocates of semantic and cognitive linguistics have employed Gestalt methods to articulate meaning and comprehension in the examination of discourse. They conclude with Gestaltists that the processes of meaning and comprehension start with perception.

Inclusio: A literary device in which a particular phrase, event, or statement appears at the beginning and end of a narrative or poetic sequence, sandwiching the rest of the prose or poetry between its initial and the final appearance. Thus Psalm 8 begins and ends with the phrase, "O Lord, our Sovereign, how majestic is your name in all the earth!" (vv. 1 and 9).

Involvement theory: Use of eight major mechanisms by the author/storyteller: rhythm, repetition, figures of speech, indirection and ellipsis, tropes, detail and imagery, dialogue, and narratives. These mechanisms allow the reader to make inferences about and interpret the text and to be more closely drawn into the world created by the storyteller.

Labeling: Putting a positive or negative name on something or someone that will then create a social identity for the person who is labeled. This in turn will influence his or her behavior and, unless the label is somehow removed or invalidated, will become the basis for or expectation of how that person will act within society.

Liminal: Having ambiguous, indeterminate, or intermediate status based on a change of character or identity. If a woman becomes a widow, her social status is transformed from a recognizable social identity to one that has very different associations — she is neither wife nor eligible virgin. A threshold or gate is liminal because it is a transition point rather than a destination.

Mental space theory: According to this method, mental spaces and connections are built up as discourse unfolds. Mental spaces can be thought of as temporary containers or locations for relevant information about a particular object. These packets of understanding are constructed during the course of dialogue; they are unique and temporary in the sense that they relate to a particular ongoing discourse.

Metaphor: A phrase that uses analogy to communicate meaning. Metaphors conceptualize emotions or feelings by explaining or interpreting one thing in comparison with another.

Metonymy: A figure of speech in which reference is made to something or someone by naming one of its attributes. This allows for representation of meaning by focusing on a single aspect or condition of an object, such as the body, to make a point.

O-space: The internal interactional space that represents the portion of space that persons in discourse occupy and that physically separates them while engaged in interaction.

Positioning theory: An approach that replaces the fairly rigid social category of "role" with the more flexible designation of "position." It recognizes the existence of the ever-changing range of possible positions within the social realm and in space. In some applications it examines the varying skills of individuals as well as the ethics of manipulating others.

Recursive frame analysis: An approach assuming that talk unfolds upon itself as we attempt to make sense of conversations. Context and text are in turn contextualized by other contexts and text. Since words are woven together to create contexts, frames are configured to create a shape or contour to the conversation.

Schema: Cognitive structures, rather like mental templates or "frames" that represent a person's knowledge about objects, people, or situations that are derived from prior experience and knowledge and thereby simplify reality, setting up expectations about what is probable in relation to particular social and textual contexts. In a literary context schema theory attempts to explain the narrative gaps in a story that are left by a storyteller who has a shared knowledge of the setting of the story and is guided by the application of relevant social and textual schemas.

Socially-shared cognition: The way in which people jointly construct knowledge about other people and places, giving them social identity and significance. This process also occurs when a group of people recognizes and collectively creates a meaning for a visual cultural icon (e.g., Santa Claus).

Sociolinguistics: The study of the aspects of linguistics applied toward the connections between language and society and the way language is used in different social situations. Sociolinguistics ranges from the study of dialects within a given region to the analysis of dialogue between men and women. Sociolinguistics takes note of humor inherent in human speech and examines how a dialect can describe the age, sex, and social class of the speaker. In so doing, it codes the social function of a language.

Space of resistance: A physical or mental sanctuary within which an individual can escape, at least temporarily, from the claims of others or the need to interact according to established social patterns or practices.

Bibliography

Abu-Lughod, Lila. "The Romance of Resistance: Tracing Transformations of Power Through Bedouin Women." *American Ethnologist* 17 (1990) 41-55.

Afsaruddin, Asma. "Introduction: The Hermeneutics of Gendered Space and Discourse." In *Hermeneutics and Honor: Negotiating Female "Public" Space in Islamic/ate Societies,* 1-28. Cambridge, MA: Harvard University Press, 1999.

Alter, Robert. *The Art of Biblical Narrative.* New York: Basic Books, 1981.

Amit, Yairah. "A Prophet Tested: Elisha, the Great Woman of Shunem, and the Story's Double Message." *BibInt* 11 (2003) 279-94.

Anbar, Moshe. "'L'aire à l'entrée de la porte de Samarie' (1 R. XXII 10)." *VT* 50 (2000) 121-23.

Arnold, Bill T. "Word Play and Characterization in Daniel 1." In *Puns and Pundits: Word Play in the Hebrew Bible and Ancient Near Eastern Literature,* ed. Scott B. Noegel, 231-48. Bethesda: CDL, 2000.

Auld, A. Graeme. "Prophets Shared — But Recycled." In *The Future of the Deuteronomistic History,* ed. Thomas Römer, 19-28. Leuven: Leuven University Press, 2000.

———. "Tamar between David, Judah and Joseph." *Svensk exegetisk årsbok* 65 (2000) 93-106.

Austin, Paddy. "Politeness Revisited: The Dark Side." In *New Zealand Ways of Speaking English,* ed. Allan Bell and Janet Holmes, 277-93. Clevedon: Multilingual Matters, 1990.

Avalos, Hector I. "The Comedic Function of the Enumerations of Officials and Instruments in Daniel 3." *CBQ* 53 (1991) 580-88.

Bal, Mieke. "One Woman, Many Men, and the Dialectic of Chronology." In *Lethal Love: Feminist Literary Readings of Biblical Love Stories,* 89-103. Bloomington: University of Indiana Press, 1987.

169

Baldwin, Joyce G. *Daniel.* TOTC. Downers Grove: InterVarsity, 1978.

Barber, Annice I. "Chaining Spaces." *Journal of Linguistic Anthropology* 15 (2005) 194-217.

Bar-Efrat, Shimon. "Love of Zion: A Literary Interpretation of Psalm 137." In *Tehillah le-Moshe: Biblical and Judaic Studies in Honor of Moshe Greenberg,* ed. Mordechai Cogan, Barry L. Eichler, and Jeffrey H. Tigay, 3-11. Winona Lake: Eisenbrauns, 1997.

Barr, James. "The Symbolism of Names in the Old Testament." *British Journal of Religious Literature* 52 (1969) 11-29.

Bartor, Asnat. "The 'Juridical Dialogue': A Literary-Judicial Pattern." *VT* 53 (2003) 445-64.

Bavelas, Janet Beavin, Christine Kenwood, and Bruce Phillips. "Discourse Analysis." In *Handbook of Interpersonal Communication,* ed. Mark L. Knapp and John A. Daly, 102-29. 3rd ed. Thousand Oaks: Sage, 2002.

Becking, Bob. "Chronology: A Skeleton Without Flesh? Sennacherib's Campaign as a Case-Study." In *"Like a Bird in a Cage": The Invasion of Sennacherib in 701 BCE,* ed. Lester L. Grabbe, 46-72. JSOTSup 363. London: Sheffield Academic, 2003.

Bender, Barbara. "Time and Landscape." *Current Anthropology* 43 (2002) 103-12.

Berdoulay, Vincent. "Place, Meaning, and Discourse in French Language Geography." In *The Power of Place,* ed. John A. Agnew and James S. Duncan, 124-39. Boston: Unwin Hyman, 1989.

Berger, Arthur Asa. *Cultural Criticism: A Primer of Key Concepts.* Thousand Oaks: Sage, 1995.

Berquist, Jon L. "Constructions of Identity in Postcolonial Yehud." In *Judah and the Judeans in the Persian Period,* ed. Oded Lipschits and Manfred Oeming, 53-66. Winona Lake: Eisenbrauns, 2006.

——. "Critical Spatiality and the Construction of the Ancient World." In *"Imagining" Biblical Worlds: Studies in Spatial, Social, and Historical Constructs in Honor of James W. Flanagan,* ed. David M. Gunn and Paula M. McNutt, 14-29. JSOTSup 359. London: Sheffield Academic, 2002.

Bird, Phyllis A. "The Harlot as Heroine: Narrative Art and Social Presupposition in Three Old Testament Texts." *Semeia* 46 (1989) 119-39.

Bishop, Ryan. "There's Nothing Natural about Natural Conversation: A Look at Dialogue in Fiction and Drama." *Oral Tradition* 6 (1991) 58-78.

Blenkinsopp, Joseph. *Ezra-Nehemiah.* OTL. Philadelphia: Westminster, 1988.

Block, Daniel I. *The Book of Ezekiel: Chapters 1-24.* NICOT. Grand Rapids: Wm. B. Eerdmans, 1997.

Boden, Deirdre. *The Business of Talk: Organizations in Action.* Cambridge, MA: Polity, 1994.

Bodner, Keith. "The Locutions of 1 Kings 22:28: A New Proposal." *JBL* 122 (2003) 533-43.

Bos, Johanna W. H. "Out of the Shadows: Genesis 38; Judges 4:17-22; Ruth 3." In *Reasoning with the Foxes: Female Wit in a World of Male Power,* ed. J. Cheryl Exum and Bos, 37-67. Semeia 42 (Atlanta: Scholars, 1988).

Boyle, Marjorie O'Rourke. "The Law of the Heart: The Death of a Fool (1 Samuel 25)." *JBL* 120 (2001) 401-27.

Brensinger, Terry L. "Compliance, Dissonance and Amazement in Daniel 3." *EvJ* 20 (2002) 7-19.

Brueggemann, Walter. "Narrative Intentionality in 1 Samuel 29." *JSOT* 43 (1989) 21-35.

Bummitt, Mark, and Yvonne Sherwood. "The Tenacity of the Word: Using Jeremiah 36 to Attempt to Construct an Appropriate Edifice to the Memory of Robert Carroll." In *Sense and Sensitivity: Essays on Reading the Bible in Memory of Robert Carroll,* ed. Alastair G. Hunter and Phillip R. Davies, 3-29. JSOTSup 348. Sheffield: Sheffield Academic, 2002.

Burgoon, Judee K., and Gregory D. Hoobler. "Nonverbal Signals." In *Handbook of Interpersonal Communication,* ed. Mark L. Knapp and John A. Daly, 240-99. 3rd ed. Thousand Oaks: Sage, 2002.

Carpenter, Eugene. "Exodus 18: Its Structure, Style, Motifs and Function in the Book of Exodus." In *A Biblical Itinerary: In Search of Method, Form and Content: Essays in Honor of George W. Coats,* 91-108. JSOTSup 240. Sheffield: Sheffield Academic, 1997.

Carroll, Robert P. *Jeremiah.* OTL. Philadelphia: Westminster, 1986.

————. "Manuscripts Don't Burn — Inscribing the Prophetic Tradition: Reflections on Jeremiah 36." In *"Dort ziehen Schiffe dahin ...": Collected Communications to the XIVth Congress of the International Organization for the Study of the Old Testament, Paris 1992,* ed. Matthias Augustin and Klaus D. Schunck, 31-42. Frankfurt am Main: Peter Lang, 1996.

Chase, William G., and Michelene T. H. Chi. "Cognitive Skill: Implications for Spatial Skill in Large-Scale Environments." In *Cognition, Social Behavior, and the Environment,* ed. John H. Harvey, 111-36. Hillsdale, NJ: Lawrence Erlbaum, 1981.

Chenail, Ronald J. "Recursive Frame Analysis." *Qualitative Report* 2 (1995) 34-43; and http://www.nova.edu/ssss/QR/QR2-2/rfa.html.

Cicourel, Aaron V. "The Interpenetration of Communicative Contexts: Examples from Medical Encounters." In *Rethinking Context: Language as an Interactive Phenomenon,* ed. Alessandro Duranti and Charles Goodwin, 291-310. Cambridge: Cambridge University Press, 1992.

Ciolek, T. Matthew, and Adam Kendon. "Environment and the Spatial Arrangement of Conversational Encounters." *Sociological Inquiry* 50 (1980) 237-71.

Clifford, Richard J. "Genesis 38: Its Contribution to the Jacob Story." *CBQ* 66 (2004) 519-32.

Clines, David J. A. "Michal Observed: An Introduction to Reading Her Story." In *Telling Queen Michal's Story: An Experiment in Comparative Interpretation,* ed. Clines and Tamara Cohn Eskenazi, 24-63. JSOTSup 119. Sheffield: JSOT, 1991.

Coats, George W. "Self-Abasement and Insult Formulas." *JBL* 89 (1970) 14-26.

Cogan, Mordechai. *1 Kings.* AB 10. New York: Doubleday, 2001.

————, and Hayim Tadmor. *II Kings.* AB 11. Garden City: Doubleday, 1988.

Collins, John J. *Daniel.* Hermeneia. Minneapolis: Fortress, 1993.

Cook, Guy. *Discourse and Literature: The Interplay of Form and Mind.* Oxford: Oxford University Press, 1994.

Cook, Stephen L. "The Tradition of Mosaic Judges: Past Approaches and New Directions." In *On the Way to Nineveh: Studies in Honor of George M. Landes,* ed. Cook and S. C. Winter, 286-315. Atlanta: Scholars, 1999.

Cooley, Charles Horton. *Human Nature and the Social Order.* New York: Scribner's, 1902.

Cosgrove, Denis E. *Social Formation and Symbolic Landscape.* Madison: University of Wisconsin Press, 1998.

Coulson, Seana. "Mental Space Theory." http://hci.ucsd.edu/coulson/LOT/chap1/node10.html (2002).

Cryer, Frederick H. "David's Rise to Power and the Death of Abner: An Analysis of 1 Samuel xxvi 14-16 and Its Redaction-Critical Implications." *VT* 35 (1985) 385-94.

Cutting, Joan. *Pragmatics and Discourse.* 2nd ed. New York: Routledge, 2008.

Daly, John A. "Personality and Interpersonal Communication." In *Handbook of Interpersonal Communication,* ed. Mark L. Knapp and Daly, 133-80. 3rd ed. Thousand Oaks: Sage, 2002.

Davies, Bronwyn, and Rom Harré. "Positioning and Personhood." In *Positioning Theory: Moral Contexts of Intentional Action,* ed. Harré and Luk van Langenhove, 32-52. Oxford: Blackwell, 1999.

Day, John. "Shear-Jashub (Isaiah vii 3) and 'the Remnant of Wrath' (Psalm lxxvi 11)." *VT* 31 (1981) 76-78.

Dearman, J. Andrew. "My Servants the Scribes: Composition and Context in Jeremiah 36." *JBL* 109 (1990) 403-21.

Deleuze, Gilles. *Foucault.* Minneapolis: University of Minnesota Press, 1988.

Dersley, Ian, and Anthony Wootton. "Complaint Sequences Within Antagonistic Argument." *Research on Language and Social Interaction* 33 (2000) 375-406.

Dévényi, Jutka. *Metonymy and Drama: Essays on Language and Dramatic Strategy.* Lewisburg: Bucknell University Press, 1996.

Dijk-Hemmes, Fokkelien van. "The Great Woman of Shunem and the Man of God: A Dual Interpretation of 2 Kings 4:8-37." In *A Feminist Companion to Samuel and Kings,* ed. Athalya Brenner, 218-30. Sheffield: Sheffield Academic, 1994.

Dion, Paul Eugène. "The Horned Prophet (1 Kings xxii 11)." *VT* 49 (1999) 259-61.

Drew, Paul, and John Heritage. "Introduction." In *Conversation Analysis.* Vol. 1: *Turn-Taking and Repair,* ed. Drew and Heritage, xxi-xxxvii. London: Sage, 2006.

Durkheim, Emile. *Elementary Forms of the Religious Life.* New York: Macmillan, 1915; repr. Glencoe: Free Press, 1965.

Eide, Hilde, V. Vicenç Quera, Peter Graugaard, and Arnstein Finset. "Physician-patient Dialogue Surrounding Patients' Expression of Concern: Applying Sequence Analysis to RIAS." *Social Science and Medicine* 59 (2004) 145-55.

Eliade, Mircea. *The Sacred and the Profane.* New York: Harcourt, Brace, 1959.

Ellwood, Iain. *The Essential Brand Book.* 2nd ed. London: Kogan Page, 2002.

Esler, Philip F., ed. *Ancient Israel: The Old Testament in Its Social Context.* Minneapolis: Fortress, 2006.

Evans, Vyvyan, and Melanie Green. *Cognitive Linguistics: An Introduction.* Mahwah: Lawrence Erlbaum, 2006.

Exum, J. Cheryl. *Fragmented Women: Feminist (Sub)versions of Biblical Narratives.* Valley Forge: Trinity Press International, 1993.

Fauconnier, Gilles. *Mappings in Thought and Language.* Cambridge: Cambridge University Press, 1997.

———. *Mental Spaces: Aspects of Meaning Construction in Natural Language.* Cambridge: Cambridge University Press, 1994.

———, and Mark Turner. *The Way We Think: Conceptual Blending and the Mind's Hidden Complexities.* New York: Basic Books, 2002.

Fewell, Danna Nolan. *Circle of Sovereignty: A Story of Stories in Daniel 1-6.* JSOTSup 72. Sheffield: Almond, 1988.

———. "Sennacherib's Defeat: Words at War in 2 Kgs 18:13-19:37." *JSOT* 34 (1986) 79-90.

Fishbane, Michael. *Biblical Interpretation in Ancient Israel.* Oxford: Oxford University Press, 1985.

Fisher, B. Aubrey, and Katherine L. Adams. *Interpersonal Communication: Pragmatics of Human Relationships.* 2nd ed. New York: McGraw-Hill, 1994.

Fokkelman, Jan P. "Genesis." In *The Literary Guide to the Bible,* ed. Robert Alter and Frank Kermode, 36-55. Cambridge, MA: Belknap, 1987.

Foucault, Michel. *The History of Sexuality.* Vol. 1: *An Introduction.* New York: Pantheon, 1978.

Freshwater, Dawn. "The Poetics of Space: Researching the Concept of Spatiality Through Relationality." *Psychodynamic Practice* 11 (2005) 177-87.

Frick, Frank S. "Ritual and Social Regulation in Ancient Israel: The Importance of the Social Context for Ritual Studies and a Case Study — The Ritual of the Red Heifer." In *"Imagining" Biblical Worlds: Studies in Spatial, Social, and Historical Constructs in Honor of James W. Flanagan,* ed. David M. Gunn and Paula M. McNutt, 219-32. JSOTSup 359. London: Sheffield Academic, 2002.

Fried, Lisbeth S. "'You Shall Appoint Judges': Ezra's Mission and the Rescript of Artaxerxes." In *Persia and Torah: The Theory of Imperial Authorization of the Pentateuch,* ed. James W. Watts, 63-89. SBLSymS 17. Atlanta: SBL, 2001.

Frymer-Kensky, Tikva. *In the Wake of the Goddesses: Women, Culture and the Biblical Transformation of Pagan Myth.* New York: Free Press, 1992.

Furman, Nelly, "His Story Versus Her Story: Male Genealogy and Female Strategy in the Jacob Cycle." In *Narrative Research on the Hebrew Bible,* ed. Miri Amihai, George W. Coats, and Anne M. Solomon, 141-49. Semeia 46. Atlanta: Scholars, 1989.

Garcia, Angela. "Dispute Resolution Without Disputing: How the Interactional Organization of Mediation Hearings Minimizes Argument." *American Sociological Review* 56 (1991) 818-35.

Geertz, Clifford. "Thick Description: Toward an Interpretative Theory of Culture." In *The Interpretation of Culture: Selected Essays,* 3-30. New York: Basic Books, 1973.

Geoghegan, Jeffrey C. "Israelite Sheepshearing and David's Rise to Power." *Bib* 87 (2006) 55-63.

Gergen, Kenneth J. *Realities and Relationships: Soundings in Social Construction.* Cambridge, MA: Harvard University Press, 1994.

Gerstenberger, Erhard S. *Leviticus.* OTL. Louisville: Westminster/John Knox, 1996.

Gill, Rosalind. "Discourse Analysis: Practical Implementation." In *Handbook of Qualitative Research Methods for Psychology and the Social Sciences,* ed. John T. E. Richardson, 141-56. Leicester: British Psychological Society, 1996.

Gívon, Talmy. "Coherence in Text vs. Coherence in Mind." In *Coherence in Spontaneous Text,* ed. Morton Ann Gernsbacher and Gívon, 59-115. Amsterdam: Benjamins, 1995.

Goffman, Erving. *Forms of Talk.* Philadelphia: University of Pennsylvania Press, 1981.

———. *Frame Analysis.* New York: Harper & Row, 1974.

———. *The Presentation of Self in Everyday Life.* Garden City: Doubleday Anchor, 1959.

———. *Relations in Public: Microstudies of the Public Order.* New York: Basic Books, 1971.

Golledge, Reginald G., and Robert J. Stimson. *Spatial Behavior: A Geographic Perspective.* New York: Guilford, 1997.

Goodman, Nelson. *Languages of Art: An Approach to a Theory of Symbols.* Indianapolis: Bobbs-Merrill, 1968.

Goodwin, Charles. "Conversation Analysis." *Annual Review of Anthropology* 19 (1990) 283-307.

Green, Barbara. "Enacting Imaginatively the Unthinkable: 1 Samuel 25 and the Story of Saul." *BibInt* 11 (2003) 1-23.

Greenfield, Meg. "Political Flip-Flops." *Newsweek* 114/18 (30 October 1989) 88.

Greenstein, Edward L. "Jethro's Wit: An Interpretation of Wordplay in Exodus 18." In *On the Way to Nineveh: Studies in Honor of George M. Landes,* ed. Steven L. Cook and S. C. Winter, 155-71. Atlanta: Scholars, 1999.

Gunn, David M., and Dana Nolan Fewell. *Narrative in the Hebrew Bible.* New York: Oxford University Press, 1993.

———, and Paula M. McNutt, eds. *"Imagining" Biblical Worlds: Studies in Spatial, Social, and Historical Constructs in Honor of James W. Flanagan.* JSOTSup 359. London: Sheffield Academic, 2002.

Gupta, Akhil, and James Ferguson. "Beyond 'Culture': Space, Identity, and the Politics of Difference." *Cultural Anthropology* 7 (1992) 6-23.

Habermas, Jürgen. *The Structural Transformation of the Public Sphere: An Inquiry into a Category of Bourgeois Society.* Cambridge, MA: MIT Press, 2001.

Hallam, Richard S. "Some Constructionist Observations on 'Anxiety' and Its History." In *Constructing the Social,* ed. Theodore R. Sarbin and John I. Kitsuse, 139-56. London: Sage, 1994.

Halliday, M. A. K., and Ruqaiya Hasan. *Cohesion in English.* London: Longman, 1976.

Halpern, Baruch. *David's Secret Demons: Messiah, Murderer, Traitor, King.* BIW. Grand Rapids: Wm. B. Eerdmans, 2001.

Hardin, James W. "Understanding Domestic Space: An Example from Iron Age Halif." *NEA* 67 (2004) 71-83.

Harré, Rom. "Images of the World and Societal Icons." In *Determinants and Controls of Scientific Development,* ed. Karin D. Knorr, Hermann Strasser, and Hans G. Zilian, 257-83. Dordrecht: Reidel, 1975.

Harris, James Ian. "The King as Public Servant: Towards an Ethic of Public Leadership Based on Virtues Suggested in the Wisdom Literature of the Old Testament." *JTSA* 113 (2002) 61-73.

Hartley, John E. *Leviticus.* WBC 4. Dallas: Word, 1992.

Hatav, Galia. "(Free) Direct Discourse in Biblical Hebrew." *HS* 41 (2000) 7-30.

Hatfield, Elaine, and Richard L. Rapson. "Love and Attachment Processes." In *Handbook of Emotions,* ed. Michael Lewis and Jeannette M. Haviland-Jones, 654-62. 2nd ed. New York: Guilford, 2000.

Hawk, L. Daniel. "Strange Houseguests: Rahab, Lot, and the Dynamics of Deliverance." In *Reading Between Texts: Intertextuality and the Hebrew Bible,* ed. Danna Nolan Fewell, 89-97. Louisville: Westminster/John Knox, 1992.

Heath, Christian. "Talk and Recipiency: Sequential Organization in Speech and Body Movement." In *Structures of Social Action: Studies in Conversation Analysis,* ed. J. Maxwell Atkinson and John Heritage, 247-65. Cambridge: Cambridge University Press, 1984.

Hill, John. "The Construction of Time in Jeremiah 25 (MT)." In *Troubling Jeremiah,* ed. A. R. Pete Diamond, Kathleen M. O'Connor, and Louis Stulman, 146-60. JSOTSup 260. Sheffield: Sheffield Academic, 1999.

Hobbs, T. Raymond. "Hospitality in the First Testament and the 'Teleological Fallacy.'" *JSOT* 95 (2001) 3-30.

———. "Man, Woman, and Hospitality — 2 Kings 4:8-36." *BTB* 23 (1993) 91-100.

———. *2 Kings.* WBC 13. Waco: Word, 1985.

Hoffman, Yair. "Aetiology, Redaction and Historicity in Jeremiah xxxvi." *VT* 46 (1996) 179-89.

Holladay, William L. *Jeremiah 1.* Hermeneia. Philadelphia: Fortress, 1986.

———. *Jeremiah 2.* Hermeneia. Philadelphia: Fortress, 1989.

Hollway, Wendy. "Gender Difference and the Production of Subjectivity." In *Changing the Subject: Psychology, Social Regulation and Subjectivity,* ed. Julian Henriques, et al., 227-63. London: Methuen, 1984.

Holmes, Janet, Maria Stubbe, and Bernadette Vine. "Constructing Professional Identity: 'Doing Power' in Policy Units." In *Talk, Work and Institutional Order: Discourse in Medical, Mediation, and Management Settings,* ed. Srikant Sarangi and Celia Roberts, 351-85. Berlin: Mouton de Gruyter, 1999.

Homan, Michael M. "Date Rape: The Agricultural and Astronomical Background of the Sumerian Sacred Marriage and Genesis 38." *SJOT* 16 (2002) 283-92.

Houtman, Cornelius. "Ezra and the Law: Observations on the Supposed Relation between Ezra and the Pentateuch." *OtSt* 21 (1981) 91-115.

Howie, David. "Preparing for Positive Positioning." In *Positioning Theory: Moral Contexts of Intentional Action,* ed. Rom Harré and Luk van Langenhove, 53-59. Oxford: Blackwell, 1999.

Huddlestun, John R. "Divestiture, Deception, and Demotion: The Garment Motif in Genesis 37-39." *JSOT* 98 (2002) 47-62.

———. "Unveiling the Versions: The Tactics of Tamar in Genesis 38:15." *JHS* 3 (2001): http://www.arts.ualberta.ca/JHS/Articles/article_19.htm

Humphreys, W. Lee. "A Life-Style for Diaspora: A Study of the Tales of Esther and Daniel." *JBL* 92 (1973) 211-23.

Hurowitz, Victor. "Inside Solomon's Temple." *BRev* 10/2 (1994) 24-37, 50.

Hutchby, Ian, and Robin Wooffitt. *Conversation Analysis: Principles, Practices and Applications.* Cambridge: Polity, 1998.

Isserlin, B. S. J. "Epigraphically Attested Judean Hebrew, and the Question of 'Upper Class' (Official) and 'Popular' Speech Variants in Judea During the 8th-6th Centuries B.C." *AJBA* 2 (1972) 197-203.

Jackson, Melissa. "Lot's Daughters and Tamar as Tricksters and the Patriarchal Narratives as Feminist Theology." *JSOT* 98 (2002) 29-46.

Jahandarie, Khosrow. *Spoken and Written Discourse: A Multi-disciplinary Perspective.* Stamford: Ablex, 1999.

Johnstone, Barbara. "Discourse Analysis and Narrative." In *The Handbook of Discourse Analysis,* ed. Deborah Schiffrin, Deborah Tannen, and Heidi E. Hamilton, 635-49. Malden: Blackwell, 2001.

Jones, Rebecca L. "'Older People' Talking As If They Are Not Older People: Positioning Theory as an Explanation." *Journal of Aging Studies* 20 (2006) 79-91.

Kamp, Albert. *Inner Worlds: A Cognitive Linguistic Approach to the Book of Jonah.* Biblical Interpretation 68. Leiden: Brill, 2004.

Kaplan, Robert B., and William Grabe. "A Modern History of Written Discourse Analysis." *Journal of Second Language Writing* 11 (2002) 191-223.

Keel, Othmar, and Christoph Uehlinger. *Gods, Goddesses, and Images of God in Ancient Israel.* Minneapolis: Fortress, 1998.

Kendon, Adam. "The F-Formation System: The Spatial Organization of Social Encounter." *Man-Environment Systems* 6 (1976) 291-96.

Kenney, J. Scott. "Victims of Crime and Labeling Theory: A Parallel Process?" *Deviant Behavior* 23 (2002) 235-65.

Kessler, John. "Persia's Loyal Yahwists: Power Identity and Ethnicity in Achaemenid Yehud." In *Judah and the Judeans in the Persian Period,* ed. Oded Lipschits and Manfred Oeming, 91-121. Winona Lake: Eisenbrauns, 2006.

———. "Sexuality and Politics: The Motif of the Displaced Husband in the Books of Samuel." *CBQ* 62 (2000) 409-23.

Kessler, Martin. "The Significance of Jer 36." *ZAW* 81 (1969) 381-83.

Klawans, Jonathan. *Purity, Sacrifice, and the Temple: Symbolism and Supersessionism in the Study of Ancient Judaism.* Oxford: Oxford University Press, 2006.

Klein, Lillian R. "Michal, the Barren Wife." In *Samuel and Kings,* ed. Athalya Brenner, 37-46. A Feminist Companion to the Bible, 2nd ser. 7. Sheffield: Sheffield Academic, 2000.

Kövecses, Zoltán. "Anger: Its Language, Conceptualization, and Physiology in the Light of Cross-Cultural Evidence." In *Language and the Cognitive Construal of the World,* ed. John R. Taylor and Robert E. MacLaury, 191-96. Berlin: Mouton de Gruyter, 1995.

———. *Emotion Concepts.* Berlin: Springer-Verlag, 1990.

————. *Language, Mind, and Culture: A Practical Introduction.* Oxford: Oxford University Press, 2006.

Kramarae, Cheris, Candace West, and Michelle M. Lazar. "Gender in Discourse." In *Discourse as Social Interaction,* ed. Teun A. van Dijk, 2:119-43. London: Sage, 1997.

Kruger, Paul A. "A Cognitive Interpretation of the Emotion of Anger in the Hebrew Bible." *JNSL* 26 (2000) 181-93.

Kuper, Hilda. "The Language of Sites in the Politics of Space." In *The Anthropology of Space and Place: Locating Culture,* ed. Setha M. Low and Denise Lawrence-Zúñiga, 247-63. Malden: Blackwell, 2003.

Laberge, Léo. "The Woe-Oracles of Isaiah 28-33." *Eglise et théologie* 13 (1982) 157-90.

Lakoff, George. *Women, Fire, and Dangerous Things: What Categories Reveal about the Mind.* Chicago: University of Chicago Press, 1990.

————, and Mark Johnson. *Metaphors We Live By.* Chicago: University of Chicago Press, 1980.

————, and Zoltán Kövecses. "The Cognitive Model of Anger Inherent in American English." In *Cultural Models in Language and Thought,* ed. Dorothy Holland and Naomi Quinn, 195-221. 6th ed. Cambridge: Cambridge University Press, 1995.

Lambe, Anthony J. "Genesis 38: Structure and Literary Design." In *The World of Genesis: Persons, Places, Perspectives,* ed. Philip R. Davies and David J. A. Clines, 102-20. Sheffield: Sheffield Academic, 1998.

————. "Judah's Development: The Pattern of Departure-Transition-Return." *JSOT* 83 (1999) 53-68.

Langacker, Ronald W. *Foundations of Cognitive Grammar,* 1: *Theoretical Prerequisites.* Stanford: Stanford University Press, 1987.

————. "Possession and Possessive Constructions." In *Language and the Cognitive Construal of the World,* ed. John R. Taylor and Robert E. MacLaury, 51-79. Berlin: Mouton de Gruyter, 1995.

Langenhove, Luk van, and Rom Harré. "Introducing Positioning Theory." In *Positioning Theory: Moral Contexts of Intentional Action,* ed. Harré and Luk van Langenhove, 14-31. Oxford: Blackwell, 1999.

Lapchick, Richard. "Sports and Public Behavior." In *Public Discourse in America: Conversation and Community in the Twenty-First Century,* ed. Judith Rodin and Stephen P. Steinberg, 71-79. Philadelphia: University of Pennsylvania Press, 2003.

Laughlin, John C. H. "The Remarkable Discoveries at Tel Dan." *BAR* 7/5 (1981) 20-37.

Lee, Benjamin. *Talking Heads: Language, Metalanguage, and the Semiotics of Subjectivity.* Durham: Duke University Press, 1997.

Lee, Christopher J., and Albert N. Katz. "The Differential Role of Ridicule in Sarcasm and Irony." *Metaphor and Symbol* 13 (1998) 1-15.

Lefebvre, Henri. *The Production of Space.* Oxford: Blackwell, 1991.

Leffler, Ann, Dair L. Gillespie, and Joseph C. Conaty. "The Effects of Status Differentiation on Nonverbal Behavior." *Social Psychology Quarterly* 45 (1982) 153-61.

Leggitt, John S., and Raymond W. Gibbs, Jr. "Emotional Reactions to Verbal Irony." *Discourse Processes* 29 (2000) 1-24.

Leib, Jonathan I. "Separate Times, Shared Spaces: Arthur Ashe, Monument Avenue and the Politics of Richmond, Virginia's Symbolic Landscape." *Cultural Geographies* 9 (2002) 286-312.

Lemche, Niels Peter. "Kings and Clients: On Loyalty between the Ruler and the Ruled in Ancient 'Israel.'" In *Ethics and Politics in the Hebrew Bible,* ed. Douglas A. Knight, 119-32. Semeia 66. Atlanta: SBL, 1995.

Lennon, Sharron J. "Sex, Dress, and Power in the Workplace: 'Star Trek, The Next Generation.'" In *Appearance and Power,* ed. Kim K. P. Johnson and Lennon, 103-26. Oxford: Berg, 1999.

Leuchter, Mark. *Josiah's Reform and Jeremiah's Scroll: Historical Calamity and Prophetic Response.* HBM 6. Sheffield: Sheffield Phoenix, 2006.

Levinson, Stephen C. *Space in Language and Cognition: Explorations in Cognitive Diversity.* Cambridge: Cambridge University Press, 2003.

Lewin, Ellen Davis. "Arguing for Authority: A Rhetorical Study of Jeremiah 1:4-19 and 20:7-18." *JSOT* 32 (1985) 105-19.

Lewis, Helen B. *Shame and Guilt in Neurosis.* New York: International Universities Press, 1971.

Li, Charles N. "Direct Speech and Indirect Speech: A Functional Study." In *Direct and Indirect Speech,* ed. Florian Coulmas, 29-45. Berlin: Mouton de Gruyter, 1986.

Liid, Dale C. "Fuller's Field." *ABD,* 2:859.

Lincoln, Bruce. *Authority: Construction and Corrosion.* Chicago: University of Chicago Press, 1994.

Lockwood, Peter F. "Tamar's Place in the Joseph Cycle." *Lutheran Theological Journal* 26 (1992) 35-43.

Long, Burke O. "The Effect of Divination upon Israelite Literature." *JBL* 92 (1973) 489-97.

———. *1 Kings.* FOTL 9. Grand Rapids: Wm. B. Eerdmans, 1984.

———. "The Form and Significance of 1 Kings 22:1-38." In *Isaac Leo Seeligmann Volume: Essays on the Bible and the Ancient World,* ed. Alexander Rofé and Yair Zakovitch, 3:193-208. Jerusalem: Rubinstein, 1983.

———. "Framing Repetitions in Biblical Historiography." *JBL* 106 (1987) 385-99.

Long, Gary. "The Written Story: Toward Understanding Text as Representation and Function." *VT* 49 (1999) 165-85.

López, Maricel Mena. "Wise Women in I Kings 3-11." In *The Many Voices of the Bible,* ed. Sean Freyne and Ellen van Wolde, 24-32. London: SCM, 2002.

Low, Setha M., and Denise Lawrence-Zúñiga. "Locating Culture." In *The Anthropology of Space and Place: Locating Culture,* ed. Low and Lawrence-Zúñiga, 1-48. Malden: Blackwell, 2003.

Lundbom, Jack R. *Jeremiah: A Study in Ancient Hebrew Rhetoric.* 2nd ed. Winona Lake: Eisenbrauns, 1997.

Lyotard, Jean-François. *The Postmodern Condition: A Report on Knowledge.* Minneapolis: University of Minnesota Press, 1984.

McCarter, P. Kyle, Jr. "The Ritual Dedication of the City of David in 2 Samuel 6." In *The Word of the Lord Shall Go Forth: Essays in Honor of David Noel Freedman in Celebration of His Sixtieth Birthday,* ed. Carol L. Meyers and M. O'Connor, 273-78. Winona Lake: Eisenbrauns, 1983.

———. *II Samuel.* AB 9. Garden City: Doubleday, 1984.

Macaulay, Ronald K. S. *The Social Art: Language and Its Uses.* New York: Oxford University Press, 1994.

———. *Talk That Counts: Age, Gender, and Social Class Differences in Discourse.* Oxford: Oxford University Press, 2005.

Magary, Dennis R. "Answering Questions, Questioning Answers: The Rhetoric of Interrogatives in the Speeches of Job and His Friends." In *Seeking Out the Wisdom of the Ancients: Essays Offered to Honor Michael V. Fox on the Occasion of His Sixty-fifth Birthday,* ed. Ronald L. Troxel, Kelvin G. Friebel, and Magary, 283-98. Winona Lake: Eisenbrauns, 2005.

Matthews, Victor H. "The Anthropology of Clothing in the Joseph Narrative." *JSOT* 65 (1995) 25-36.

———. "Entrance Ways and Threshing Floors: Legally Significant Sites in the Ancient Near East." *Fides et Historia* 19/3 (1987) 25-40.

———. "Female Voices: Upholding the Honor of the Household." *BTB* 24 (1994) 8-15.

———. "Hospitality and Hostility in Genesis 19 and Judges 19." *BTB* 22 (1992) 3-11.

———. *Judges and Ruth.* NCambBC. Cambridge: Cambridge University Press, 2004.

———. "The King's Call to Justice." *BZ* 35 (1991) 204-16.

———. *Old Testament Themes.* St. Louis: Chalice, 2000.

———. *Old Testament Turning Points: The Narratives That Shaped a Nation.* Grand Rapids: Baker, 2005.

———. "The Social Context of Law in the Second Temple Period." *BTB* 28 (1998) 7-15.

———. *Studying the Ancient Israelites.* Grand Rapids: Baker, 2007.

————. "Traversing the Social Landscape: The Value of the Social Scientific Approach to the Bible." In *Theology and the Social Sciences,* ed. Michael Horace Barnes, 214-36. Annual Publication of the College Theology Society 46. Maryknoll: Orbis, 2001.

————. "The Unwanted Gift: Implications of Obligatory Gift Giving in Ancient Israel." In *The Social World of the Hebrew Bible,* ed. Ronald Simkins and Stephen Cook, 91-104. Semeia 87. Atlanta: SBL, 1999.

————, and Don C. Benjamin. "Amnon and Tamar: A Matter of Honor (2 Sam 13:1-38)." In *Crossing Boundaries and Linking Horizons: Studies in Honor of Michael C. Astour on His 80th Birthday,* ed. Gordon D. Young, Mark Chavalas, and Richard E. Averbeck, 345-72. Bethesda: CDL, 1997.

————. *Old Testament Parallels: Laws and Stories from the Ancient Near East.* 3rd ed. Mahwah: Paulist, 2006.

————. *Social World of Ancient Israel, 1250-587 B.C.E.* Peabody: Hendrickson, 1993.

Mayer, Walter. "Sennacherib's Campaign of 701 BCE: The Assyrian View." In *"Like a Bird in a Cage": The Invasion of Sennacherib in 701 BCE,* ed. Lester L. Grabbe, 168-200. JSOTSup 363. London: Sheffield Academic, 2003.

Mays, James L. *Micah.* OTL. Philadelphia: Westminster, 1976.

Meier, Samuel A. *Speaking of Speaking: Marking Direct Discourse in the Hebrew Bible.* VTSup 46. Leiden: Brill, 1992.

Menn, Esther Marie. *Judah and Tamar (Genesis 38) in Ancient Jewish Exegesis.* JSJSup 51. Leiden: Brill, 1997.

Merwe, Christo H. J. van der. "Biblical Exegesis, Cognitive Linguistics, and Hypertext." In *Congress Volume, Leiden 2004,* ed. André Lemaire, 255-80. VTS 109. Leiden: Brill, 2006.

Meschonnic, Henri. "Translating Biblical Rhythm." In *Biblical Patterns in Modern Literature,* ed. David H. Hirsch and Nehama Aschkenasy, 227-40. BJS 77. Chico: Scholars, 1984.

Meyers, Carol. *Exodus.* NCambBC. Cambridge: Cambridge University Press, 2005.

Miller, Cynthia L. *The Representation of Speech in Biblical Hebrew Narrative: A Linguistic Analysis.* HSS 55. Atlanta: Scholars, 1996.

Miller, J. Maxwell, and John H. Hayes. *A History of Ancient Israel and Judah.* 2nd ed. Louisville: Westminster/John Knox, 2006.

Miscall, Peter D. "Biblical Narrative and Categories of the Fantastic." In *Fantasy and the Bible,* ed. George Aichele and Tina Pippin, 39-51. Semeia 60. Atlanta: Scholars, 1998.

Moberly, R. W. L. "Does God Lie to His Prophets? The Story of Micaiah ben Imlah as a Test Case." *HTR* 96 (2003) 1-23.

————. "To Speak for God: The Story of Micaiah ben Imlah." *Anvil* 14 (1997) 243-53.

Morschauser, Scott. "'Hospitality', Hostility and Hostages: On the Legal Background to Genesis 19:1-9." *JSOT* 27 (2003) 461-85.

Murphy, Roland E. *Proverbs*. WBC 22. Nashville: Nelson, 1998.

Na'aman, Nadav. "The Deuteronomist and Voluntary Servitude to Foreign Powers." *JSOT* 65 (1995) 37-53.

Niehoff, M. "Do Biblical Characters Talk to Themselves? Narrative Modes of Representing Inner Speech in Early Biblical Fiction." *JBL* 111 (1992) 577-95.

Noble, Paul R. "Esau, Tamar, and Joseph: Criteria for Identifying Inner-biblical Allusions." *VT* 52 (2002) 219-52.

Nunan, David. *Introducing Discourse Analysis*. London: Penguin, 1993.

Perinbanayagam, R. S. *Discursive Acts*. New York: Aldine de Gruyter, 1991.

Person, Raymond F., Jr. *In Conversation with Jonah: Conversation Analysis, Literary Criticism, and the Book of Jonah*. JSOTSup 220. Sheffield: Sheffield Academic, 1996.

————. *Structure and Meaning in Conversation and Literature*. Lanham: University Press of America, 1999.

Pexman, Penny M., and Kara M. Olineck. "Does Sarcasm Always Sting? Investigating the Impact of Ironic Insults and Ironic Compliments." *Discourse Processes* 33 (2002) 199-217.

Porter, Stanley E., and Jeffrey T. Reed. *Discourse Analysis and the New Testament: Approaches and Results*. JSNTSup 170. Sheffield: Sheffield Academic, 1999.

Potter, Jonathan. "Discourse Analysis and Constructionist Approaches: Theoretical Background." In *Handbook of Qualitative Research Methods for Psychology and the Social Sciences*, ed. John T. E. Richardson, 125-56. Leicester: British Psychological Society, 1996.

————. *Representing Reality: Discourse, Rhetoric and Social Construction*. London: Sage, 1996.

Prouser, Ora Hprn. "Suited to the Throne: The Symbolic Use of Clothing in the David and Saul Narratives." *JSOT* 71 (1996) 27-37.

Rad, Gerhard von. *Genesis*. OTL. Philadelphia: Westminster, 1961.

Ramsey, George W. "Speech-Forms in Hebrew Law and Prophetic Oracles." *JBL* 96 (1977) 45-58.

Rappaport, Roy A. *Ritual and Religion in the Making of Humanity*. Cambridge: Cambridge University Press, 1999.

Resnick, Lauren B. "Shared Cognition: Thinking as Social Practice." In *Perspectives on Socially Shared Cognition*, ed. Resnick, John B. Levine, and Stephanie D. Teasley, 1-20. Washington: American Psychological Association, 1991.

Richardson, Tim, and Ole B. Jensen. "Linking Discourse and Space: Towards a

Cultural Sociology of Space in Analysing Spatial Policy Discourses." *Urban Studies* 40 (2003) 7-22.

Roach-Higgins, Mary E., and Joanne B. Eicher. "Dress and Identity." In *Social Science Aspects of Dress: No Directions,* ed. Sharron J. Lennon and Leslie Davis Burns, 29-38. ITAA Special Publication 5. Monument, CO: International Textile and Apparel Association, 1993.

Roberts, Kathleen J., and Paul Volberding. "Adherence Communication: A Qualitative Analysis of Physician-Patient Dialogue." *AIDS* 13 (1999) 1771-78.

Rock, Irvin. "Comment on Asch and Witkin's 'Studies in Space Orientation II.'" *Journal of Experimental Psychology: General* 121 (1992) 404-6.

Rodman, Margaret C. "Empowering Place: Multilocality and Multivocality." In *The Anthropology of Space and Place: Locating Culture,* ed. Setha M. Low and Denise Lawrence-Zúñiga, 204-23. Malden: Blackwell, 2003.

Rofé, Alexander. "The Vineyard of Naboth: The Origin and Message of the Story." *VT* 38 (1988) 89-104.

Rook, John. "Making Widows: The Patriarchal Guardian at Work." *BTB* 27 (1997) 10-15.

Roth, Martha T. *Law Collections from Mesopotamia and Asia Minor.* SBLWAW 6. Atlanta: Scholars, 1995.

Rudman, Dominic. "Is the Rabshakeh Also Among the Prophets? A Rhetorical Study of 2 Kings xviii 17-35." *VT* 50 (2000) 100-10.

Sabat, Stephen, and Rom Harré. "Positioning and the Recovery of Social Identity." In *Positioning Theory: Moral Contexts of Intentional Action,* ed. Harré and Luk van Langenhove, 87-102. Oxford: Blackwell, 1999.

Sacks, Harvey. "Everyone Has to Lie." In *Sociocultural Dimensions of Language Use,* ed. Mary Sanches and Ben G. Blount, 57-80. New York: Academic, 1975.

———. *Lectures on Conversation,* ed. Gail Jefferson. Oxford: Blackwell, 1992.

———. "Notes on Methodology." In *Structures of Social Action: Studies in Conversation Analysis,* ed. J. Maxwell Atkinson and John Heritage, 21-27. Cambridge: Cambridge University Press, 1984.

———. "On Doing 'Being Ordinary.'" In *Structures of Social Action: Studies in Conversation Analysis,* ed. J. Maxwell Atkinson and John Heritage, 413-29. Cambridge: Cambridge University Press, 1984.

———, Emanuel A. Schlegel, and Gail Jefferson. "A Simplest Systematics for the Organization of Turn-Taking for Conversation." *Language* 50 (1974) 696-735.

Sakenfeld, Katharine Doob. *Just Wives? Stories of Power and Survival in the Old Testament and Today.* Louisville: Westminster/John Knox, 2003.

Schart, Aaron. "Combining Prophetic Oracles in Mari Letters and Jeremiah 36." *JANES* 23 (1995) 75-93.

Scheff, Thomas J. "Shame and Conformity: The Deference-Emotion System." *American Sociological Review* 53 (1988) 395-406.

————. "The Structure of Context: Deciphering *Frame Analysis*." *Sociological Theory* 23 (2005) 368-85.

————. "Toward a Sociological Model of Consensus." *American Sociological Review* 32 (1967) 32-46.

————, and Suzanne M. Retzinger. *Emotions and Violence: Shame and Rage in Destructive Conflicts.* Lexington, MA: Lexington, 1991.

Schegloff, Emanuel A., and Harvey Sacks. "Opening Up Closings." *Semiotica* 8 (1973) 289-327.

Schiffrin, Deborah. "Discourse Markers: Language, Meaning, and Context." In *The Handbook of Discourse Analysis,* ed. Deborah Schiffrin, Deborah Tannen, and Heidi E. Hamilton, 54-75. Oxford: Blackwell, 2001.

————. "Narrative as Self-Portrait: Sociolinguistic Constructions of Identity." *Language and Society* 25 (1996) 167-203.

Seale, Leroy F. "Emerging Questions: Text and Theory in Contemporary Criticism." In *Voice, Text, Hypertext: Emerging Practices in Textual Studies,* ed. Raimonda Modiano, Seale, and Peter Schillingsburg, 3-21. Seattle: University of Washington Press, 2004.

Seitz, Christopher R. *Theology in Conflict: Reactions to the Exile in the Book of Jeremiah.* BZAW 176. Berlin: de Gruyter, 1989.

Shields, Rob. "Knowing Space." *Theory, Culture & Society* 23 (2006) 147-49.

Shotter, John, and Kenneth Gergen. "A Prologue to Constructing the Social." In *Constructing the Social,* ed. Theodore R. Sarbin and John I. Kitsuse, 1-19. London: Sage, 1994.

Shoval, Noam, and Michal Isaacson. "Application of Tracking Technologies to the Study of Pedestrian Spatial Behavior." *The Professional Geographer* 58 (2006) 172-83.

Shweder, Richard A., and Jonathan Haidt. "The Cultural Psychology of the Emotions: Ancient and New." In *Handbook of Emotions,* ed. Michael Lewis and Jeannette M. Haviland-Jones, 397-414. 2nd ed. New York: Guilford, 2000.

Simkins, Ronald, and Stephen Cook, eds. *The Social World of the Hebrew Bible.* Semeia 87. Atlanta: SBL, 1999.

Slugoski, Ben R., and William Turnbull. "Cruel to Be Kind and Kind to Be Cruel: Sarcasm, Banter and Social Relations." *Journal of Language and Social Psychology* 7 (1988) 101-21.

Smith, Neil, and Setha Low. "Introduction: The Imperative of Public Space." In *The Politics of Public Space,* ed. Low and Smith, 1-16. New York: Routledge, 2006.

Snyman, S. D. "A Note on *pth* and *ykl* in Jeremiah xx 7-13." *VT* 48 (1998) 559-63.

Soggin, J. Alberto. "Judah and Tamar (Genesis 38)." In *Of Prophets' Visions and the*

Wisdom of Sages, ed. Heather A. McKay and David J. A. Clines, 281-87. JSOTSup 163. Sheffield: Sheffield Academic, 1993.

Soja, Edward W. *Thirdspace: Journeys to Los Angeles and Other Real-and-Imagined Places.* Cambridge, MA: Blackwell, 1996.

Sperber, Dan, and Deirdre Wilson. *Relevance: Communication and Cognition.* Cambridge, MA: Harvard University Press, 1986.

Spina, Frank A. "Israelites as *gērîm,* 'Sojourners,' in Social and Historical Context." In *The Word of the Lord Shall Go Forth: Essays in Honor of David Noel Freedman in Celebration of His Sixtieth Birthday,* ed. Carol L. Meyers and M. O'Connor, 321-35. Winona Lake: Eisenbrauns, 1983.

Spitzberg, Brian H., and William R. Cupach. "Interpersonal Skills." In *Handbook of Interpersonal Communication,* ed. Mark L. Knapp and John A. Daly, 564-611. 3rd ed. Thousand Oaks: Sage, 2002.

Stangor, Charles, and Mark Schaller. "Stereotypes as Individual and Collective Representations." In *Stereotypes and Stereotyping,* ed. C. Neil Macrae, Stangor, and Miles Hewstone, 3-37. New York: Guilford, 1996.

Steinsaltz, Adin. *Biblical Images: Men and Women of the Book.* New York: Basic Books, 1984.

Sternberg, Meir. *The Poetics of Biblical Narrative: Ideological Literature and the Drama of Reading.* Bloomington: Indiana University Press, 1985.

Stone, Ken. "Gender and Homosexuality in Judges 19: Subject-Honour, Object-Shame?" *JSOT* 67 (1995) 87-107.

Sweetser, Eve, and Gilles Fauconnier. "Cognitive Links and Domains: Basic Aspects of Mental Space Theory." In *Spaces, Worlds, and Grammar,* ed. Fauconnier and Sweetser, 1-28. Chicago: University of Chicago Press, 1996.

Talmy, Leonard. "Force Dynamics in Language and Cognition." *Cognitive Science* 12 (1988) 49-100.

Tannen, Deborah. "Introducing Constructed Dialogue in Greek and American Conversational and Literary Narrative." In *Direct and Indirect Speech,* ed. Florian Coulmas, 311-32. Berlin: Mouton de Gruyter, 1986.

————. *Talking Voices: Repetition, Dialogue, and Imagery in Conversational Discourse.* Cambridge: Cambridge University Press, 1989.

Tarlin, Jan William. "Tamar's Veil: Ideology at the Entrance to Enaim." In *Culture, Entertainment and the Bible,* ed. George Aichele, 174-81. JSOTSup 309. Sheffield: Sheffield Academic, 2000.

Taylor, John R. "Introduction: On Construing the World." In *Language and the Cognitive Construal of the World,* ed. John R. Taylor and Robert E. MacLaury, 1-21. Berlin: Mouton de Gruyter, 1995.

Thompson, J. A. *The Book of Jeremiah.* NICOT. Grand Rapids: Wm. B. Eerdmans, 1980.

Tonson, Paul. "Mercy Without Covenant: A Literary Analysis of Genesis 19." *JSOT* 95 (2001) 95-116.

Toorn, Karel van der. "Female Prostitution in Payment of Vows in Ancient Israel." *JBL* 108 (1989) 193-205.

———. "In the Lions' Den: The Babylonian Background of a Biblical Motif." *CBQ* 60 (1998) 626-40.

———. "The Significance of the Veil in the Ancient Near East." In *Pomegranates and Golden Bells: Studies in Biblical, Jewish, and Near Eastern Ritual, Law, and Literature in Honor of Jacob Milgrom*, ed. David P. Wright, David Noel Freedman, and Avi Hurvitz, 327-39. Winona Lake: Eisenbrauns, 1995.

Towner, W. Sibley. "Daniel 1 in the Context of the Canon." In *Canon, Theology, and Old Testament Interpretation*, ed. Gene M. Tucker, David L. Petersen, and Robert R. Wilson, 285-98. Philadelphia: Fortress, 1988.

Tracy, Karen. "Discourse." In *Studying Interpersonal Interaction*, ed. Barbara M. Montgomery and Steve Duck, 179-96. New York: Guilford, 1991.

Turner, John C. *Rediscovering the Social Group: A Self-Categorization Theory*. Oxford: Blackwell, 1987.

Tybout, Alice M,. and Tim Calkins, eds. *Kellogg on Branding: The Marketing Faculty of the Kellogg School of Management*. Hoboken: Wiley, 2005.

Tyner, James A. "Self and Space, Resistance and Discipline: A Foucauldian Reading of George Orwell's *1984*." *Social and Cultural Geography* 5 (2004) 129-49.

Walsh, Jerome T. "The Contexts of 1 Kings xiii." *VT* 39 (1989) 355-70.

Weinfeld, Moshe. "Ancient Near Eastern Patterns in Prophetic Literature." *VT* 27 (1977) 178-95.

———. "The King as the Servant of the People: The Source of the Idea." *JJS* 33 (1982) 189-94.

Weisberg, Dvora E. "The Widow of Our Discontent: Levirate Marriage in the Bible and Ancient Israel." *JSOT* 28 (2004) 403-29.

Wenham, Gordon J. *Genesis 16-50*. WBC 2. Dallas: Word, 1994.

West, Paige, James Igoe, and Dan Brockington. "Parks and Peoples: The Social Impact of Protected Areas." *Annual Review of Anthropology* 35 (2006) 251-77.

Westenholz, Joan Goodnick. "Tamar, *Qĕdēšā, Qadištu*, and Sacred Prostitution in Mesopotamia." *HTR* 82 (1989) 245-65.

White, Hugh C., ed. *Speech Act Theory and Biblical Criticism*. Semeia 41. Decatur: Scholars, 1988.

Wieringen, Archibald L. H. M. van. *The Implied Reader in Isaiah 6-12*. Biblical Interpretation 34. Leiden: Brill, 1998.

Wildavsky, Aaron. "Survival Must Not Be Gained through Sin: The Moral of the Joseph Stories Prefigured Through Judah and Tamar." *JSOT* 62 (1994) 37-48.

Wiseman, Donald J. *Nebuchadnezzar and Babylon*. Schweich Lectures 1983. Oxford: Oxford University Press, 1985.

Wolde, Ellen van. "Cognitive Linguistics and Its Application to Genesis 28:10-22." In *One Text, a Thousand Methods*, ed. Patrick Chatelion Counet and Ulrich Berges, 125-48. Boston: Brill, 2005.

———. "A Leader Led by a Lady: David and Abigail in I Samuel 25." *ZAW* 114 (2002) 355-75.

———. "Who Guides Whom? Embeddedness and Perspective in Biblical Hebrew and in 1 Kings 3:16-28." *JBL* 114 (1995) 623-42.

Woodhouse, Robert. "The Biblical Shibboleth Story in the Light of Late Egyptian Perceptions of Semitic Sibilants: Reconciling Divergent Views." *JAOS* 123 (2003) 271-89.

Wooffitt, Robin. *Conversation Analysis and Discourse Analysis: A Comparative and Critical Introduction*. London: Sage, 2005.

Wright, David P. "Music and Dance in 2 Samuel 6." *JBL* 121 (2002) 201-25.

Wright, G. R. H. "The Positioning of Genesis 38." *ZAW* 94 (1982) 523-29.

Wrong, Dennis H. *Power: Its Forms, Bases, and Uses*. New Brunswick, NJ: Transaction, 1995.

Yadin, Azzan. "Goliath's Armor and Israelite Collective Memory." *VT* 54 (2004) 373-95.

Zebrowitz, Leslie A. "Physical Appearance as a Basis of Stereotyping." In *Stereotypes and Stereotyping*, ed. C. Neil Macrae, Charles Stangor, and Miles Hewstone, 79-120. New York: Guilford, 1996.

Zick, Timothy. "Speech and Spatial Tactics." *Texas Law Review* 84 (2005) 581-651.

Žižek, Slavoj, ed. *Mapping Ideology*. London: Verso, 1994.

Subject Index

Scripture Index